Beyond the Jordan
Studies in Honor of W. Harold Mare

Dr. Glenn A. Carnagey, Sr., Editor
Glenn Carnagey, Jr., Associate Editor
Dr. Keith N. Schoville, Associate Editor

Wipf & Stock Publishers
Eugene, Oregon

Wipf & Stock Publishers
199 West 8th Avenue, Suite 3
Eugene, OR 97401

Beyond the Jordan
Studies in Honor of W. Harold Mare
Copyright©2005 by Near East Archaeological Society
ISBN: 1-59752-069-1
Publication Date: February 2005

10   9   8   7   6   5   4   3   2   1

Dr. W. Harold Mare

Table of Contents

Preface

There is a famous saying: "Man proposes but God disposes." The truth of that wisdom is applicable to the publication of this volume in honor of W. Harold Mare. It has been in production for too many years. The process was initiated a number of years ago by several members of the Near East Archaeological Society. The project was placed in the hands of Dr. Glenn A. Carnagey, Sr., who had served for many years as the editor of the *Near East Archaeological Society Bulletin.* Although Dr. Carnagey labored faithfully on the volume, deteriorating health interfered with the process. I was asked by the NEAS Board of Directors to facilitate the project, and I assisted Glenn in the editing process. At the same time, his son, Glenn, Jr., was actively involved in the preparations as well. Then, the unexpected happened–Glenn, Sr., died unexpectedly in the spring of 2003. Due to the myriad responsibilities which his father's death imposed upon Glenn, Jr., the work languished for well over a year. To relieve him of further work on the volume, the responsibility for the final pre-publication preparations was given to me in July, 2004.

On behalf of the contributors, I want to express the apologies of the NEAS Board for this long delay. At the same time, I want to express appreciation for the editors who have labored on the project. But now, for the rest of the story!

W. Harold Mare had been recovering from ill health and was well enough in the spring of 2004 to return to another season in the field excavating his site, Abila of the Decapolis in northeastern Jordan. To our shock and dismay, he died in a vehicle accident while there. We do have this consolation, however; he was aware of the volume in preparation and knew of the contributors and their contributions well before his death.

In light of these events, the Board of Directors of the NEAS were determined to see this project through to completion. It is our intent that it honor both Harold and Glenn. To this end, I have included below obituaries for both scholars. Dr. Edwin Yamauchi prepared the obituary for Dr. Mare for publication in *Biblical Archaeology Review:*

> W. Harold Mare, the director of the excavations at Abila was killed in a car accident near his site in Jordan on June 21. Though Mare could walk only with difficulty, he had been determined to introduce David Chapman, his designated successor, to the site. Mare, who was asleep at the time, was instantly killed one month before his 86th birthday. After Mare's body had

1

been returned to the States, memorial services were held in his honor at the Covenant Presbyterian Church in St. Louis on July 2.

Chapman wrote that when Mare was not able to sleep, he spent the time in prayer. Darlene Brooks Hedstrom marveled at Mare's energy, up everyday at 4:30 a.m. to arouse the other staff. Mike Fuller recalled, "Harold was always cheerful and rarely lost his temper." Robert Cooley described Mare as always energetic and enthusiastic. John Davis wrote, "His passion for his work and his humility were obvious to both Arab and American workers."

Mare dug at sites such as Tekoa, Heshbon, and Khirbet Radanna before he began his own excavation at Abila of the Decapolis in 1980. Mare gave annual reports to the Archaeological Institute of America, the American Schools of Oriental Research, and the Near East Archaeological Society. He also wrote entries on Abila in various reference works, and published preliminary reports in such journals as *Aram,* the *Annual of the Department of Antiquities of Jordan,* and the *Bulletin of the Near East Archaeological Society.* John D. Wineland's 1996 Miami University Ph.D. dissertation, was published in 2001 in the British Archaeological Reports series as *Ancient Abila: An Archaeological History.*

Mare served as the president of the Near East Archaeological Society from 1971 to 1992, and as president of the St. Louis society of the Archaeological Institute of American during 1978-79. He was one of the translators of the *New International Version,* and contributed the commentary on First Corinthians in *The Expositor's Bible Commentary.* He wrote *Mastering New Testament Greek* (1975), and *The Archaeology of the Jerusalem Area* (1987). A Festschrift, *Beyond the Jordan,* in his honor will be published by Wipf & Stock.

Mare was born in Portland, Oregon, on July 23, 1918. His hard work on a farm prepared him well for the rigors of excavations in later life. He received the B.A. in 1941 and the M.A. in 1946 from Wheaton College. After graduating from Faith Theological Seminary in 1945, he received his Ph.D. in classical archaeology from the University of Pennsylvania in 1961.

Mare served as a pastor for ten years in Colorado and North Carolina, before he became a founding member of Covenant Theological Seminary in St. Louis and a professor of New Testament there from 1963 to 1984. Even in his retirement, he continued to teach at the seminary.

He was predeceased by his wife Betty in 2002. Mare is survived by five children, Myra, Sally, Nancy, Harold, Jr., and Judith, and their families.

The obituary for Glenn Carnagey follows:

Dr. Glenn A. Carnagey led a full life unto the Lord, accomplishing those assignments that God chose to give him with zeal and enthusiasm.

Preface

Born on September 13, 1938 in Hammond, Indiana, he was the son of Walter and Helen Carnagey. His family later moved to a farm in Arkansas for several years, prior to moving to Houston where he graduated from Milby High School.

He was a highly educated man, obtaining a BA in English from the University of Texas, and a MA and PhD in English at the University of Tulsa. A teacher throughout his life, his first experience was with emotionally disturbed children. From there, he taught nuclear weapons as an officer in the US Army, and in subsequent years taught English courses at the University of Tulsa, American Christian College, and several other universities. Together with his brother, Dale, he established Wakefield Academy in Tulsa, OK, to provide an excellent educational alternative for children.

However, the focus of his life was always teaching the word of God. He obtained a ThM from Dallas Theological Seminary, where he distinguished himself by receiving the Chafer Award in Apologetics, and was ordained by Berachah Church. He pastored several churches throughout his life, including: Faith Bible Church of Dallas, TX (1964-1965), Candlelight Bible Church of Houston, TX (1965-1966), Grace Bible Church of Muskogee, OK (1968-1972), Patrian Bible Church of Tulsa, OK (1972-1988), South Tulsa Bible Church (1990- 1991) and Grace Community Church of Golden Valley, MN (1993-1996). Dr. Carnagey also had the burden and desire to train additional men to teach God's word. While pastor at Patrian Bible Church, he founded and became president of the Tulsa Seminary of Biblical Languages, whose graduates continue to serve around the country.

Dr. Carnagey had a tremendous interest in biblical archaeology, with a strong conviction that the physical evidence discovered through this work would help convince others of the truth revealed in God's word. He assisted in numerous archaeological digs in Israel and Jordan from 1978 to 2000 as a ceramic typologist, and was a board member and Bulletin editor for the Near Eastern Archaeological Society. He delivered numerous papers, and most recently completed a Festschrift of significant articles provided by field archaeologists.

During his later years, Dr. Carnagey retired from the pastoral profession due to health issues, but continued to serve as a beloved Sunday School teacher and was blessed to teach his own grand-children, as well as others. Dr. Carnagey was called home to God's presence on April 24, 2003, in Minneapolis, MN, while enroute to Spokane to attend a pastor's conference. He is survived by his wife of 43 years, Nan Carnagey; his elder son, Glenn, Jr. and wife, Cindy, children Sarah, Adam and Christina Carnagey; his younger son John and wife Kim, children Walter, Rebecca, Alan and Tresona Carnagey. He is predeceased by his brother, Dale Carnagey, and survived by his sister, Phyllis Wisneski.

Finally, I want to acknowledge the invaluable help which I have received from Paul J. Ray, Jr., editor of the *Near East Archaeological Society Bulletin* for his technical assistance, to Jim Tedrick of Wipf & Stock who gave me helpful encouragement and direction, and particularly for putting me in touch with Kimberly Medgyesy, who expertly put the final touches on the manuscript prior to publication. And there were others, here unnamed but not forgotten, who gave me sound advice.

I am sorry that some of the graphics will not be up to the standard I sought, but there was no way to obtain higher resolution copies, particularly in the case of the pottery drawings. Any other errors can be attributed to me.

Keith N. Schoville
September, 2004

Dr. W. Harold Mare, Professor and Archaeological Director

A Biography and Commentary On His Life
Dr. Reuben G. Bullard, Professor
Archaeological Geologist
Cincinnati Bible College & Seminary, University of Cincinnati

Many lives are beyond contact with us. Some other lives are tangential to our own, yet a few lives impact our own in a highly significant way. From the very moment I came to know Dr. Mare, his energy, drive, motivation, spiritual warmth and sense of personal purpose and destiny were highly evident to me. This contact has touched my life and that of my colleagues and stu-dents in many ways. And that is the story I am about to tell.

I was in the company of Dr. Wilkie Winter in 1972 at a St. Louis meeting of the Near East Archaeological Society when I first met Harold. The activity and efficiency of his personality as he spoke and acted upon the business at hand caught my attention. This was no common man, but one who knew exactly where he wanted and purposed to go. Not only was Harold outgoing and personable, he was also a warmhearted individual. He would put his arm around the person to whom he was talking and/or while walking, in an embrace of "brotherhood" and encouragement. I had rarely seen such overt enthusiasm, even amongst those of my own Faith, but it surely gave assurance that he very much wanted you "with him." This was no common man, but one who knew exactly where it was obvious to him that God wanted his life.

We were invited to his home to continue discussion of our affairs where he proudly introduced us to his family. They were a natural part of his life in St. Louis and overseas. He was then and is now an outgoing man giving his energies to his seminary and to the discipline of historical research in the Bible, its language and its people as evidenced through an investigation of the remains of its culture. Harold is driven by a great archaeological drive and motivation. This is the background for many things that took place in the years hence. The single characteristic that typifies W. Harold Mare is his personality. He has shown a direct, on-target approach to all issues at hand with a strong and very firm determination involved in the pursuit of his goals, especially those in connection with archaeological objectives. He led with a broad vision, which he applied in his administrative oversights, whether as Professor of

New Testament at Covenant Seminary or with the responsibilities of the President of the Near East Archaeological Society or as the director of the Abila Expedition in northern Jordan. Other significant aspects of the life of Harold Mare are the staunch personal Faith he manifests in everything he touches: prayer at meals, and the enthusiastic teaching of his Sunday School class in the Presbyterian Congregation where he is active. This spiritual aspect of his life was also present during our research seasons in Jordan.

A total objectivity to intellectual honesty is a patent trait exhibited by Dr. Mare in all of our research designs in planning, execution and publication. There was no room for any duplicity or cover-ups. Although all of us who possessed certain personal biases as Christians, at times secretly hoped for a strong cultural witness to the First Century of the Decapolis of the Christian Era, most of the architectural picture is Roman, Byzantine and Omayyad. All of us kept true to the historical data that was found without any idea of presenting something contrary to the truth of our finds.

A highly frustrating situation hung over our work between our research seasons. A more- than-one-time event in our biennial work phases was the theft of our architectural members [capitals, columns and cut building stones] before Harold could bring about restoration of the structures discovered. This also applied to the robbing of original well-supplied tombs, mostly on the east side of the valley of the Wadi Quailibah (Quelbah on the local highway sign). All of these activities by certain Jordanians deeply pained him, not only for his own sense of moral propriety but also for losses to the Kingdom of Jordan. These stolen antiquities would never be seen in Jordan's developing museums or as restored basilicas on the site for visitors to the land to enjoy and study.

Nevertheless, his quest for the culture of Abila has continued through such events of adversity. Harold Mare has never taken his eyes and heart off this challenging city-site, unlike certain other field archaeologists who move from site to site without an appropriate publication obligation to each. Some researchers have passed from this life with the special material and data understanding of an ancient city (Biblical, at times) in their minds only—with irreparable loss to all who hunger for those special historical-cultural insights.

Covenant Seminary quite fittingly has given its honored Professor high support and respect. I had the privilege of addressing an audience gathered on that campus to celebrate the opening of the W. Harold Mare Institute for Biblical and Archaeological Studies that had just been completed there on October 23, 1999. That address which summarizes certain particulars of this biography deserves to be included here:

DEDICATION CEREMONY
BIBLICAL AND ARCHAEOLOGICAL STUDIES INSTITUTE
Covenant Theological Seminary
St. Louis, Missouri
23 October, 1999
By Dr. Reuben G. Bullard

It is with great pleasure that I am speaking to the occasion of the dedication of this wonderful facility. The Institute and Museum, erected in the honor of one of the living giants of 20th Century research in the archaeology of the Bible, Dr. W. Harold Mare, stands before us at Covenant Seminary as a fitting credit to this theological institution. There is no other person in my awareness who deserves this celebration more than the fine professor and scholar of this seminary. I have worked with international scholars from well-known universities and seminaries at highly famous sites throughout the Near East and Mediterranean for nearly forty years. Dr. Mare stands above them all in his faith in God and in the insistence upon the historical veracity of His Word. His zeal for the dynamics of research discovery at archaeological sites is surely unmatched.

I began my academic relations with archaeological colleagues on an international scale in 1963 with my work on the finds of Dr. Nelson Glueck, former Director of the American Schools of Oriental Research in Jerusalem and who was well known for his surveys in Jordan and the Negev and excavation at Tell el Kaleifah, possibly Ezion Geber of the time of Solomon. Although a Reformed Jew, Dr. Glueck led a dedicated research life both in the city and in the desert. Among other directors with whom I have worked of this high caliber are Dr. David Soren, University of Arizona and Dr. W. Harold Mare, Covenant Theological Seminary. Harold Mare especially is to be praised for his high sense of moral life style in a context where, often far away from home, excavation participants may experience strong sexual temptations.

One dig with which I had a lengthy association had a well-known reputation for being a near-brothel at which only a conservative Jew and I were the strong staff critics. Dr. Mare brought a clear Christian conscience and morality to the leadership of the Abila Excavations, of which those of us at Cincinnati are most proud.

As a field archaeologist, he labored at Heshbon in Jordan[1], and later as President, he sought a fitting site for the Near East Archaeological Society to sponsor at Colossae in Turkey. When frustrated at uncooperative Turkish authorities, he took his efforts to Jordan and researched the viability of a little known city-site in the northern part of that Biblical Land. Harold's efforts were greeted with great enthusiasm and cooperation by the Antiquities administrators of the Hashemite Kingdom of Jordan. Nearly single-handedly, he moved forward without the underwriting of ACOR whose liberal staffing was adversarial to Dr. Mare's conservative theological posture. He mounted a highly successful expedition to Abila of the Decapolis a few kilometers south of Syria.

Professor Mare revealed his ability as Director to attract skilled and intellectually qualified students, Biblical and church historians, Biblical scholars, linguists, Arabic culture investigators, knowledgeable artistic specialists, photographers, ceramacists, stratigraphers, surveyors, architects, cartographers, anthropologists, tomb and skeletal specialists, entomologists, botanists, pedologists, geomorphologists, geologists and field archaeologists.

Without the levels of funding under which other major digs operate, this amazing enterprise accomplished more in significant finds and architectural features than many others. The number of basilica or church foundations (presently, five) brought to light may soon rival that of Pella and possibly Jerash, also. [Story: the second basilica at Abila, Umm el Amad, was first considered as a likely Roman temple, but when the covering soil fell off part of a capital or upper member of a column, a cross became visible. A surprisingly beautiful church building came out of the digging by the late Dr. Wilkie Winter and his team. (He looked forward to seeing this Covenant archaeological facility and wanted to be here.).]

Other spectacular results of Dr. Mare's 20 years of persistent biennial investigations are painted tombs [Harold has had to get to these ahead of efficient tomb robbers], long water tunnels which brought water to the center of the city, a well-preserved Roman bridge, a viaduct connecting two upper portions of the city, an amazing street, east-west direction, surfaced with durable basalt pavers and many other architectural features, ceramics and objects.

Aside from these material remains, this archaeological enterprise has generated the impetus for a large number of undergraduate degrees, several masters level and at least two doctorate degrees. The students and staff have been measurably blessed by the cultural remains which have afforded vital research and publication data for mostly Roman and Byzantine historical period clarifications and understanding. I have taken note of the pattern of relationships in academic institutions between those scholars whose specialty is the text, whether Biblical or secular-historical, and those whose specialty is field research in the backgrounds of that text through the years. Any control and direction of department or college or seminary funds may reveal significant antipathy between these fields. The extent of activity that colleagues who work in textual areas, ranging from faculty to administration, exhibit in channeling institutional research resources *from field research activities* has been significant. I have observed this practice in three institutions. The manifest exception to this human behavior has been a number of praiseworthy institutions. Among these, and at the top, stands Covenant Theological Seminary, its administration, faculty, staff, and phenomenal supporters of archaeological research. The highest praise, in my mind, must go to this school and to all these people, to whom a salute and a tribute should pass. This new building, the W. Harold Mare Institute for Biblical and Archaeological Studies, therefore, is a grand attestation of very proper thought and consideration!
I find this occasion to be an exceptional event in the history of American academia and I am honored to have been a part of it.

[Dr. John Davis, Grace Theological Seminary, followed with his own tribute to Dr. Mare on this occasion.]

Post Celebration Comment
A fuller biography of Dr. W. Harold Mare will reveal a person whose love of God is foremost, a feature of his life underscored by a rich faith. These facets of his personality never blinded him to the objective goals of his work in the field. For Harold, faith never erased fact, nor, in his mind did it ever have to. Some of those

who came to work under the directorship of Dr. Mare felt that their own conceptions and contributions were not always received as well as they desired. I know the personality traits of Professor Mare about which they speak. He can be strongly opinionated and dogmatic about the direction of the excavation from dig season to dig season. My liaison and encounter record with Harold is otherwise. After reasoning together with him, at times more than once, most objectives that I envisioned for the expedition were put in place. I have seen him show deep concern and love for every participant taking part in the expedition."

Letter

Dear Harold, 30 October 1999

Greetings in the wonderful Name of our Lord and Savior Jesus Christ!!! What a terrific celebration in commemoration of the W. Harold Mare Institute of Biblical and Archaeological Studies! No other academic community has so honored any of its living celebrated personnel. Perhaps the Siegfried Horn Institute at Andrews is a second, but Dr. Horn had passed on to his reward. You are in sound mind, body and spirit and are going to achieve great things for the Lord at Abila, at Covenant Seminary and church at and through the Institute during those years the Lord will grant you.

The Harold and Betty Mare Family

The members of this family, Harold, Betty and five children, never appeared to me as individuals who had divergent goals and objectives. Those whom I met and with whom I worked were dedicated to those objectives on which Harold's career focused. My observations in their home, at Covenant and at Abila lead me to conclude that Betty and Myra, their oldest child, were as much a part of Biblical world research as Harold. This daughter showed high interest and strong devotion in the archaeological enterprise of her father (as is often the pattern in many families with the oldest son or daughter). Myra gave her energies to summer research activities with a level of zeal that rivaled that of her father during off-season investigation activity, when the staff was smaller than that of the regular biennial field research expeditions.

Not many experienced a family life-style so driven by a dedication that was both intellectual and spiritual. The quest of opening up and illuminating the world of the Bible has been the common objective of this special family. I write this at a time when the discord and centripetal forces at work in our 21st Century culture rip apart families in the malaise of unfaithfulness and divorce. The tie that binds the Mare family is as strong as any could be, and that tie is Faith (belief in the Father, Son and Holy Spirit), Hope (actualized by determination to accomplish the nearly impossible), and Love (of God, family, and his academy (Covenant Seminary)! Evidence of the motivation and drive that Harold, with the backing discussed above, is manifest in the tragic fire that destroyed the Mare home in 1982. Harold did not miss a single responsibility as professor at Covenant, as President of NEAS and as one of the strong supporters of archaeology in the St. Louis community.

The Harold and Betty Mare family has appeared to me as a deeply spiritual and

Beyond the Jordan

strongly unified home with a church-centered life-style. I have had a fine relationship with Mrs. Mare in our excavation facilities at Hartha, especially during the 2000 season. I saw a devotion to her husband and he to her. Sometimes Betty Mare extended her work effort for the excavation beyond the limits that other spouses would have. I have had great concern and sympathy for this lady watching her manage the dig registration when she was in considerable pain and having to seek relief from heavy sedatives during the 2000 season. She held that activity to be her life's work no matter what situation arose. She, like her daughter Myra, gave summers to special activities to further important research goals. At the time of this writing (January 30, 2002), the Lord has seen fit to take Betty home, thus sparing her further suffering. We shall all miss her!

Our present concern goes out now also for Dr. Mare. He required critical bypass (quintuple) surgery on the 16th of January during the finalization of this document. This emergency was compounded by pneumonia fever that followed upon his operation. Dr. Bullard spoke to Harold on the 16th of March when he related that he had just come to the decision that the 2002 Abila Expedition must be cancelled because of the developing political unrest in the Near East. He was deeply moved by the possibility of danger to our volunteer students, veteran workers and staff. I fully concurred with this conclusion, but I could hear the sadness in his voice for a lost archaeological research opportunity, the first such cancellation in 22 years. We pray that this opportunity will not be his last.

I believe that I am as qualified as anyone to write about Dr. Mare's embrace of all the young and aspiring "Biblical Archaeologists" as any other person. As the designer (along with colleagues) of the Near East Antiquities program for undergraduates and the Near Eastern Antiquities graduate program in the Cincinnati Bible Seminary,[2] I welcomed a site that promised an alternative to the many pre-Christian world remains where I had worked prior to Abila. Dr. W. Wilkie Winter, Dr. Lewis A. Foster and Professor Robert Drake participated in the planning and execution of these Bible Backgrounds degree minors for our students at Cincinnati.

Later, our College and Seminary administration and trustees, largely under the prompting of Dr. W. Wilkie Winter with my full support had taken up a ten-season commitment to a consortium relationship with the Abila expedition in 1982. This was a $3,000-level participation option that afforded some faculty archaeological field research privileges including travel and lodging. Although the level of support that granted valuable publication rights was $5,000, Harold graciously permitted publicity and publication opportunities to me, a generous and considerate move on his part. Our participation venue granted open opportunities to our students, on both College and Seminary levels.[3]

This was especially encouraging because we had been building up and urging our Cincinnati students to become involved in campus studies in Bible Backgrounds (both lecture and lab), the options of Bible Land Travel Studies (These covered most of the Mediterranean countries.), and the participation in archaeological excavations that were offered from our campus. Consequently, nearly fifty of our students, college and seminary, along with four faculty, encouraged by the writer, participated in the staffing of the Abila Expedition mostly, but also other expeditions[4] for regular research seasons and investigations. Student skills, ranging from photography and drafting to curation and registration supplemented the actual digging that most were doing there. My students from the University of Cincinnati deserve special mention for their contributions to Abila and other sites as well.

A number of degrees were earned, both on the undergraduate and graduate levels, at CBC&S from their research at Abila. Not to be forgotten, two of my students (Dr. John Wineland and Dr. Robert Smith) earned their doctorates under Dr. Edwin Yamauchi at Miami University (of Ohio) in connection with their research at Abila and associated areas of study. Others pursued Bachelor degrees in "Ancient Near Eastern Studies" and Master degrees in "Antiquities."[5] Cincinnati scholars have contributed significantly to the total accomplishments of the biennial expeditions of Dr. Harold Mare and his team at the Abila site.

I am pleased to report that these field research operations at this city-site have revealed the existence of five churches and many other Roman and Byzantine cultural attributes (I should not neglect to mention that we have materials that represent the time span from the Bronze Age to Turkish occupation, too).

Anecdotes:
1) An Unholy Gearshift
Once upon a time in the 1880s I was told that Harold was driving an American Center of Oriental Research vehicle on the streets of Irbid with a fellow archaeologist, probably Bas van Elderen (from whom this tale may have come). All went well until Harold endeavored to negotiate a difficult grade whereupon using all his energies to shift gears, he literally pulled the gearshift out of its mechanism with a total paralysis of the station wagon. Hehad to leave the vehicle parked along the streets of Irbid with the assistance of the Police waiting for the ACOR officials to come and fix it.

2) Christmas in New York
Harold, Wilkie Winter, and several other colleagues were in New York for Archaeological Institute of America meetings in the late 1970's. For some reason we wanted to attend services in a grand old New York City house of worship. Harold knew exactly where to steer our group, taking us to a church with highly festive decorations for the Christmas season. This ecumenical venture stands vivid in our memories of a city that was more reminiscent of an "old fashioned Yule time" celebration.

3) Virgin Water Tunnels
Harold had a high regard for the young graduate scholar, Michael Fuller of Washington University, St. Louis. He had come into the Abila Expedition organization early, and when I came with 9 students on the tail end of a four-week tour of the "Biblical Roman World," Michael took pride in his discoveries and showed an apparent

"ownership" of his work himself in my presence with airs of authority that seemed at times to transcend those of Dr. Mare. I valued the remarkable skills of this young man and encouraged him in his drafting/mapping work. He had discovered our two amazing water tunnels (at least portions thereof not visited by any of our team before). Three of my students were as eager as Michael to explore the ramparts of our large city-site. In doing so they found a puteus, or "man-hole" cover and shaft leading into the latest of the pair of tunnels. They were so excited over their find (perhaps unaware of the Fuller find) that they invited me to take a tour of the water tunnels. Although not as agile as they, I descended into the man-made underground "aqueduct." We toured and photographed portions of the excavation cut in chalk bedrock, where in places Byzantine crosses were carved into the walls. Even a section of smoothed wall rock was painted white with red lettered Greek words painted on it. [Bastiaan van Elderen later translated this epigraphy from a document copy that my student, Craig Stanforth, had carefully lettered.] I made some geological observations and we left. Well, I don't think that the archaeological world has ever heard anything like the consequent vocal venting of rage and storming. Michael charged that my students had "raped his virgin" in going into the feature that he regarded, apparently, as his private domain. I have never ever beheld a colleague who coveted a find to the extent that he regarded it as his, personally. [It surely in no wise belonged to any one of us on the expedition, but to the Kingdom of Jordan and to the Abila Archaeology Corporation of St. Louis. I had to pour oil on troubled waters.]

4) The Harolds

During our 1984 season at Abila, we had four staff members whose names were John. Harold always referred to the excavation dig quarters' restroom as "Johns." As time went by the irritation generated by this reference boiled over and, led by Dr. John Davis, a plot was hatched whilst Harold was taking his siesta. The facilities were hung with signs stating that these were henceforth to be termed "The Harolds." Stringers of crepe paper lined the way from the pottery reading table to the renamed facilities along with balloons and some confetti. As soon as Dr. Mare arose and arrived at the afternoon's pottery reading area[6] he was informed that a special event had transpired that he would want to see. And amid sounds of mock trumpets we all marched to the newly labeled restrooms. Well, we never could fully tell just how Harold regarded the "Harolds," and I am certain he made some slips, but he abstained from addressing the facilities as "johns" for the remainder of the '84 season.

5) Training in Classical Architecture

Once, during a discussion in a preparatory 1988 meeting with our new student volunteers and staff at the Area D basilica at Abila, Dr. Mare pointed to the restored columns standing on the stylobate of the building foundations. "These are not to be called pillars," he said, "which are attached support features. Supports that are freestanding are to be termed columns." He remarked that his professor of architecture at the University of Pennsylvania had so emphatically instructed him. This attention to architectural detail was another hallmark of this Professor and Director of excavations.

Faculty at Covenant Theological Seminary

His students, colleagues and administration at Covenant Seminary in St. Louis have showed an outstanding, even amazing, appreciation for Dr. Mare, as was made evident by the erection of the Institute of Biblical Archaeology, cited above, on the school campus. At that time I related my deep satisfaction at this demonstration of affection and tribute to their beloved professor and archaeologist.

A reaffirmation of this scholar and researcher is seen in an event that took place on the 9th of November, 2001. Dr. Mark Chavalas, University of Wisconsin, La Crosse, presented two lectures in archaeology, in honor of Dr. Mare at Covenant in the Rayburn Chapel. After the second lecture in the evening, the climax of the day took place when an unveiling of a portrait of this beloved Professor occurred. Rarely does an institution so fully honor any of its individual faculty in such a manner and to this extent.

The preparation for his life's work as a Professor of New Testament and Biblical Archaeological Excavator is evident in his collegiate study track of ministerial, academic and research functions:

1) W. Harold Mare was born on July 23, 1918 in Portland, Oregon

2) Graduated from Wheaton College with the Highest Honors; Member of the Wheaton College Scholastic Honor Society, 1941

3) Graduate Fellow in History, Wheaton College, Wheaton, Illinois, 1941-43

4) Instructor, Classical Greek, Wheaton, summer 1942

5) Ministerial activity in Illinois, 1942
Ministerial activity in Denver, Colorado, 1953-60
Ministerial activity in Charlotte, North Carolina, 1960-63

6) Instructor, New Testament, Faith Theological Seminary, Wilmington, DE, 1947-53

7) Director and Professor, Near East School of Archaeology, Jerusalem 1964

8) Professor of Classics, Chair, Department of Classics, Covenant College, 1963-65

9) Professor, Near East Institute of Archaeology, Jerusalem, summer 1970

10) Professor of New Testament, Covenant Theological Seminary, St. Louis, Missouri (West Bank), Israel, 1963-1972

11) Professor, Archaeological School and Excavations at Raddana, Ramallah 1972 research season

12) Core Staff member, Heshbon Excavations, Siegfried Horn, Director. 1974-76 research seasons

13) Colossae Expedition exploration activity in Turkey with Dr. Donald Burdick, an attempt to obtain permission from Turkish Antiquities authorities to set up an excavation base at Honac, Lycus Valley. 1975-81

14) Staff, Regional Archaeological Research team in Central Moab, Jordan, Maxwell Miller, Director,.research season. 1979

15) Director, Abila of the (Jordanian) Decapolis Excavations, Quailibah (Spring), Hartha, northern Jordan. 1980

16) Celebrated as "Professor Emeritus" of Covenant Theological Seminary. 1982

17) Director and Curator, The Archaeological Institute, Covenant Theological Seminary, St. Louis. 1980-1998

18) Director and Curator of the new W. Harold Mare Institute of Biblical Archaeological Studies, Covenant Theological Seminary, 1999 [see Dedication above in this biography]

19) Active membership in The Near East Archaeological Society; The Evangelical Theological Society; The Archaeological Institute of America [St. Louis Society 1972- 78; President 1978-1980], American Schools of Oriental Research, The Classical Club, St. Louis [president 1982-92] and the Missouri Numismatic Society.

Harold has shown a constant, untiring and highly productive agenda in his career and work. This characteristic of life has been a hallmark during all the thirty years I have had the stimulating pleasure of knowing this scholar and researcher. He has exhibited a prodigious output as his activity vita reveals (above and see bibliography following). An example of this vigor is the brochure of the 2002 Expedition to Abila of the Jordanian Decapolis that arrived eleven months ahead of the 15 June 2002 departure date. The amazing aspect of this is the future planning and output in his 83rd year of life!

Dr. W. Harold Mare, Professor and Archaeological Director

President of Near East Archaeological Society [1971 to 1992]

Dr. Mare guided the Society effectively and dynamically. He participated with others in the reorganization of the Society. His agendas challenged and directed the Board of Directors very effectively. There was joy of energy and service in equipping him and the others of us for Biblical archaeology. Many shared his vision of historical, literary and archaeological exploration of the Biblical World. Most regarded the co-laboring with Harold an honor and a privilege.

Harold's tenure as Society President saw some of the most vigorous activity I have ever observed in the various professional affiliations I have experienced. A few of the events will illustrate. He called business meetings in New York, Dallas, New Orleans, St. Louis, Atlanta, San Diego, Chicago, San Francisco and Kansas City, Kansas and others at regular scheduled times. He called special executive meetings at odd hours, such as at 6:00 A.M. and 10:00 P.M. These meetings were breakfasts, lunches and dinners with Harold holding forth with business all the while as we ate. Of course, there were "normal" gatherings for the usual conduct of business for which he called and for which there was an agenda. While there was always a pressing sense of urgency about our business, Harold was very fair about allowing every voice to be heard. Business was done and in those areas where our staff functioned well, all moved well. If there was ever any concern about his direction, it usually came from those of us who were doing less than he and who may have felt a modicum of jealousy.

As president of NEAS, the initial quest of Dr. Mare was to establish a field research base for a New Testament city-site. He sought to secure excavation permission and rights to the untouched site of Colossae in western Turkey. This involved scouting out the recognized site near the modern town of Honac and face-to-face meetings with antiquities and government personnel. Our late colleague, Dr. Donald Burdick accompanied Harold in much of the venture.

A number of contacts were made with the Turkish Antiquities Department from whom they sought appropriate government approval. Every possible venue was explored. He solicited support from diplomatic connections, both Turkish and the United States. After several years, his efforts did not yield any fruition for a permit to excavate Colossae in the Lycus Valley near Honac. The author knows of no permission granted to any investigator or investigating institution as of early 2002.

He served as president of the Near East Archaeological Society with an expectancy of promoting activities that could bring back the primary objective of field research that the first President, Dr. Joseph Free (Wheaton), had carried out. The aim of this activity was to restore research legitimacy to this Society. There arose, however, serious discussion about meaningful relationship between the two. Early activity of the Society involved Wheaton and their personnel.

After the death of Dr. Joseph Free, this activity became less prominent. Harold and others strove to revitalize this research and publication activity. The relevance of support to the Society revolved about the meaning of the term "Endorsement," and the implication that this dig was to be the foremost research work of the Society. How would the Board regard other research ventures by Society members, individually

15

or collectively?

NEAS business included discussions about the endorsement of excavations by the society. The conclusion, however, came about that endorsement terminology was not proper inasmuch as other institutions of the Society membership may want such recognition coupled with the hint of any potential support incumbent upon the organization. We settled on a statement of "expedition endorsement," implying only that the society recognizes a worthy research endeavor by bonafide members and their institutions. Publications by members would be received and published as the society's resources allowed.

After a period of some two years, Harold and a selected team of archaeologists planned a site survey of a ruin upon which Gottlieb Schumacher, a German geographer and surveyor, had chanced about 5 km south of the Yarmouk River in the 1880's. He regarded it as probably a Decapolis city-site named Abila.[7] After a field survey of the area in 1980 with the aid of Dr. W. Wilkie Winter and Michael Fuller along with members of Harold's family, it was recognized as a major Graeco-Roman urban center. The Jordanian authorities, unlike their Turkish counterparts, fully embraced Dr. Mare's excavation research design. He was given full permission to make oversight decisions required for a full-fledged field operation. Ultimately, there was no special link between the Society over which Harold Mare was President and the Expedition over which he was Director. Thus, any impropriety was clearly avoided.

The most important matter to emerge from Harold's field activity was the publication of the excavation reports and documents m the Society's Bulletin. The exact function of the Near East Archaeological Society Bulletin had never been fully established m the minds of several Board Members. It has been printed in California, Chicago, Tulsa, Oklahoma, and now, at Andrews University, Berrien Springs, Michigan. Some clarity was tendered by John Wineland (President: 1998-2001) and Dr. Glenn A. Carnagey Sr. as assisted by Glenn Carnagey, Jr. (Journal Editor: 1990-1996 assisted after two major strokes by his son), but now it is in the hands of our colleagues at Berrien Springs (Journal Editor: David Merling) and (Book Review Editor: Paul Ray). It has been revamped and we look for more excellent content with regular timing.

A special aspect of the excavation leadership of Dr. Mare is his strong presence at pottery reading time—4 P.M. on digging days. He has acquired a reading skill ranging from the Late Bronze Age into the Arabic Periods. During several seasons across the twenty-one year operations of the Abila Expedition several pottery experts have been on staff from whom Harold also profited.[8] A keen, perceptive field archaeologist, he immediately recognizes a valuable historical find and expends all the time necessary to see it properly recorded stratigraphically, cleaned, registered, photographed, drawn and published.

In an effort to establish a viable relationship with ASOR[9] and CAP, the Committee on Archaeological Policy, Harold Mare applied to the "judges" of this "guardian" of officially recognized excavations in the Middle East. He was patently disappointed (and discouraged and visibly shaken) as I saw him in our meetings in New Orleans some 20 years ago. Although Harold Mare was wrongly regarded as an ultraconservative Biblical professor, he surely was not in any sense an extremist. His research propriety was duly honest. He did not yield to the rejections of ASOR's CAP (which some regarded as a "Good Ol' Boy" network). He seems not to have been "liberal" enough to be considered capable of carrying on legitimate research like they did. All of this negative energy, however, directed toward Harold was futile.

He made firm and lasting friends of the Jordanian Antiquities authorities who fully accepted his credentials as a first-rank excavator. His work at Hisban in the 1970s had opened the door to their trust of his work in Jordan. He could not understand why his work was not accepted by CAP, and I also observed that, since the Jordanian authorities had approved this research, the decision of CAP would have no effect on his opportunity in that country. Indeed, the Jordanian sanction of Harold's research has continued to this day.[10]

I have listened to a number of complaints about Dr. Mare, mostly from my students whom I have invited to Abila. The complaints usually centered upon Harold's unwillingness to listen to their ideas and suggestions. I discovered that he will listen to petitions and other points of view when offered in a friendly (warm) manner and explained, keeping in mind advantages they would give both to the Director and to the excavation process. I will not deny or cover up those complaints, but I know that understanding the personality of the Director and finding that beneficial "FRAME OF MIND" on the part of both parties DOES YIELD POSITIVE OUT-COMES with Harold Mare. Essentially, his operating mind-set stands unless, like the New Testament widow before the judge (Luke 18:1-5), a persistent plea can lead to a change of his mind. This happened a number of times when he had a little time to think about an issue before coming around to anyone who helps him see that this or that would benefit the expedition.

He exhibited an adequate and fair posture in facing the challenge of the issues of life, work and faith. He was and is fair to other conservatives who have some variation in theology, faith and practice. He came to and participated in dig personnel worship services on Sunday evenings [while courteously refraining from certain activities that were not a part of his personal practice].

Mare's oversight of the operations is, in my mind, a manifestation of his administrative genius. All excavation directions, orders and commands were primarily in his hands. Because of critical budgetary limitations[11] he believed it to be mandatory that he controls every penny of the funds he so enthusiastically raised from those providers who wanted to support the Expedition. His hands were on almost every function and operation of the excavation process.

That frugality was a source of mild humor, from time to time. Remarks were made that Harold purchased and oversaw every roll and the use of bathroom tissue, certainly a function most directors refer to the Camp Manager. We often were unaware of how narrow a survival margin he had on which to exist, and he did so with unbelievable perseverance that is most virtuous.

At times, Dr. Mare exhibits an open joviality, especially at dinner when seated at the head of our long table graced with adequate wholesome foods of which little often remains. I personally enjoyed these times at the dig table. Those moments afforded some very significant personal insights and the occasion to discuss his personal concerns and in what way I might help him in the excavation research enterprise. Harold personally served as the "Dig alarm clock" using various devices to awaken the staff—Biblical verses, usually,—as he walked within earshot of sleepers (but had he had the ability to sound a ram's horn, I have no doubt that would have been employed also). His field vehicle went to the field ahead of the arrival time for the staff that was transported from our lodging and work quarters by bus. It was the same for end-of-dig day rides. He even made two trips at a time for the senior staff. Harold involved himself in every function of the excavation operations, carrying on a vigilant presence at each of the dig foci during every morning's operations.

Care and concern for the elderly and ailing staff was a hallmark of the oversight that W. Harold Mare allowed for himself. Throughout the twenty-one years of my involvement along with that of my students and others on the dig Dr. Mare brought those who became sick to treatment during the season.[12] Hospital runs by automobile for those who needed doctors care were administered by him, even to the extent of going all the way to the hospital at Mafraq[13]. I never saw him in a state of exhaustion.

High interest in the scientific investigations that may accrue to a fuller, more accurate story of the site's history was brought to bear everywhere in the excavation process. Considerable effort was expended by Dr. Mare to secure and assist a scientific staff for the Expedition. He went to exceptional ends to invite scientific and anthropological specialists who could enhance the accomplishments of the whole research picture of Abila and its environment.

Harold accepted the contribution of tomb painting specialists from Wilfrid Laurier University of Waterloo, Ontario, for whom he provided the means to carry on their studies in 1982. This artistic work was published. Entomologist (insect specialist) Marshall Magner and his wife Ernestine joined the team in 1988. Their collection of specimens was large and comprehensive and their research was published in the NEAS Bulletin. Ethno-archaeologist, John Shoup (an associate of Michael Fuller) conducted investigations into the Arabic family and tribal structure of the ethnic profiles residual after the conquest of the Abila urban complex in the 7th Century. The transition of the dynamics of the peoples of the area is most evident in the architectural remains from both anthropologies: the Byzantine demise & the Omayyad beginnings.[14]

Pedologist and Clay Mineralogist, Clarence Meninga, of Calvin College, Michigan, requested permission of me to join our scientific staff in 1992. I regarded his specialty as a fine asset to the profile of scientific workers for the elucidation of clays in Abila history. However, his research has yet to be published. Sadly, and briefly, Clarence disagreed with the common publication standards of the Abila Expedition and other Middle East excavations and withdrew his association from the work.

The writer became a part of the Abila Expedition from the very start as a Cincinnati Bible College and Cincinnati Christian Seminary colleague and proxy to Dr. Wilkie

Winter in 1980 and 1982. I staunchly supported this field research venture because of its potential for being a prominent Graeco-Roman city-site, and one that could add to our understanding of the New Testament and Early Christian (pre-Islamic) world. We were pleased to discover that the site also covers considerable Bronze and Iron Age remains along with Hellenistic deposits. A clear Arabic presence is obvious as well. My contributions focused on the area of Archaeological Geology, and I was assigned the responsibility of the scientific research oversight of our investigations. Dr. Mare has always shown an excitement that was no less than my own when we were doing field traverses and reconnaissance. He literally stood upon precipices nearly 1000 feet above the Yarmuk River in the 2002 field season with the curiosity and fulfillment of any scientist. He was heartily elated when we discovered basaltic lava flows south of the Yarmuk on the level of the upland plateau that presented a proximal source for the black building stones of Abila streets and church buildings.

Throughout the early years of Classical and Near Eastern archaeology in the 19th and 20th Centuries, "treasure hunts" took place for the great museums of Europe and America. Subsequently, as archaeology assumed a more responsible conduct, the primary objectives of stratigraphic excavators centered upon architectural, ceramic and objective finds. Little, if any, attention was given to the sediment composition, sedimentation, the composition of lithics and building stones, metallurgy, hydro-geology, botanical and faunal materials, bedrock stratigraphy and structure, geomorphology and historical geography of site environments. These have been the research goals of this writer since the early 1960s, The generous aid of Dr. Nelson Glueck, President of Hebrew Union College, Cincinnati, Ohio, made possible the doctoral work of the writer at Tell Gezer in Israel. The Core Staff[15] at this site of excavations sought to build their research on the Wheeler-Kenyon method of stratigraphy, which we endeavored to amplify with our work. Associate specialists did innovative advance work with flotation procedures for seeds, grains and very small bones.

Harold Mare of Covenant Seminary also held a vision of the benefits of scientific investigations at both Colossae and Abila from the very beginning of research efforts there. I was enthusiastically invited to be a staff member of the former and then the latter.[16]

A keen, perceptive field archaeologist and historian, Dr. Harold Mare immediately recognized the value of historical finds. These took on for him special significance in their environmental, stratigraphic and geological context. He expended all the time necessary to see them properly recorded stratigraphically, cleaned, registered. photographed, drawn and published. He afforded me all the encouragement any specialist could desire.

The Zeal of Harold Mare for Raising Up Young Scholars

The difficulty of inspiring new and young scholars to consider vocational or even avocational careers in Biblical archaeology is characteristic of our time in the latter part of the 20th Century of research history. Many Christian and Jewish seminary students who came to their institutions for studies preparatory for their respective ministries do not presently seem to show the level of interest in archaeology that I have seen earlier in my career. That historical research zeal is nearly absent, which "called" a Dr. George Ernest Wright, a Dr. Nelson Glueck, a Dr. W. Harold Mare or a Dr. Willard Wilkie Winter [many others[17] could be cited, also]. These scholars viewed, as does the writer, Biblical archaeological research as a healthy and vital support for Biblical history. (By this, I am not saying that these needed Bible backgrounds as a substitute for faith, but rather for its rewarding amplification and illustration of many phases of Biblical history and geography.[18]

A variant of theology distinguishes Covenant Theological Seminary from The Cincinnati Bible College and Seminary,[19] but they are both staunchly conservative Biblically and driven by deep historical commitments to evangelical theological tenets. That variant of theology is meaningful to both Harold and me, nevertheless the "tie that binds" us in our common evangelical Faith is very strong, too. Here, Wilkie Winter (deceased, 1998)[20] and I stood, bound in evangelical ties with Harold and our other evangelical colleagues.

We, and our colleagues in the Near East Archaeological Society (established by Dr. Joseph Free of Wheaton College in 1958 as a union of evangelical scholars), have not, and are not, seeking to verify and sanction our respective sense of Biblical Faith. Many are aware of the position of Dr. William G. Dever who speaks for the elimination of a "Biblical Archaeology" supplanted by a "Syro-Palestinian Archaeological" concept. The recent change of title for the 100-year-old journal, Biblical Archaeologist to Near East Archaeology is a clear illustration of the effect and influence of the liberal mind even in such a prestigious organization as The American Schools of Oriental Research.[21]

I am cognizant of the desire to broaden the focus of the historic publication of ASOR to include "non-Biblical topics", but surely this could have been accomplished without the "disembowelment" of the historic focus of the BA. As an example of the previous breadth of editorial policy of this journal, an article by this writer was accepted entitled, "Geological Studies in Field Archaeology: Tell Gezer, Israel," Biblical Archaeologist, Vol. XXXIII, pp. 97-132, December 1970. There was sufficient latitude in the minds of those who guided its make up to allow for a clearly non-Biblical piece under its "Biblical" banner. Evidence of the change of editorial philosophy of the BA can be seen in an example. Under the title of Near East Archaeology a menu is presented to us that is very similar to that of a publication of the AIA [The Archaeological Institute of America]. This journal appears to have furnished a working model for the trustees of ASOR. It is Archaeology, a long-standing journal (primarily a secular publication) of the AIA. This seems to be a patent move and valid witness to a parallel trend among liberal scholars for "sanitizing" Biblical names and titles from their studies.

Postlude
This discussion is written in celebration of a beloved colleague. I requested that

the photograph of Dr. Mare be included in this Festschrift work because it was unveiled on the 9th of November 2001 at Rayburn Chapel, Covenant Theological Seminary, as a tribute to our celebrant. The occasion was highlighted by two presentations by our NEAS Board member, Dr. Mark W. Chavalas, University of Wisconsin, La Crosse. The vitality to be seen in this photograph has scarcely lessened since I was first introduced to Harold in the early 1970's. Our co-labors have yielded many blessings, not only for us but for our students and institutions as well. This labor of appreciation and honor has given the author many hours of deep pleasure and satisfaction.

Publications

After the completion of his doctoral dissertation, "The Greek Bomos" [altar] in classical Greek Literature," Harold Mare published a large number of articles across the productive years of his life. The focus of his writing has been on New Testament Greek, taught from a Classical Attic perspective.[22] From 1964 to the present (into 2002) he has also written profusely in Biblical and archaeological research. This has been especially about discoveries made by members of the expedition at Abila, a testimony to his desire to set before his peers the product of student and colleague labors. Dr. Mare's creativity and activities and mind have come alive in word and print, and in many ways "ad Gloria Deum".

Curriculum Vita
A partial list of the publication activity of W. Harod Mare

Ph. D. Dissertation (University of Pennsylvania): *A Study of the Greek Bomos [Altar] in Classical Greek Literature.*

Books:
1. I Corinthians notes in the *NIV Study Bible, New International Version* (Grand Rapids: Zondervan, 1985).
2. *The Archaeology of the Jerusalem Area* (Grand Rapids: Baker, 1987).
3. I Corinthians, Zondervan Study Bible, K. L. Barker and J. Kohlenbaker eds. (Nashville: Thomas Nelson, 1994).
4. I Corinthians, *Expositor's Bible Commentary* (Grand Rapids: Zondervan, 1995).
5. Study Notes on the *New Geneva Study Bible*
6. Co-translator with Wilbur B. Wallis of the Book of Acts for the International Version of the Bible, and member of the Intermediate Editorial Team of the New International Version of the Bible
7. *Mastering New Testament Greek* (Grand Rapids: Baker Book House, 1979; Eugene, Oregon: Wipf and Stock, 2000.
8. *Backgrounds of the Bible, Matthew through Revelation* (Fearn, Tain; Scotland: Christian Focus Publications, Ltd., 2003).

Beyond the Jordan

Among the numerous articles:

A. Numbers of articles published in:
1. *The Anchor Bible Dictionary,* D. W. Freedman, ed. (New York: Doubleday, 1992), "Abila," and a number of articles on Jerusalem.
2. *Annual of the Department of Antiquities of Jordan* (Amman, Jordan: Department of Antiquities):
    a. "Background and Analytical Description of Abila of the Decapolis and the Methodology Used in the 1980 Survey," *ADAJ,* 1982.
    b. "Abila of the Decapolis 1982 Excavation and Regional Survey," *ADAJ,* 1983.
    c. "The 1984 Season at Abila of the Decapolis," *ADAJ,* 1986.
    d. "The 1986 Season at Abila of the Decapolis," *ADAJ,* 1988.
    e. "The 1988 Season at Abila of the Decapolis," *ADAJ,* 1991.
    f. "The 1990 Season at Abila of the Decapolis," *ADAJ,* 1992.
    g. "The 1992 Season at Abila of the Decapolis," *ADAJ,* 1995.
    h. "The Marble Statue of the Greek Huntress Artemis," 1997.
    i. "The 1996 Season at Abila of the Decapolis," *ADAJ,* 1998.
    j. "The 1997 Qualibah/Abila of the Decapolis," *ADAJ,* 1998
3. *Eerdman's Dictionary of the Bible,* D. N. Freedman, ed. (Grand Rapids: Eerdmans, 2000). Articles on "Decapolis" and various cities of the Decapolis: "Abila," "Gadara," "Gerasa," "Hippos," "Pella," and "Scythopolis."
4. *The Grace Journal* (Winona Lake, IN: Grace Seminary).
    a. "The Smallest Mustard Seed—Matthew 13:32," GJ, Vol. 9, No. 3, Fall, 1968.
    b. "The Greek Altar in the New Testament and Inter-Testament Periods," *GJ,* Vol. 10, No. 1, Winter, 1969.
    c. "Teacher and Rabbi in the New Testament Period," *GJ,* Vol. 11, No. 3, Fall, 1970.
    d. "The New Testament Concept Regarding the Regions of Heaven with Emphasis on 2 Corinthians 12:1-4," *GJ,* Vol. No. 2, Winter, 1970.
    e. "The Holy Spirit in the Apostolic Fathers," *GJ,*Vol. 13, No. 2, Spring, 1972.
    f. "Guiding Principles for Historical Grammatical Exegesis," *GJ,* Vol. 14, No. 3, Fall, 1973.
5. *The International Standard Bible Encyclopedia,* revised, G. W. Bromily, et al. eds., vol. 1 (Grand Rapids: Eerdmans, 1979), Contributor.
6. *Journal of the Evangelical Theological Society*
    a. "Paul's Mystery in Ephesians 3," *JETS,* vol. 8, no. 2, Spring, 1965.
    b. "Prophet and Teacher in New Testament Period," *JETS,* Summer, 1966.
    c. "Pauline Appeals to Historical Evidence," *JETS,* Summer, 1
    d. "Church Functionaries: The Witness in the Literature and Archaeology of the New Testament and Church Periods," *JETS,* Vol.13, Part 4, Fall, 1970.

    e.   "The Role of the Note-Taking Historian and His Emphasis on the Person and Word of Christ," *JETS*, Vol. 15, Part 2, Spring, 1972.

    f.   "The Cultural Mandate and the New Testament Gospel Imperative," *JETS*, Vol. 16, No. 3, Summer, 1973

    g.   Book Review of E. M. Meyers and J. F. Strange. *Archaeology: the Rabbis and Early Archaeology* (Nashville: Abingdon, 1981) for *JETS*, Vol 25, No., 1, March 1982

    h.   Book Review of J. A. Thompson, *The Bible and Archeology*, 3rd ed. (Grand Rapids: Eerdmans, 1982), *JETS*, Vol. 26, No. 2, June, 1983.

    i.   Book Review of E. M. Blaiklock and R. K. Harrison, eds. *The New International Dictionary of Biblical Archaeology* (Grand Rapids: Zondervan for *JETS*, vol. 28. no. 4, winter, 1985.

    j.   Book Review of *Major Cities of the Biblical World*, R. K. Harrison, ed. (Nashville: Thomas Nelson, 1985) for *JETS*, Vol. 29, no. 4, December 1986.

7.   *The Near East Archaeological Society Bulletin*

    a.   "Geographical Locations in the Jerusalem Area in the Time of Christ," *Near Eastern Archaeology* (Bulletin of the Near East Archaeological Society), Vol. 7, Nos. 2,3,4, Summer-Winter, 1964.

    b.   "Archaeology and Literary Evidence Regarding Building Remains and Worship in the Early Church, *NEASB*, New Series, No. 1, 1971.

    c.   "The Problem of the Three Walls of Jerusalem," *NEASB*, New Series, no. 3, 1973.

    d.   "More Selected Bibliography of Current Archaeological Books," *NEASB*, New Series, No. 2, Fall, 1973.

    e.   "The 1974 Excavation at Tell Heshbon and Its Bearing of the Date of the Exodus," *NEASB*, 1975.

    f.   "More Selected Bibliography of Current Archaeological Books," *NEASB*, No. 4, January 1973.

    g.   Book Review on Harry Thomas Frank, *Bible, Archaeology, and Faith* (Nashville: Abingdon) for *NEASB*, Fall, 1975.

    h.   "Archaeological Prospects at Colossae." paper given at the Evangelical Theological Society, Dec., 1975, published in *NEASB*, Spring, 1976.

    i.   "Selected Bibliography of Archaeological Books," *NEASB*, August, 1977.

    j.   "The 1980 Survey of Abila of the Decapolis: Background Survey Techniques, Ce ramic Analysis, Archaeological History and Architectural Features," (coauthor), *NEASB*, New Series, nos. 17-18, 1981

    k. "The Abila Excavation: The Second Campaign at Abila of the Decapolis (1982), Director's Report," *NEASB*, New Series, No. 21, Spring, 1983.

    l. "The Abila Excavation. The Third Campaign at Abila of the Decapolis (1982), Director's Report," Analysis of Coins, 1984 (coauthor), *NEASB*, New Series, No. 24, Winter, 1985.

m. The 1986 Abila of the Decapolis Excavation: Director's Report," *NEASB,* New Series, No. 2, Winter, 1988.

n. "Coins from the l986 Excavation at Abila of the Decapolis," (coauthor), *NEASB,* New Series 30, Winter, 1988.

o. "l988 Abila of the Decapolis Excavation: Director's Report," *NEASB,* New Series 31, Summer 1988.

p. "Coins from the 1988 Excavation at Abila of the Decapolis," (coauthor), *NEASB,* nos. 32-33, Winter, 1989.

q. "The Sixth Campaign at Abila of the Decapolis: The Abila Excavation— The Director's Preliminary Report," *NEASB,* New Series, No. 34, Spring, 1990 (published 1991).

r. "Coins" from the 1990 Excavation at Abila of the Decapolis," (coauthor), *NEASB,* New Series, No. 35, Fall, 1990 (published Fall, 1991).

s. "The Abila Excavation: The 1992 Seventh Campaign of the Abila of the Decapolis, the Director's Report," *NEASB,* New Series 37, Fall, 1992.

t. "The 1994 Abila Excavations at Abila of the Decapolis - The Director's Preliminary Report on the Eighth Campaign," *NEASB,* No. 39-40, 1995.

u. "Abila of the Decapolis: Ninth Season of Excavation: 1995 Special Under ground Aqueduct Excavation," *NEASB,* New Series, No. 41, 1996.

v. "1994 Abila Coin Report," (coauthor) *NEASB,* New Series 41, 1996.

w. "Coins from the 1995 Excavation at Abila of the Decapolis," (coauthor), *NEASB,* New Series, No. 41, 1996.

x. "The l996 Season of Excavation at Abila of the Decapolis," (coauthor) *NEASB,* Vol. 42, 1997.

y. "Restoration of the Area E Cruciform Church at Abila of the Decapolis," (coauthor), *NEASB,* Vol. 42, 1997.

z. "Restoration of the Area E Cruciform Church at Abila," *NEASB,* vol. 44, 1999.

8. *The New International Dictionary of Biblical Archaeology* (Grand Rapids:Regency, Zondervan, 1983). "Abila", "Jerusalem, New Testament," "Mount of Olives." and a number of other articles.

9. *Studies in the History and Archaeology of Jordan* (Amman, Jordan: Department of Antiquities).

a. "Internal Settlement Patterns in Abila." *SHAJ,* IV, 1992.

b. "The Technology of the Hydrological System at Abila of the Decapolis." *SHAJ,* V, 1992.

c. "Abila of the Decapolis in the Roman Period: A Time of Revitalization and Expansion," *SHAJ,* VII, 2001.

10. *Wycliffe Bible Encyclopedia,* CF. Pfeiffer, H.E. Vos, and J. Rea, eds. (Chicago: Moody Press, 1975), Contributor "Weights, Measures, and Coins," "Travel and Communication," "Tempt, Temptation," "Tribe," and a number of other articles.

Dr. W. Harold Mare, Professor and Archaeological Director

11. *The Zondervan Pictorial Encyclopedia of the Bible,* 5 vols. (Grand Rapids, Zondevan, 1975). "Cosmogony," "Dress," "Eye Paint" and 42 other articles.

B. Also articles in:
1. *Akkadica, Archaeology of Jordan, II* (Brussels, Belgium, Musees Royaux d'art et d'histoire, 1989, "Field Report on Qailibah/Abila of the Decapolis."
2. *American Journal of Archaeology,* Archaeological Newsletter
   a. "The Underground Aqueducts at Abila of the Decapolis," *AJA,* Archaeological Newsletter, April 1992.
   b. "Report on the 1992 Abila of the Decapolis Excavation," *AJA,* Archaeological Newsletter, April 1993.
   c. "Report on the 1994 Abila of the Decapolis Excavation," *AJA,* Archaeological Newsletter, April 1995.
3. *Andrews University Seminary Series.*
   a. Analytical report on 1974 excavation of Area C of Area C of the 1974 Hesh bon, Jordan, Archaeological Expedition, Summer, 1974, *AUWW,* Vol. XIV, No. 1, Spring 1976, pp. 63-78.
   b. Analytical Report on 1976 excavation of Area C of the 1976 Heshbon, Jordan, Archaeological Expedition, Summer, 1976, *AUSS,* Winter, Vol. XVI, No.1, 1978.
4. *Annual Bulletin on the Archaeology of Jordan, Liber Annuus* (Jerusalem:Studium Biblicum Franciscum).
   a. "The 1982 Abila Excavation and Regional Survey," *LA,* 1983.
   b. "The 1984 Season of Excavation at Abila of the Decapolis, Quailibah, Northern Jordan," *LA,* 1985.
   c. "The 1990 Season of Excavation at Abila of the Decapolis," *LA,* 1990.
5. *Antike Welt* (Berlin, Germany) (Printed by Philipp Von Zabern,MainzamRhein), 2002, "Abila of the Decapolis."
6. *ARAM* periodical
   a. "Abila: A Thriving Greco-Roman City of the Decapolis," *ARAM* Vol. 4, (Ox ford: University of Oxford), 1993.
   b. "The Christian Church of Abila of the Decapolis of the Yarmouk Valley System in the Umayyid Period," *ARAM* Vol. 5, 1994.
   c. Abila and Palmyra: Ancient Trade and Trade Routes from Southern Syria into Mesopotamia, *ARAM,* Vol. 7, 1995.
7. *Archiv fur Orientforschung* (Tubingen, 1986). "Abila of the Decapolis."
8. *Artifax.* "The 1999 Excavation and Restoration of the Abila 6th Century Cruciform Cathedral."
9. *Bible and Spade,* Spring, 1974. "The Walls of Jerusalem and the Place of the Crucifixion and Burial of Jesus."
10. *Bible Press* "The Grace of God," June 13, 1965.
11. *Biblical Archaeologist*
    a. "1980 Survey of the Decapolis," *BA,* 45, Summer, 1981, pp. 179-180.

b.   "Tomb Finds at Abila of the Decapolis," *BA,* Winter, 1981.

12. *Biblical History* (Empire Press).

   a.   Book Review on G. I. Davies, Megiddo in the Cities of the Biblical World (Lutterworth Press, 1986) *BH,* Vol. 1, No. 4, December 1987.

13. a.   Book Review on F. F. Bruce, *New Testament History* (New York:Doubleday, 1971), *Christianity Today,* Vol. 15 August 27, 1971

   b.   Book Review of Peter Toon, *Jesus Christ is Lord* (Judson Press, 1979), *CT,* Vol. 25, No. 1, January 2,1981.

14. *Current Issues in Biblical and Patristic Interpretation: Studies in Honor of Merrill C. Tenney,* Gerald Hawthorne, ed. (Grand Rapids: Eerdmans, 1975). "A Study of the New Testament Concept of the Parousia."

15. *The Gospels Today: A Guide to Some Recent Developments,* J. H. Skilton,ed. (Philadelphia: Skilton House Publishers: The Sowers, 1990). "Genre Criticism and the Gospels."

16. *Holman Bible Handbook,* J. S. Dockery, ed. (Nashville: Holman BiblePublishers), 1992). "Biblical Archaeology."

17. *Interpretation and History: Essays in Honour of Allan A. MacRae,* R. L.Harris, ed. (Singapore: Christian Life Publishers, 1986). "The Work Ethic of the Gospel and Acts."

18. *Journal of Roman Archaeology,* Vol. 10,1997. A Roman Tomb at Abila of the Decapolis," (coauthor with Robert W. Smith).

19. *National Missions Reporter* (Bible Presbyterian Church)

   a.   "God and Country," *NMR,* Vol. 6, No. 2, February, 1953.

   b.   "How Love I Thy Law!", Vol. 6, No. 8, October, 1953.

20. *New Dimensions in New Testament Study,* R. N. Longenecker and M. C. Tenney, eds. (Grand Rapids: Zondervan, 1974) "The Pauline Work Ethic."

21. *The New Encyclopedia of Archaeological Excavations in the Holy Land,* E. Stern, ed. (Jerusalem: Israel Exploration Society, Simon and Shuster, 1992). "Abila"

22. *The Oxford Encyclopedia of Archaeology in the Near East,* E. M. Meyers,ed. (New York: Oxford University Press, 1997). "Abila"

23. *The Presbyterian Journal*

   a.   "Turn the Other Cheek?" *PJ,* Vol. XXVIII, No. 9, July 2, 1969.

   b.   "Excavations Confirm Early Church in the Decapolis, *PJ,* Vol XLI, No. 21, September 22, 1982.

   c.   Book Review of E. M. Blaiklock, The Archaeology of the New Testament (Nashville, Thomas Nelson, 1984) for *Presbyterian Journal,* 1985.

24. Presbyterian: Covenant Seminary Review

   a.   Book Review of J. Massyngberde Ford, *Revelation, Anchor Bible* (New York: Doubleday, 1975).

   b.   "Buswell as Educator, Vol. II, Nos. 1-2, 1076.

   c.   "The Christian and His Material Possessions (Part I)," *Presbyterion,* Vol. V, No. 1, Spring 1979.

d. "The Christian and His Material Possessions (Part II)," *Presbyterion,* No. 2, Fall 1979.
e. Book Review of D. F. Wells, *The Person of Christ* (Westchester, IL: Crossway Books, 1984.
f. Book Review of H. W. House and T. Ice, *Dominion Theology: Blessing or Curse? (An Analysis of Christian Reconstructionism)* Portland, Oregon: Multnomah Press, 1988).
25. *The Reformed Presbyterian Reporter,* (Reformed Presbyterian Church, EvangelicalSynod), Contributor.
26. *Review Biblique*
    a. "The Abila of the Decapolis Excavation and Regional Survey," *RB,* 1983.
    b. "The 1986 Abila of the Decapolis Excavation," *RB.*
    c. Article of the 1900 excavation at Abila of the Decapolis, *RB.*
27. *Salt* (Covenant Seminary Student Theological Journal)
    a. "The Heart of Christmas," *Salt,* Vol. 3, Issue 3, December, 1972.
    b. "The Wise Men, the Star and Jesus," *Salt,* Vol. 5, Issue 3, December, 1974.
28. *Syria,* LXX, 1993, Fascicles 1-2 (Librairie Orientaliste) "Abila of the Decapolis Excavations," *Syria,* LXX, 1993.
29. *The Westminster Theological Journal*
    a. "Acts 7: Jewish or Samaritan in Character?" *WTJ,* Vol. XXXIV, No. 1, November 1971, pp. 1-21.
    b. " The Meaningful Language of the New Testament," *WTJ,* Vol. XXXVII, No. 1, Fall 1974, pp. 95-105.
    c. Book Review of G. Cornfeld and D. N. Freedman, Consulting Editor, Archaeology and the Bible: Book by Book (San Francisco: Harper and Row, 1976) for *WTJ,* Vol. XLVI, No. 1, Spring, 1984.

Postlude

The measure of a scholar's work is the impact he/she has had on the lives of others. The positive affirmations I have received about Harold from his students and colleagues are numerous across the times I have been received at Covenant Seminary and at Abila.

This discussion is written in celebration of a beloved colleague. Our co-labors have yielded many blessings, not only for us but for our students and institutions as well. This labor of appreciation and honor has given the author many hours of deep pleasure and satisfaction.

The special personality of Dr. W. Harold Mare will always hold a unique place in the minds and hearts of all of us who have known and worked with him. He is not a casual and lightly motivated man, but rather he attacks with all his mental, physical and spiritual constitution those issues and actions that are vital to him. I will confess that, for Wilkie Winter and me, the last 20 years of his life and mine would have been

27

very different for us without Harold Mare. The lives of our students who caught the thrill of Biblical field exploration have been deeply affected, even redirected, by their experiences in the expeditions Harold conducted.

I have found a further, deeper fulfillment in my research quest to study, analyze and apply the relationship of material and natural science to the environment of a city-site, such as is Abila, made possible by the field research discovery of Dr. W. Harold Mare. The people of antiquity lived closer than we to the material necessities of their lives: clays for writing and for seals, for mud bricks and mortar and for roofs. Clays, in antiquity, were the material of the near universal packaging medium, and the substance of most lamp making. Moreover, Abila gave us special appreciation for the architecture and masonry of Roman and Byzantine times. Even that worship service that John Wineland conducted in the partially restored structure of our Area "D" Umm el Amad basilica during our 1988 season gave us a momentary connection with the early Christians who also worshiped there.

I could then appreciate the laborious quarrying and transportation and erection of the basalt and limestones of the columns of that church. The amazingly beautiful mottled *opus sectile* and the unique mosaic floorings of the church and the adjoining buildings saw the light of day again (excavated by my son, Rick and daughter, Cathy, and others who were invited by Harold and supervised by Wilkie[23]). Identification and research of all the provenance of these lithics gave me a new chapter in my archaeological geological career and publications.

Three visits of Dr. Harold Mare to the campus of CBC&S in Cincinnati were each memorable occasions. We brought him here to speak about his research and to be our honored guest in our Abila Expositions in the 1980s and '90s with special sessions in Foster Hall and exhibits in the George Mark Elliot Library. Two of the school's chapel sessions across these decades featured Decapolis archaeology and its historical witness.

On behalf of all ten field research staffs of the Abila Expeditions across the past 20 years, we say, "Thank you very, very much, Dr. Mare, our greatly special Mudir." You have been a notable inspiration on the horizon of our lives!

NOTES

[1] In the summer of 1970, I was invited by Dr. Siegfried Horn to research and write about the archaeological geology of the area of Heshbon [Hisbon] south of Madaba in Jordan. Before we could leave for the field, the Amman 6th Circle house rented by ASOR (American Schools of Oriental Research in Jordan) as its research headquarters, we came under fire [the building was hit several times.] by the Palestinians who were gathering hostages in their assault on King Hussein's regime. After being under house arrest for 7 days by them, the American Red Cross negotiated our liberation, flying us out of Amman to Beirut and then to Athens. My wife was called by the American Embassy that reported our safety from there. [The research carried out in 1971 was reported as the "Geological Study of the Heshbon Area, Jordan," *Andrews University Seminary Studies,* Vol. X, July, 1972, No. 2,

[2] This terminology was the corporate name for these two divisions of the Institution. The

undergraduate level was renamed as the Cincinnati Christian Seminary in 1973. The school name became the Cincinnati Bible College & Seminary in 1987.

[3] In 1998 The CBC&S consortium contract with the Abila Expedition was terminated by the Administration, probably on account of the death of Dr. Winter. Although I deeply regretted this termination, there was no reconsideration, and I offered this consortial window to the Religious Studies Program where it was received with favor at the $5000 participation level.

[4] Our students and alumni have been engaged in archaeological research in Israel, Jordan, Egypt, Cyprus, Turkey, Greece, Italy and Carthage (Tunisia).

[5] See my "Report on the History of the Archaeological Activity of the Cincinnati Bible College and Seminary" in preparation.

[6] Here, a large table held the pottery excavated the previous day where it was "read" for identification by the type and its period of history. The ceramic material is designated by the archaeological time frame that has an equivalent historical time range. [Other venues of dating are coins (after 600 B.C.) seals, metallic compositions, inscriptions and other written remains (aside from radio-metrics).]

[7] I had completed a consulting assignment that had taken me out of Jordan for more than a week in 1984. Upon my return, John Wineland asked me to examine a limestone fragment having one side with writing on its flat surface. Its Greek uncials viewed with a flashlight at night spelled out "ABILA" among other unclear words.

[8] Certain invited experts [Ms. Lenson and others] worked on the discovered materials, but there arose issues of control of the excavation process. This left Dr. Mare discouraged for a short time as he refused to yield the direction of the project to which he had dedicated his life and his institution.

[9] ASOR has been a liaison among a number of institutions with certain faculty that has been interested principally in the archaeology of Bible Lands for over 100 years. The honored aegis of historically (and scientifically) valid field research has held its banner high until a recent embrace of the broader field of general anthropological archaeology.

[10] Many of us regarded CAP's decision about Dr. Mare's Archaeological research in Jordan to be influenced by his open espousal of conservative Biblical views and, in their minds, historically unreliable ones. Those associated with him all through the years recognize his staunch devotion to full objectivity in his work, even if counter to his personal preferences. [I, personally, have co-labored and consulted with most of the CAP members of that time, and I held them in high regard, professionally. I was disappointed in their action.]

[11] The Abila Expedition never had NEH, NSF or endowed institutional funding. Peer review would encounter resistance by those who regarded Harold Mare's conservative frame of mind as unscientific and perhaps not fully responsible to interpretive objectivity. This was fully coun-ter to the personality and *modus operandi* of Dr. Mare. He based his research on that which was discovered and not on any personal bias or religious skewing of his material. That is not to say he did not want to have finds that would reinforce his hopes for historically correlative cultural dates. I have never seen or heard of a single incident of factual deception in connection with any stratigraphic context or in-situ artifact. [Permit me the liberty of affirming that I have witnessed various levels of deception on the part of certain Biblically liberal directors (who shall remain unnamed) through 34 years of my relations with them].

[12] Laura Ward, Ada Braun, Roger Noble, and Mark ("Cap") Damaron, were among the students from my institutions, the UC and CBC&S, who received special care. There have been others such as Dr. Harold Stigers and Dr. (M.D.) Robert Kyle who fell during their fieldwork activities and were properly attended.

[13] The Mafraq humanitarian (mission) hospital is a wonderful oasis "in the desert." Dr. and Mrs. Mare "recover" physically, mentally, and spiritually here on the weekends. The staff may find rest or additional research opportunities at the Expedition headquarters [This has given me an opportunity to exercise my cooking skills, too!] The option of touring sites and visiting museums is also a viable learning activity.

[14] Could this be a form of that which today is called "ethnic cleansing"?

[15] Dr. William Dever, Dr. Darrell Lance, Anita Furshpan Walker, Dr. Dan Cole, Dr. John Holliday, Dr. Lawrence Stager, Dr. Seymore Gitin, Drs. Eric and Carol Myers, Dr. Randy Osborne, Dr. John Worrell and others.

[16] Early in the author's work with excavations, he was invited to do consulting analytical work on a number of sites in Israel, Jordan, Cyprus, Tunisia (Carthage), Italy and Greece. These analytical procedures involved an understanding of material culture, human and natural agents of activity and processes that yield the structural residues in ancient sites. The writer's work has ranged from a single villa to a temple and the large urban complexes of Carthage, Curium (Cy-prus) and Abila.

[17] Dr. Sara Fudge and Mark Ziese of CBC&S deserve exceptional mention here.

[18] Discussion of the activities of "Biblical Archaeologists" in the early days of their research, say, from Sir Flinders Petrie through the first half of the 20th Century to those scholars who followed Nelson Glueck and George Ernest Wright has focused on an invalid charge by certain liberals who followed them. The allegation by some of their students that these earlier workers were driven by a strong desire to prove the Bible and as such, their efforts were and are flawed, is a misjudgment of their research intentions. This writer finds such contentions of these younger scholars (who attain their livelihood from institutions that were established historically on programs based upon a traditional conservative belief) unfair and irresponsible. The attacks I have seen, heard and read upon their former teachers and scholars who devoted their lives to understanding the "world of the Bible" is a sad commentary on some modern educational traditions. One must view his study and research on the basis of where he is in the time-stream of knowledge and understanding. Indeed, we stand on the shoulders of those who precede us and value their contribution to our own intellectual journey in life.

[19] The Cincinnati Bible College & Seminary is an institution established in 1924 by men and women who were watching liberal and "modernistic-minded" individuals move into prominent positions of power and influence in colleges and seminaries supported by Church of Christ, Christian Church and Disciples of Christ congregations across the land. The divisive issues centered upon matters of inspiration and the viability of the Bible, of the reality of miracles and even the historicity and deity of Christ. As a consequence there arose a number of Bible colleges and graduate schools (seminaries), the constitutions of which upheld those conditions of Faith that sustained the "catholic Christian church" from the days of the Apostles. Indeed, "Here I stand"!

[20] See my forthcoming Biography of Dr. Willard Wilkie Winter.

Dr. W. Harold Mare, Professor and Archaeological Director

[21] My postgraduate and post-doctoral career was closely associated with both Dr. Glueck and Dr. Wright, both of whom invited me to conduct scientific consultations about Tell el Kaleifah and Tell Gezer, Shechem (Tell Balatah) and Idalion. I value their wisdom and Biblical posture that I experienced on numerous occasions. I regard them as giants of their respective Faiths and beliefs. [Later note on this discussion—Our own vision should be solid enough to appreciate the different virtues that each of us holds dear. I affirm that after 9/11/2001 violent terrorist attacks took place upon our society and country where both Jews and Christians live in peace and harmony (I have been the recipient of support through years of research in Israel from Hebrew Union College/Jewish Institute of Religion in Cincinnati and New York.)]

[22] This was the method of instruction employed by Professor Rupert C. Foster of Cincinnati Bible Seminary, also. He regarded this language tool to be the best historical basis and most easily refocused in the Hellenistic Koine structure of New Testament Greek.

[23] Elsewhere, Dr. Robert Smith, mentioned above, first supervised the digging in the eastern part of Area A. Howard Bullard excavated the first tabun oven in these deposits where, yet later on, this area was turned over to Dr. Glenn Carnagey along with Susan Lopez as assistant area director, and later on full Area Director where EBI, EBII, EBIII, and EBIV were found - the only site in all of Jordan or Israel to have such a complete spectrum of Early Bronze ceramic remains. This area came to be designated as Area AA. John Wineland found his basilica in Area A, east of the EB remains to the west. Dr. Wineland did a superb job of excavating, defining and publishing this great basilica of Area A. At the bottom of his excavation in the apse of the church, more levels of EB pottery were found, which have yet to be placed into the order of Early Bronze pottery at Abila. But this will have to wait until further excavation and examination of the pottery. The robbing of architectural members of this notable church has seriously affected its restoration. We may accomplish the "resurrection" of this structure only through artistic painting.

31

Not Just a Building, It's a Monument

An address celebrating the dedication of Covenant Seminary's new building, 'The W. Harold Mare Institute for Biblical and Archaeological Studies' on Oct. 23, 1999.
John J. Davis, Th.D., D.D.
Professor of Hebrew and Old Testament
Grace Theological Seminary
Winona Lake, IN 46590

I am honored and delighted to be part of this very special occasion that brings us together. I have known Dr. Mare for more than 35 years and have worked with him on various archaeological projects. He is a man of intellectual skill, moral integrity, focused tenacity and biblical godliness, the latter being the most significant. I congratulate Covenant Theological Seminary for its sense of vision and commitment to serious biblical disciplines for making this building a reality. In the few moments I have with you, I want to focus on the fact that what stands here is not just a building, but a monument.

1. It, Like All the Buildings On This Campus, Is a Monument of the Grace and Glory of God.

Every building on this campus contributes to the theological education of its students, each in its special way. This building will be no exception. I have always been intrigued with the fact that the Old Testament Tabernacle was called a a "Tent of Meeting." It was where the Hebrews met their god in worship, confession and dedication. It was the place where His special presence was represented by Shekinah glory. While the chapel on this campus is where students and faculty will meet God in worship, the W. Harold Mare Institute for Biblical and Archaeological Studies is where they will come for Biblical and Archaeological Studies and where they will meet him through the facts of history. And those facts are not mere casual or incidental footnotes to our faith, but are at the very foundations of our Christian heritage.

2. This Building is a Monument to Dr. Harold Mare.

Over the years, Dr. Mare has distinguished himself as a competent scholar, skilled archaeologist, and a spiritual father to men and women in Christian ministries around the world. He is an accomplished author whose works in New Testament related studies has had a significant impact on young scholars as well as those of us whose hair is gray or missing. Those in the latter category should not despair, remembering that God does not marble tops on cheap furniture.

His tireless efforts in excavating Abila for eleven successful seasons will surely be noted in the annals of Jordanian archaeology as one of the outstanding achievements of this century. The information gained from this site is significant for its scope —— Early Bronze Age through, and beyond, the Byzantine period —— and its depth. Important light is being shed on New Testament times and culture in northern Jordan. The discovery of five churches at the site is remarkable, indeed.

This has all become archaeological reality because of the determination by Dr. Mare to get the job done. His energy in this regard is boundless. I can recall well when discovering an unrobbed Early Roman tomb with a very significant assemblage of artifactual material and bones, I had serious concerns about the security of this remote site. Dr. Mare's solution was that "We will work around the clock until the tomb is completely and carefully excavated." He joined us working throughout the night to see that happen.

This marvelous building, then, is a Monument to the Grace and Glory of God. Second, it is a monument to the archaeological achievements of Dr. Harold Mare. Now finally, I want to suggest that ——

3. It is a Monument to the Historical Foudations of Our Christian Faith.

There are some theologians who have suggested that it doesn't really matter whether the history of the Bible is real or accurate, it is the existential encounter with the lofty sentiments of the text that lead us to ultimate moral ideals that really count.

Such suggestions are clearly out of touch with what the prophets and apostles had to say. Virtually all sermons recorded in the Old Testament are based on historical assumptions of reality. For example, when Joshua spoke to Israel at Shechem near the end of his life, as recorded in Joshua 24, he assumed the historic realities of Abraham's special call, the blessing of his children, the deliverance of the Israelites from Egypt and their victories in Canaan. After reminding the Hebrews of these events, he challenged them to "...fear the LORD and serve Him in sincerity and truth, and put away the gods which your fathers served beyond the river and in Egypt and serve the Lord." If these events were but randomly collected myths, the spiritual challenge would hardly have had any power or impact.

The apostle Paul, takes a similar view of historical facts in his admonitions of I Cor. 10: 11-12 which read, "Now these things happened to them as an example and they were written for our instruction upon whom the end of the ages have come. Therefore, let him who thinks he stands take heed lest he fall."

The "these things' of which Paul spoke included the exodus from Egypt and subsequent wilderness journey (vv. 1-10). It is very important to note that Paul says that "these things happened to them." They are historic realities upon which our faith and spiritual deportment are based.

It seems that the Apostle Paul almost anticipated modern anti-historical and existential notions when he suggested in I Cor. 15 that if the resurrection of Jesus was not an actual historical, geographical, and biological event, we have no theology and, as a matter of fact, our "faith is vain and we are still in our sins" (I Cor, 15:17). God's self-disclosure took place in and through historical events. They are, therefore, critically important to a reasonable faith.

Someone has said, if one does not know the facts, argument is to no avail, and if one does know the facts, argument is unnecessary. The epigram might be too general, but one thing is clear and that is that facts are indispensable to justify belief (Zaharias 1990: 1). They are essential in understanding the revelatory and redemptive processes in Scripture.

Archaeological enterprise at its best discovers and interprets facts, organizes them into meaningful information that ultimately leads us to truth. Truth, as I understand it, is correspondence to reality. Scripture is a quality of a proposition or a propositional correspondence to reality.

Education, when functioning at its best, should be the pursuit of truth. It's what our world desires and needs.

Remember the probing question of Pilate, "What is truth?" (John 8:38). Our generation struggles with that question and has erroneously concluded that all truth is relative and changing, or that sincerity is as important as truth.

I'm glad my doctor does not subscribe to the latter sentiment. When my physician pre-scribes medicine, I expect him to be right, not just sincere!

Then there are the avant-garde progressive student bodies whose progressive student bodies roam through the smoldering ruins of the administration buildings and sing joyfully,

> Mine eyes have seen the glory of the
> > burning of the schools,
> We are torturing the teachers,
> > And breaking all the rules.
> We broke into the field house
> > and smashed the swimming pools.
> Our truth goes marching on.

Archaeology is a delicate process of both discovery and destruction that must be carried out with thoughtful discipline. The archaeologist cannot re-work his experiment as the natural scientist can. Since artifactual and structural materials are being removed, the digging must be conducted with stratigraphic discipline, careful observation and accurate recording.

The goal of all of this is not just to prove the historical reliability of recorded events in the Bible (although it has done that), but to accurately reconstruct the world of the Bible. So the larger contribution of archaeology is therefore, in hermeneutics rather than apologetics. There are, after all, considerable limitations to empirical evidence of this type.

It is fascinating to look back over the past century of archaeological exploration and see its early brutal and often embarrassing attempts at artifactual recovery.

Who can forget the fact that Giovanni Battista Belzoni used palm trees as battering rams to open an Egyptian tomb? Then he states, "Every step I took I crushed a mummy in some part or other" (Ceram 1966: 141). In one early European report it was noted that "where necessary, the dolmens were blasted, the circles of stones removed . . . (Wheeler 1954: 113).

Today, the situation is dramatically different. Field archaeology is a multi-discipline enterprise. Photographers, ceramacists, architects, entomologists, numismatists, paleo-botanists and zoologists, osteologists, paleographers, artists, computer data processing specialists and the ever popular and not to be forgotten, geologists make up the team.

The results of the modern dig shed light on a wide range of issues that are eminently relevant to the student of Scripture. From these explorations we know about the architectural traditions and methods of a biblical culture, as well as the characteristics of daily life. What kind of food they ate, the nature of their economy, their civil and religious practices, and how they buried their dead are all included in the reconstructed profiles of Ancient Near Eastern populations. The geographical , topographical and geological character of a site can often account for its survival or demise.

The objects that are on display in this beautiful new building are not mere ambiguous curiosities from the past, but the evidential material upon which we establish historical and cultural realities.

But contemporary biblical archaeology at its best is not only concerned with the issues of historiography and historicity, but in effective biblical exposition. It puts flesh and bones on ancient peoples, it recreates the landscapes on which they lived and sheds invaluable light on their customs and religious life.

The intense struggles of Jonah over proposed ministry in Nineveh is best understood against the background of certain Assyrian military activities. Those practices have come to light through excavated materials.

Ashur-Nasirpal II (883 - 859), who ruled about a century before Jonah's visit, had this to say about the treatment of defeated foreigners:

> The heads of their warriors I cut off, and formed them into a pillar next to their city. Their young men and maidens I burned in the fire.
> I built a pillar next to the city gate and I flayed (alive) all the chief men who had revolted and I covered the pillar with their skins. Some I walled off within the pillar, some I impaled upon the pillar on stakes . . . I cut off the limbs of officers who had rebelled." (Finegan 1959: 202-3).

The same language appears in the seventh century B. C. Inscriptions of Ashur-banipal (668-627).

A bronze relief from the days of Shalmaneser III (858 - 824 B.C.) that adorned the palace at Balawat shows severed heads and bodies impaled on stakes.

The discovery of these materials through archaeological research illustrates the practical hermeneutical and homoletical application of such discoveries.

So then, archaeology is indispensible in the establishment and illumination of certain historical events. It is with a new and profound confidence that we can say with the Apostle Paul, "'these things happened to them.' They are historical realities.

Indeed, a century of Middle Eastern archaeology has demonstrated that the history of the Bible is eloquent in form and accurate in substance.

But our work is not done. Many scholars have become the morticians of truth rather than the ministers of truth, and the frustration and suffering of a fallen world is deepened.

If people express ontological despair by saying they don't really know who they are and why they are here, it is because they have been the intellectual victims of cosmological confusion. When we miss the mark on the issue of origins, it should be no surprise that our present existence is robbed of true meaning and significance.

If modern intellectual pursuits have produced cosmological error and ontological con-fusion, can teleological uncertainty be far behind? How can one speak of a sure and meaningful future against the background of these disturbing conclusions?

The apostle Paul reminds us that in Christ we have the ultimate answer to the heart of scientific and philosophical inquiry. In Col. 1:16 he states that "All things have been created by him and for him." In this he answers the scientific question "How" and the philosophical question "Why".

The most exciting years of archaeological research may still be ahead. New visions, new techniques and new applications will surely yield rich rewards for those who engage in the process.

Against the background of the nature of our Christian faith, the presence of this building on the campus of a theological seminary is most appropriate. And the name on this unique monument is a reminder that it is the hard work of committed and competent men and women that make archaeological discoveries a reality.

This is a wonderful day in which we dedicate, not just a building, but a monument. It is a monument to the grace and glory of our Lord and also a monument to the notable achievements of Dr. Harold Mare. Finally, it is a monument to the historical foundations of the Christian faith.

REFERENCES

Ceram, C. W. ed.,
1966 *Hands on the Past,* New York: Knopf.
Finegan, J
1959 *Light from the Ancient Past.* London: Oxford University Press.
Wheeler, M.
1954 *Archaeology from the Earth.* Baltimore: Penguin.
Zacharias, R.
1990 *A Shattered Visage: The Real Face of Atheism.* Grand Rapids: Baker.

Crucifixion, Bodily Suspension, and Jewish Interpretations of the Hebrew Bible in Antiquity

David W. Chapman
Covenant Theological Seminary

Ever since Yigael Yadin published his famous reevaluation of the Qumran Nahum Pesher (Yadin 1971), there has been significant (and sometimes heated) discussion about whether the Hebrew phrase תלה על־עץ ("hung upon a tree") implied crucifixion in the Temple Scroll and in the Nahum Pesher. This debate has also involved analyses of rabbinic and targumic treatments of some key pentateuchal material (especially of Deut 21:22-23). The discussion is all the more sensitive given the appropriate caution that comes when one is called upon to answer the question, "did Jewish people in antiquity support crucifixion as a legal penalty?" My goal here is *not* to solve these hotly contested issues. Rather I would suggest that significant progress could be gained by asking a different question. Namely, "how were Old Testament texts which spoke about human bodily suspension received in the late Second Temple and early rabbinic eras?" This involves reframing the discussion from debates about who historically supported crucifixion, to asking more broadly how biblical texts were received and retransmitted in Jewish antiquity.

There are in the Hebrew Bible several notable instances where individuals are hung aloft as part of the death penalty. So in Genesis, Joseph is called upon in prison to interpret the dreams of Pharaoh's cupbearer and his baker. The butler is told he will be freed, but the baker will have his head removed from him and he will be hung on a tree (Gen 40:19; cf. 40:22; 41:13). Similarly, in the book of Esther, Haman attempts to hang Mordecai on a tree as part of his execution, but the tables are turned and Haman is instead hung in Mordecai's place (Esth 7:9-10; cf. 2:23; 5:14; 6:4; 7:9; 8:7; 9:13-14, 25). There are several other examples of people who face similar deaths—both those who are explicitly "hung on a tree" (Deut 21:22-23; Josh 8:29; 10:26) and those whose death, apart from such specific terminology, may well involve some form of suspension (Num 25:4; 2 Sam 4:12; 21:6, 9, 12-13; possibly Lam 5:12).

This paper claims that later Jewish interpreters frequently apply technical human bodily suspension terminology to these passages, and this evidences an ongoing tendency to actualize biblical penal suspension texts by associating them with forms of human bodily suspension (including crucifixion) that were common in the Hellenistic and Roman world. The concept of "actualization" has been fruitfully

Beyond the Jordan

employed elsewhere in the discussion of Jewish retransmission of biblical tradition, especially in analyses of the Septuagint by such figures as Seeligmann, Hanhart, Koenig, and van der Kooij (e.g. Kooij 1997: 513-529). The term "actualization" can be taken in at least two ways: First, as an attempt by a later Jewish interpreter to identify certain contemporary events as predicted (or paralleled) in any given biblical text (an obvious example being the *pesherim* literature at Qumran). This is not the definition I am working with for this paper. Rather, I would follow a second definition and identify "actualization" in this context as the reading of the biblical text through the lens of a later interpreter's cultural assumptions. The ultimate contention of this paper is that the series of Old Testament texts which refer to penal bodily suspension were naturally associated in later Jewish tradition with the forms of penal bodily suspension which the interpreters themselves knew and witnessed in their own Hellenistic and/or Roman context.

Of course, this is not a phenomenon that is limited to Jewish tradition. Herodotus recounts the narrative of Polycrates of Samos who was first killed in an unspeakable way, and then attached to a stake (*Hist.* 3.125). Herodotus uses the term ἀνασταυρό ω to refer to this suspension. The sequence and grammar of the Greek verbs in Herodotus is significant—first Polycrates is killed and only afterwards is he suspended. However, later Hellenistic and Roman historical traditions about Polycrates increasingly associated his death with crucifixion (e.g. Lucian, *Cont.* 14; Philo, *Prov.* 2.24-25), thus actualizing this famous execution to more contemporary forms of suspension (see further Hengel 1977: 24n.).

Before proceeding further it would be wise to step back and inquire into the range of meaning of a few key crucifixion terms from antiquity—such Greek verbs as ἀνασκολοπίζω and ἀνασταυρόω and such a Hebrew verb as צלב and its Aramaic equivalent. I have spent considerable space elsewhere analyzing these terms (Chapman 2000: 8-26), and we only have space for a quick summary.

In most modern thought, in part due to the influence of Christian art and culture, crucifixion has a particular shape—namely a shape known technically as a *crux immissa* (†) to distinguish it from other ancient cross forms. Furthermore, "crucifixion" for us inevitably implies a means of execution where a live person is affixed to wood. However, it would be dangerous to read such assumptions into our study of ancient texts, especially when Seneca can refer to the varieties of shapes of crucifixion crosses he has seen. Or, more to our particular subject, note that Josephus can report the monstrous incident outside Jerusalem during the Jewish revolt where Roman soldiers "out of rage and hatred amused themselves by nailing their prisoners in different postures," affixing them to σταυροί. The shape of the cross may not have been what distinguished "crucifixion" in antiquity. In a similar fashion we must ask whether ancient authors assumed that crucifixion involved living people being executed via suspension, or whether the victims could already be dead prior to being hung.

In terms of ancient crucifixion terminology, if we focus first on the Greek words we observe that ἀνασταυρόω, which is Josephus' favorite term for the act of crucifying, can also be used by Josephus when he reports that "they crucified" the

38

dead bodies of Saul and his sons "to the walls of the city of Bethsan" (*Antiquities* vi.374; τὰ δὲ σώματα ἀνεσταύρωσαν πρὸς τὰ τείχη τῆς Βηθσὰν πόλεως). Nevertheless, most often for Josephus ἀνασταυρόω does indeed refer to death by crucifixion, as is clear when Antiochus Epiphanes crucifies his opponents while they are still alive and breathing. Later Josephus employs this term of king Alexander Jannaeus, who crucifies his opponents and slaughters their wives and children before them while they are still living (*Ant.* 13.380). Perhaps more frequently associated with a means of producing death is the term ἀνασκολοπίζω. This term clearly refers to crucifixion in most instances in Philo (e.g. *Flacc.* 83-85; *Jos.* 96-98; *Post.* 61), yet in earlier Greek literature ἀνασκολοπίζω and its cognate noun σκόλοψ may designate impalement as opposed to pinning or tying someone to a cross. The connecting feature for both ἀνασταυρόω and ἀνασκολοπίζω, as can be seen in Josephus and Philo and can be widely shown in other contemporary Greek authors, is that these words do refer in a technical fashion to executionary bodily suspension. However, these terms alone do not necessarily indicate whether that bodily suspension was the actual means of death (this is at least the case with ἀνασταυρόω), and by themselves they do not tell you the shape of the object upon which the person was hung. Therefore, if one's concern is to confidently ascertain the exact shape of the cross, or whether the victim was affixed to it alive or already dead, one must look to contextual indicators to prove one's case. Often such contextual indicators were not the concern of the author.

Entering now in a very brief space into the debated arena of the meaning of the Hebrew verb צלב and its Aramaic counterpart, I would argue that צלב in these two languages partakes of a similar range of referents as the Greek words just discussed. In some circumstances it can clearly refer to an act of crucifixion in the modern sense of the word. This is quite evident when Jewish narratives tell of the authorities (i.e. the Romans) executing a ל יסטים (a "brigand"), for the Romans commonly did this by means of affixing the living criminal to a cross. Yet elsewhere צלב can refer to a post mortem penalty.

Now, while we must be very careful not to commit the semantic fallacy of word/concept identification, and while we must also recognize that related words in different languages may bear distinct ranges of meaning, I still would suggest that these words evidence a striking cross-cultural phenomenon. That is, in the late Hellenistic and Roman eras Greek, Hebrew, and Aramaic all had technical terms for human bodily suspension associated with execution. But in each case these languages often did not on the basis of these terms alone distinguish the particular form of suspension, nor did they indicate solely by these words whether the penalty was ante mortem or post mortem. It is perhaps for this reason that these words could so easily be applied to biblical passages where we might be rightly reticent to apply the modern English term "crucifixion."

Now let us turn to some particular examples where such terminology is employed in early Jewish biblical interpretation. As noted above, the chief baker is "hung on a tree" in Gen 40:19 (cf. 40:22; 41:13). In the Hebrew context of Gen 40:19 the execution appears to be one which first involves beheading and then post mortem suspension. The Septuagint, the likely base text for Philo and Josephus, follows this word order as well. One feature of this passage in Hebrew and Greek is the way that the suspended baker will become "food for birds." Such a gruesome description would likely remind readers of this text in the Hellenistic and Roman eras of the suspended bodies in their own days whose decaying flesh was left to be eaten by scavenger birds and animals. Indeed the later retellings of the Joseph narratives tend to keep the reference to birds while actualizing some of the other features of the text.

Philo employs the Greek term ἀνασκολοπίζω ("impale" or "crucify") when he speaks of this text (*Jos.* 96–98; *Som.* 2.213). Of great interest in Philo's rendering in *Jos.* 96 is the fact that he reverses the order of the Hebrew text, requiring the suspension to precede the beheading. The natural reading of Philo would therefore imply that the person was crucified alive (using ἀνασκολοπίζω), and that decapitation was added after the baker was already suspended. A few decades later Josephus renders the same narrative with ἀνασταυρόω (*Ant.* 2.72–73), omitting altogether the "lifting of the head" clause. Josephus' lack of reference to decapitation naturally leaves the reader with the impression that the baker was affixed to the tree alive. And this crucifixion reading receives strong support as Josephus continues to indicate that the baker will be "unable to defend himself" from attacking scavenger birds (as if he would be conscious on the cross of his inability to ward off the birds). Later, the Targumim on this passage, while including (or even heightening) the emphasis on decapitation prior to suspension, nonetheless continue the pattern of applying technical terms for human bodily suspension by employing צְלַב (and, in Targumim Onqelos and Neofiti, the noun cognate צְלִיבָה).

This Genesis text thus provides a striking example of where later Jewish traditions make use of technical terms to represent a biblical bodily suspension text. Of course, once the text is so interpreted, the ancient reader of the interpretation would be left to understand the new Greek or Aramaic term in light of their own experience of the meanings of those words. And the slightly revised contexts in Philo and Josephus would most likely have called for direct comparisons to the crucifixions that were occurring in their day.

Moving to the book of Esther, the Hebrew text repeatedly emphasizes Haman's scheme to have Mordecai hung on a tree, but his nefarious plan is reversed and Haman himself and his ten sons are instead hung on the tree. As early as the two Greek versions of Esther, Haman's death was said to be caused by σταυρόω (see Esth 7:9 in the B text [= LXX], and E18 in both the A & B Greek texts). Josephus even more often employs suspension/crucifixion terms when he speaks of Haman's demise (*Ant.* 11.208, 246, 261, 267, 280). And the two main Targumim to Esther both generally speak of Haman's death using צְלַב terminology. Similarly the many rabbinic accounts continue to employ צְלַב and its cognates. At the very least we observe in these Jewish retellings of biblical narratives the actualization of suspension terminology.

To illustrate the point of this paper more clearly let us focus for the moment solely on the Greek versions of Esther. The Greek translators of Esther in the A and

B texts certainly were able to render the Hebrew phrase "hang upon a tree" with a literal Greek equivalent (such is clearly the case in their translations of Esth 2:23; 5:14; 6:4; 7:10; 8:7; 9:13-14, 25 which all use some form of the more generic κρεμά ννυμι). Yet these two Greek versions both choose at least once to employ a more contemporary Greek idiom by encapsulating the Hebrew expression with σταυρόω. The match was a good one, since σταυρόω could refer to human bodily suspension. It is not possible to know fully the cultural associations that these translators had with the term σταυρόω (i.e. whether such a term referred for them to "crucifixion" in the modern sense of the word). Yet, it is also clear that, once they had so translated the Hebrew, later Greek readers would likely have associated σταυρόω with forms of bodily suspension that they witnessed in their own culture. Such freedom for later Greek readers to actualize the now translated biblical text is increased by a lack of any clear indication in the Greek (or for that matter in the Hebrew) as to how exactly Haman died.

If one then considers the later traditions on Esther, the shift from the Hebrew to more contemporary idiom is more apparent. Thus, given that Josephus commonly associates crucifixions in his own day with σταυρός terminology, the application of such terms to Haman's demise would likely have connoted crucifixion to his readers. Finally, more overt implications of crucifixion in the death of Haman can actually be found in a few key rabbinic texts.

Outside these two texts from Genesis and Esther there are several other passages in the Hebrew Bible that refer to human bodily suspension. The phrase "hang upon a tree" also occurs in Joshua 8:29 and 10:26-27. Other words clearly indicate a bodily suspension in Ezra 6:11. And Jewish interpreters have inferred such a suspension in Lamentations 5:12-13 and in the use of יָקַע in Numbers 25:4 and 2 Samuel 21:6, 9, 13. While the evidence for actualization of the Hebrew is less spectacular in Second Temple and rabbinic Jewish treatments of these passages than we have already witnessed with regard to Genesis and Esther, one should note that most of these are rendered with צְלַב in the Targumim, thus shifting the semantic range from a general hanging (or other penalty) in the MT to a specific executionary suspension penalty in the Targumim. Briefly summarizing some other fascinating connections we note that the Septuagint and Peshitta of Lamentations 5:12 have the victims hung by their hands (plural)—a death which could seem much like ancient crucifixions. Josephus renders Ezra 6:11 with ἀνασταυρόω, and rabbinic sources employ Ezra's language in the discussion of Haman's death by suspension in Esther.

As a last example of this actualizing tendency we now turn to the more hotly contested evidence from Deuteronomy 21:22-23. In the Hebrew this passage refers to the those whose sin bears a judgment of death—such people are to be put to death and then hung on a tree, but the hanging is not to last more than a day for "a curse of God is the one who is hung" and land defilement is to be avoided. There is much that could be said about this text, but we shall focus primarily on the question of where this passage is actualized and where it is not.

Before addressing the main question three initial observations are in order. First, the key suspension words in Deuteronomy 21:22 (וְתָלִיתָ אֹתוֹ עַל־עֵץ—"and you hang him on a tree") are similar to the Hebrew phraseology found in Genesis 40-41 and in Esther. Hence, it would not be surprising if a similar actualizing tendency appears in Deuteronomy 21 as we have already witnessed in the Genesis and Esther texts.

Second, the issue arises as to whether the קִלְלַת אֱלֹהִים ("curse of God") construct in Deuteronomy 21:23 represents a subjective genitive (God does the cursing) or an objective genitive (God is the one being cursed, i.e. blasphemed). Rabbinic interpretation codified in the Talmud (also supported by Josephus, Symmachus and the Peshitta) applied this text to the blasphemer (as one who "curses God"). On the other hand, the more ancient tradition (being witnessed in the LXX, OL and known as late as *Targum Neofiti*) saw קִלְלַת אֱלֹהִים as a reference to the hung person being cursed by God. Concerning these two differing interpretations of the "curse of God" construct there are at least two consequences when one examines later traditions that are relevant to the actualizing discussion. On the one hand, human bodily suspension texts that refer to the death of either blasphemers or cursed persons may very well be citing or alluding to this passage. On the other hand, the very fact that many translators interpret this law by clarifying the "curse of God" construct (as a reference either to a blasphemer or to a curse by God) proves that Deuteronomy 21 has been actualized in the past (at least with respect to this issue). Therefore, it should not be surprising when the penalty itself ("and you hang him on a tree") is also actualized as to its contemporary significance.

Third, and most important, the order of verbs in verse 22 ("he is executed and you hang him on a tree") would most naturally imply a sequence of events with the person's death occurring prior to the bodily suspension. While it is not impossible to read the death and the suspension as simultaneous events, a post mortem penalty is the more natural read for the Hebrew.

However, while Deuteronomy 21 in Hebrew does not itself likely refer to suspension as a means of execution, it was nonetheless related by some key Jewish interpreters to contemporary suspension practiced in antiquity. This actualizing tendency was true to the extent that at least some Jewish authors could apply this passage in crucifixion contexts. Thus Philo employs strong crucifixion vocabulary in his rendering of Deuteronomy in *De Specialibus Legibus*. While Josephus elsewhere avoids crucifixion terminology in his interpretations of Deuteronomy 21:22 (*Ant.* 4.202, 264-265), nonetheless his belittling of Idumaean piety in *Bell.* 4.317 incorporates the argument that Jewish people bury their crucified malefactors before sunset. This could only, in my judgment, stem from an application of Deuteronomy 21:23 to those who receive the penalty of ἀνασταυρόω.

Rabbinic literature in some key places strongly disconnects Deuteronomy 21 from the Roman activity. Both the Sifre and the Bavli follow the natural reading of the verbal order in the Hebrew text to prove that crucifixion is not in view in Deuteronomy 21:22 (*Sifre Deut.* 221 and *b. Sanh.* 46b). While these rabbinic texts overtly distance Deuteronomy from crucifixion, nevertheless we might ask why this issue arose in the first place. Quite possibly it arose because others understood the penal suspension in this text in light of the crucifixions common in their day. In any case, no less a rabbinic figure that R. Meir is able to draw a parable based on connecting crucifixion to the Deuteronomic passage.

Finally, I note that the Temple Scroll, regardless of whether one understands this Qumran document as implying crucifixion, nonetheless displays a strong impetus to actualize the text of Deuteronomy 21 into further discussion. Indeed, as has been pointed out since Yadin, the most natural reading of Temple Scroll 64 (lines 8 and 10-11) is to see the person being first hung and then dying—overtly reversing the order of the Deuteronomy passage.

In summary, Second Temple and early rabbinic literature frequently evidences a tendency to actualize biblical human suspension texts. This is not to claim that such actualization is necessarily evident in every Jewish interpreter of every biblical suspension text. Nevertheless, a clear trend does surface in the literature. This tendency is not in any real sense surprising. It would be quite natural for people to read passages about human bodily suspension in light of their own contemporary experience, especially where the exact methods of suspension are not mentioned in the biblical text.

Indeed, given the strength of this tendency in the literature, texts that avoid such overt actualization may in fact signal a cultural sensitivity on the part of some Jewish interpreters to the possible application of crucifixion in certain contexts. The rabbis, especially after the horrors of the great failed Jewish revolts, were thus sensitive to their biblical law justifying the kind of Roman crucifixion which had been so cruelly meted out against the Jewish nation. Thus for this reason, and possibly for others, it can be observed that they distanced biblical law from mandating crucifixion (cf. *Sifre Deut.* 221 and *b. Sanh.* 46b mentioned above).

Nonetheless, such refusal to actualize some passages by some interpreters does not affect the more positive case witnessed in multiple places in Second Temple and rabbinic Jewish literature. Ancient Jewish interpreters frequently associated biblical suspension texts with the human bodily suspension practices common in their own day.

NOTES

[1] It is with great delight that I dedicate this contribution to Harold Mare—my friend, colleague and mentor at Covenant Theological Seminary and at the Archaeology Institute bearing his name. This paper provides a focused summary of portions from a chapter in my—*Ancient Perceptions of Crucifixion among Jews and Christians* (forthcoming from Mohr-Siebeck).

[2] To mention just a few works: Baumgarten (1972: 472-81); ibid. (1982: 7*-16*); Díez Merino (1976: 48-69); Fitzmyer (1978: 498-507); García Martínez (1979-1980: 221-35); Hengel (1984: 27-36); Puech (1998: 73-5); Schwartz (1992: 81-88).

[3] Ἀποκτείνας δέ μιν οὐκ ἀξίως [some MSS ἀξίω] ἀπηγήσιος Ὀροίτης ἀνεσταύρωσε· —"Having killed him (in some way not fit to be told) Oroetes then crucified him…" Text in Hude (1927); translation in Godley (1971).

[4] *"De Consolatione ad Marciam* 20.3 in Basore (1965, pp. 2:68-69). A similar point is made in Hengel (1977: 24ff.).

[5] προσήλουν δ᾽ οἱ στρατιῶται δι᾽ ὀργὴν καὶ μῖσος τοὺς ἁλόντας ἄλλον ἄλλῳ σχή ματι πρὸς χλεύην, καὶ διὰ τὸ πλῆθος χώρα τ᾽ ἐνέλειπε τοῖς σταυροῖς καὶ σταυροὶ τοῖς σώμασιν—*Bell.* v.451. Texts and translation in Thackeray et al. (1926-1965).

[6] Similarly Plutarch can depict post mortem suspension with ἀνασταυρόω (*Tim.* 22.8; *Cleom.* 39.1; cf. *De fortuna Romanorum* 325d for the impaling of dogs) where elsewhere Plutarch appears to designate death by crucifixion with this term (cf. *Fab.* 6.2-3; *Alex.* 72.3; *Caes.* 2.7; *Ant.* 81.1; *De Garrulitate* 509a; and σταυρόω in *Parallela minora* 311d-e). Polybius too can mention the suspension of living (*Hist.* 1.86.6; cf. 1.11.5; 1.24.6; 1.79.4) and of dead bodies (*Hist.* 5.54.6-7; 8.21.3).

[7] Josephus, *Ant.* 12.256 (ζῶντες ἔτι καὶ ἐμπνέοντες ἀνεσταυροῦντο). Note more broadly *Vita* 420-21, where the three crucified individuals are removed from the cross at Josephus' request (one of them survives). Also see *Ant.* 11.267 (καὶ κελεύει παραχρῆμα αὐτὸν ἐξ ἐκείνου τοῦ σταυροῦ κρεμασθέντα ἀποθανεῖν); 13.380 (cf. *Bell.* 1.97); most likely also *Ant.* 19.94; *Bell.* 3.321. In other situations the context is not necessarily determinative as to whether the σταυρός was the means of death, though often it is possible to assume so. For ἀνασταυρόω conveying crucifixion cf. Lucian, *Prom.* 1-2.

[8] Outside Philo cf. Dionysius of Halicarnasus, *Antiq. Rom.* 5.51.3; Lucian, *Prom.* 2, 7, 10; *Peregr.* 11, 13; *Philops.* 29.

[9] Impalement is associated in earlier Greek with the cognate noun σκόλοψ (see Euripides, *Electra* 898; *Iphigeneia* 1430). Later possibly Dio Chrysostom, *Orationes* 17.5.

[10] Again note my fuller treatment (Chapman 2000: 12-26). For a contrary opinion to the one listed below see Baumgarten (1982: 8*-9*). Another contrary opinion, though less decisively argued, is found in Cohn (1977: 209). Halperin (1981: 37-40) argues the opposite extreme, claiming that צלב almost always designates crucifixion.

[11] Sokoloff (1990, s.v.) in defining the Aramaic term צלב notes that it means "to impale, crucify."

[12] So *Esth. Rab.* 10:5 (note the use of nails). For earlier rabbinic Hebrew (as then developed in later texts) see e.g. *m. Yebam.* 16:3 (see also *t. Yebam.* 14:4; *b. Yebam.* 120b; *y. Yebam.* 16:3 [15c]—ransoming of a crucified man); *t. Git.* 7(5):1 (also *y. Git.* 7:1 [48c]; *b. Git.* 70b— crucified man signals for a writ of divorce); *m. Shabb.* 6:10 (also *y. Shabb.* 6:9; *b. Shabb.* 67a—nail used in crucifixion).

[13] See *b. B. Mes.* 83b; *Mek. Shirata* 7 (Lauterbach 1933-1935, vol. 2, pp. 57-58), 10 (ibid. vol. 2, pp. 79-80); *Eccl. Rab.* 7:37 [21c] on Eccl 7:26; *Esth. Rab.* 3:14 [7d] on Esth 1:12; *PRK* suppl. ii.2. And note *t. Sanh.* 9:7 discussed below.

[14] Cf. Josephus, *Bell.* 2.253. Further instances in Hengel (1977: 46-50).

[15] Especially in the Targumim. See *Tg. Onq.*, *Tg. Neof.*, and *Tg. Ps.-J.* on Gen 40:19 and on Deut 21:22; *Tg. Josh.* 10:26; possibly *Tg. Ps.-J.* on Lev. 24:23.

[16] ישא פרעה את־ראשך מעליך ותלה אותך על־עץ—"Pharaoh will lift your head from upon you and he will hang you on a tree." While De Rossi lists two MSS which omit the מעליך ("from upon you"), his own opinion tells against this shortened reading (De Rossi 1784-1798, verse cited). Further, other versions (save the Vulgate) all include this key word

44

(e.g. the LXX, Old Latin, and the Peshitta). This would tell against any modern attempt to omit "from upon you" or to view the "lift your head" phrase as metaphorical (as in the commentaries by Gunkel, Skinner, Westermann, Sarna, and Hamilton). Rather the baker appears to have his "head lifted from upon him" in the sense of being beheaded. Targum Onqelos apparently interpreted this text as requiring decapitation, and Targum Pseudo-Jonathan clearly understood 40:19 this way.

[17] ἀφελεῖ Φαραω τὴν κεφαλήν σου ἀπὸ σοῦ καὶ κρεμάσει σε ἐπὶ ξύλου.

[18] This is true of Philo, Josephus and the Targumim mentioned below.

[19] ὁ βασιλεὺς ἀνασκολοπισθῆναί σε καὶ τὴν κεφαλὴν ἀποτμηθῆναι κελεύσει—"the king will command you to be crucified and your head to be be cut off."

[20] αὐτὸν ἀνασταυρωθέντα βορὰν ἔσεσθαι πετεινοῖς οὐδὲν ἀμύνειν αὐτῷ δυνάμενον (Josephus, *Ant.* 2.73).

[21] See both *Targum Rishon* and *Sheni* on Esth 2:23; 5:14; 7:9, 10; 8:7; 9:14, 25. Also *Targum Rishon* on 6:4 and *Targum Sheni* on 5:14; 9:24. Text and translation Grossfeld (1983) and Grossfeld (1994). Translation without Aramaic text Grossfeld (1991).

[22] E.g. *Gen. Rab.* 30:8; *Exod. Rab.* 20:10; *Lev. Rab.* 28:6; *Esth. Rab.* Proem 1; 2:14; 3:15; 7:3, 10, 11; 9:2; 10:5, 15.

[23] Most noticeable is Josephus, *Ant.* 11.267 where the king "immediately ordered him [= Haman] hung from that cross in order to die'"—κελεύει παραχρῆμα αὐτὸν ἐξ ἐκείνου τοῦ σταυροῦ κρεμασθέντα ἀποθανεῖν.

[24] Ropes and nails are mentioned as part of Haman's death in *Esth. Rab.* 10:5. *Targum Sheni* (5:14) implies that the punishment of צלב was the means of death planned for Mordecai. Haman also begs for a more respectable death in *Tg. Esth. II* 7:10.

[25] So *Tg. Josh.* 8:29; 10:26; *Tg. Sam.* on 2 Sam 21; *Tg. Lam.* 5:12. Even Num 25:4 in the whole Palestinian targumic tradition is transformed into a death via צלב and explicitly connected with Deut 21:23 by the requirement to bury the bodies within the day. Rabbinic authorities connected Num 25:4 with hanging by noting that 2 Sam 21 employs the same Hebrew verb (from יקע) and involves longtime exposure and the warding off of scavenger birds (*b. Sanh.* 34b-35a).

[26] It is also worth noting the crucifixion implications in *Lam. Rab.* 5:12-13.

[27] Josephus, *Ant.* 11.17, 103. Also see *Tg. Esth. I* 7:9 and MS Paris Heb. 110 of *Tg. Esth. I & II* at Esth 3:2; *PRE*, chpt. 50.

[28] The fact that *Tg. Neof.* Deut 21:23 manifests the same application of this verse as the LXX (to the cursing of all those hung on the tree) indicates that this view did not quickly perish after the penning of the Septuagint but was still found in at least some sectors of rabbinic Judaism. This is also likely testified in 11QTemple LXIV, 12—here the hung person is cursed by both God and men (מקוללי אלוהים ואנשים תלוי על העץ).

[29] The Hebrew reads: והומת ותלית אתו על־עץ

[30] Again, we note that the Targumim typically render the Hebrew phrase with צלב and/or its cognate nouns. Though they keep the order of death followed by suspension, thus likely following the Hebrew in designating a post mortem penalty, the Targumim have certainly updated the terminology of suspension (thus actualizing the passage to at least this degree).

[31] Philo, *Spec. Leg.* 3.151-152. God, who rightly could have commanded multiple deaths

upon a single person for certain criminal acts instead "commands those who murder to be crucified" (κελεύων τοὺς ἀνελόντας ἀνασκολοπίζεσθαι). Moreover God returns to his love of mankind by saying of these people: "Do not let the sun set upon those who have been crucified, but let them be concealed in the earth, having been taken down before sunset." (μὴ ἐπιδυέτω ὁ ἥλιος ἀνεσκολοπισμένοις, ἀλλ᾽ ἐπικρυπτέσθωσαν γῇ πρὸ δύσεως καθαιρεθέντες)□my translation; text from Colson et al. (1929-1962). Note how Deut 21:23 is clearly intended in the command to bury (also in the overall context of Torah legal exposition in *Spec. Leg.*). Death by suspension is implied by the terminology, the contrast with a myriad of other deaths, and the lack of any other contextual indicators implying some other form of execution.

[32] "They [the Idumaeans] actually went so far in their impiety as to cast out the corpses without burial, although the Jews are so careful about funeral rites that even malefactors who have been sentenced to crucifixion are taken down and buried before sunset." The last phrase in Greek runs:"ὥστε καὶ τοὺς ἐκ καταδίκης ἀνεσταυρωμένους πρὸ δύντος ἡλί ου καθελεῖν τε καὶ θάπτειν.

[33] So the *Sifre*: "One might think that they will hang him alive, as in the manner which the [Roman] government does; so Scripture says, '…and he was put to death, and you hung him on a tree'" (Deut 21:22). The phrase "as the Roman government does" though omitted in some MSS, is likely original and thus is included in the Finkelstein edition (Finkelstein 1969).

[34] See *t. Sanh.* 9:7 (and cf. *b. Sanh.* 46b). The parable concerns a king whose twin brother joins a band of brigands (ל יסטייא). The twin is crucified (והיו צולבין אותו על הצלוב) and this led to a rumor that the king had been crucified. Therefore it is said, "…a curse of God is the one who is hung." Crucifixion is likely in view not only because of the Hebrew terminology but also because the twin is executed for brigandry. Note that R. Meir's interpretation assumes an objective genitive in the Deuteronomy "curse of God" construct (God is cursed).

[35] This is certainly true in the attempt in 11QTemple 64: (1) to define to whom the penalty applies (slanderers, those who surrender God's people to other nations, and who do evil against God's people; as well as those who have fled to a foreign nation and cursed God's people); (2) to articulate procedure (requiring two or three witnesses); (3) and to interpret the "curse of God" construct in Deut 21:23 (it refers to those""cursed of God and men").

[36] So line 8: ותל יתמה אותו על העץ וימת. This point is disputed by some, so Bernstein (1979: 145-166) argues that this passage in the Temple Scroll is not an exegetical midrash on Deut 21:22-23. However, the surrounding 11QTemple context involves a retelling of Deut 21, the language of Deut 21:22-23 is clearly picked up, and the additional material in the Temple Scroll all attempts to define whose sins merit a "judgment of death" in Deut 21:22. Baumgarten (1972: 472-481) argues that the death is by suspension, but the kind of suspension in question is hanging on a noose and not crucifixion. There appear good reasons to reject Baumgarten's position (cf. Chapman 2000: 15-24), but the point of this essay—that actualization is present in Jewish interpretations of biblical texts—would still be sustained in 11QTemple even if Baumgartner's position proves tenable (though admittedly with a different form of contemporary executionary suspension envisaged than crucifixion).

[37] This same tendency may actually be witnessed in Josephus, who, while he often connects biblical texts with crucifixion, is more circumspect with regard to Deuteronomy 21 and its biblical application in Joshua 8 and 10. But this should be the topic of another paper.

REFERENCES

Basore, J. W.
  1965 *Seneca Moral Essays.* 3 vols. Cambridge: Harvard University Press.
Baumgarten, J. M.
  1972 Does *TLH* in the Temple Scroll Refer to Crucifixion? *Journal of Biblical Literature* 91: 472-81.
  1982 Hanging and Treason in Qumran and Roman Law. *Eretz Israel* 16: 7*-16*.
Bernstein, M. J.
  1979 *Midrash Halakhah* at Qumran? 11QTemple 64:6-13 and Deuteronomy 21:22-23. *Gesher* 7: 145-66.
Chapman, D. W.
  2000 Perceptions of Crucifixion among Jews and Christians in the Ancient World. Ph.D. dissertation, University of Cambridge.
Cohn, H.
  1977 *The Trial and Death of Jesus.* New York: Ktav.
Colson, F. H., et al.
  1929-1962 *Philo.* 10 (+ 2 suppl.) vols. Cambridge: Harvard University Press.
De-Rossi, J. B.
  1784-1798 *Variae Lectiones Veteris Testamenti.* 4 + suppl. vols. Parma: Ex Regio Typographeo.
Díez Merino, L.
  1976 El suplicio de la cruz en la literatura Judia intertestamental. *Studii Biblici Franciscani Liber Annuus* 26: 31-120.
Finkelstein, L.
  1969 *Sifre on Deuteronomy.* New York: Jewish Theological Seminary of America.
Fitzmyer, J. A.
  1978 Crucifixion in Ancient Palestine, Qumran Literature, and the New Testament. *Catholic Biblical Quarterly* 40: 493-513.
García Martínez, F.
  1979-1980 4QpNah y la Crucifixión: Nueva hipótesis de reconstrucción de 4Q 169 3-4 i, 4-8. *Estudios Bíblicos* 38: 221-35.
Godley, A. D.
  1971 *Herodotus.* Revised ed., 4 vols. Cambridge: Harvard University Press.
Grossfeld, B.
  1983 *The First Targum to Esther: According to the MS Paris Hebrew 110 of the Bibliotheque Nationale.* New York: Sepher-Hermon Press.
  1991 *The Two Targums of Esther: Translated, with Apparatus and Notes.* Edinburgh: T & T Clark.

1994 *The Targum Sheni to the Book of Esther: a critical edition based on MS. Sassoon 282 with critical apparatus*. New York: Sepher-Hermon.

Halperin, D. J.
1981 Crucifixion, the Nahum Pesher, and the Rabbinic Penalty of Strangulation. *Journal of Jewish Studies* 32: 32-46.

Hengel, M.
1977 *Crucifixion in the Ancient World and the Folly of the Message of the Cross*. Translated by John Bowden. London & Philadelphia: SCM Press & Fortress Press.
1984 *Rabbinische Legende und frühpharisäische Geschichte: Schimeon b. Schetach und die achtzig Hexen von Askalon*. Heidelberg: Carl Winter.

Hude, K.
1927 *Herodoti Historiae*. Third edition. Oxford: Clarendon.

Kooij, A. van der
1997 Isaiah in the Septuagint. Pp. 513-29 in *Writing and Reading the Scroll of Isaiah*, vol. 2, ed. C. G. Broyles and C. A. Evans. Leiden: Brill.

Lauterbach, J. Z.
1933-1935 *Mekilta de-Rabbi Ishmael*. 3 vols. Philadelphia: Jewish Publication Society of America.

Puech, E.
1998 Die Kreuzigung und die altjüdische Tradition. *Welt und Umwelt der Bibel* 9.3: 73-5.

Schwartz, D. R.
1992 'The Contemners of Judges and Men' (11Q Temple 64:12). Pp. 81-88 in *Studies in the Jewish Background of Christianity*. Tübingen: J. C. B. Mohr (Paul Siebeck).

Sokoloff, M.
1990 *A Dictionary of Jewish Palestinian Aramaic of the Byzantine Period*. Israel: Bar Ilan University Press.

Thackeray, H. St. J., et al.
1926-1965 *Josephus*. 10 vols. Cambridge: Harvard University Press.

Yadin, Y.
1971 Pesher Nahum (4QpNahum) Reconsidered. *Israel Exploration Journal* 21: 1-12.

Elchasaites, Manichaeans, and Mandaeans in the Light of the Cologne Mani Codex

Edwin M. Yamauchi
History Department
Miami University
Oxford, OH 45056

It is both a privilege and a pleasure to dedicate this essay to an outstanding New Testament scholar, indefatigable archaeologist, and personal friend with whom I have roomed for more years than I can recount at the annual ETS/NEAS and IBR/SBL meetings. Harold Mare's leadership for many years sustained the Near East Archaeological Society. A number of my graduate students have profited by working under him at his excavations at Abila, most notably Robert Smith and John Wineland. Their experiences with him in Jordan inspired them to write their Ph.D. dissertations on early Christianity in Jordan and on Abila's history.

Jewish Christians in Jordan

Church fathers such as Origen, Epiphanius and Jerome wrote of a variety of Jewish-Christian groups who flourished in Jordan, some of whom they regarded as heretical. Of particular significance are the extensive references of Epiphanius, who was born in Palestine near Eleutheropolis (Beit Guvrin) and who later became the bishop of Salamis in Cyprus (d. 402/403). He wrote the *Panarion* or *Medicine Chest* against various heresies (Amidon).

Epiphanius mentions both the **Nazarenes**, a Jewish baptist group, and a Jewish-Christian group called the **Nazoreans**, who lived in Beroeia, Pella, and Kochaba, and who used the Aramaic language. In the New Testament the term **Nazarene** (Ναζαρηνος) appears six times (four times in Mark and twice in Luke) as an epithet describing Jesus (Mimouni). On the other hand the term **Nazoraean** (Ναζωραιος) occurs 13 times (twice in Matthew, once in Luke, three times in John and seven times in Acts). Of these instances all refer to Jesus except Acts 24:5, which refers to his followers. Both terms identify Jesus as coming from Nazareth. Matthew 2:23 sees in Jesus' epithet a fulfillment of Isaiah 11:1, which speaks "of a branch" (נצר = neṣer) arising out of the house of Jesse (i.e. David).

There is no evidence apart from Epiphanius (*Panarion* 18) for a pre-Christian, law-observing, Jewish group who called themselves Nazarenes. It is possible that he was referring to memories of a group like the Qumran community, whom most scholars have identified as the Essenes, who practiced repeated immersions. Far more problematic would be their identification with the Mandaeans, who call themselves the *nāṣōrāyā or* "observers," as there is no firm evidence of their pre-Christian existence (Yamauchi 1970).

The Nazoreans, who were found in such Jordanian sites as Pella, may have stemmed from the Jewish Christians who fled Jerusalem before the Roman siege which resulted in the destruction of the temple in 70 AD (Yamauchi 1991: 11-30). These sectarians, though they tried to live according to the Jewish Law, were relatively orthodox Christians, who accepted the virgin birth and acknowledged Paul. The church fathers speak of a "gospel" used by the Nazoreans, which may possibly be identical with the "Gospel of the Hebrews."

A less orthodox Jewish-Christian group mentioned by Epiphanius are the Ebionites, who are so named after the Hebrew word for poor (אֶבְיוֹן = *'ebyōn*). The Ebionites according to Irenaeus (*Adversus Haereses* 1.26.2) used only Matthew's Gospel, rejected the virgin birth and Paul, and observed circumcision. Origen adds that they observed the Passover. Epiphanius, who cites from a Gospel of the Ebionites, reports that they rejected the eating of meat and the duty of marriage and procreation. They prayed in the direction of Jerusalem and met in synagogues. They held that Jesus was a mere man, who was adopted as the son of God. Epiphanius also reported that the Ebionites were later influenced by the Elchasaites, a tradition which is doubted by scholars (e.g. Klijn and Reinink).

Some of the church fathers also mention a group called the Elchasaites, followers of an Elchasai (or Elxai). His name has been analyzed as based on the Aramaic phrase (חֵיל כסי) *ḥēl ksē* "hidden power." According to Epiphanius (Pan. 19) Elchasai appeared in the reign of Trajan (98-117) among the Ossaeans, who were Jews living in the Nabatean regions of Iturea, Moabitis and Arielitis in the neighborhood of the Dead Sea. At the time that he wrote there were remnants of this group still living in Nabataea and Perea near Moabitis under the name Sampsaeans.

Elchasai had originally appeared in Parthian territory and prophesied that a universal conflict would blaze up three years after the Parthian War (114-116), a prediction which was not fulfilled. Elchasaism may have originally been a Jewish movement that tried to demonstrate its allegiance to the Parthians in their conflict against the Romans (Klijn and Reinink). It was later influenced by Christians as the description of the revelation of the holy book indicates, an account which says that the revelation was brought by two gigantic angels, a male Son of God and a female Holy Spirit, each 96 Roman miles tall!

Hippolytus (*Ref.* 9.8-17; 10.25-29) reports that a follower of Elchasai named Alcibiades arrived from Apameia in Syria in Rome during the pontificate of Callistus (217-22). He claimed to have a book of revelation, obtained by Elchasai from the Seres (silk merchants?), which was dedicated to Sobiaei (from the verb צבע *ṣbʿ* "to baptize"), not a person as Epiphanius believed but to the "baptized." Alcibiades claimed to have the gift of foreknowledge from astrology. According to *Ref.* 15.3-6, those bitten by a mad dog had to go to a river, pray to the Supreme God, and invoke seven witnesses. They were baptized fully clothed. They had to say they would not sin again, nor commit adultery, nor steal.

According to Eusebius (*H.E.* 6.38), who cites Origen (ca. 247), the Helkesaites (sic) came to Caesarea and preached that it was permissible on some occasions to dissimulate. They also produced a book, which they claimed had fallen from heaven.

Isḥāq an-Nadīm in his *Kitab al-Fihrist,* i.e. "the catalogue" (10th cent.) describes a sect of "baptizers" (Arabic *Mughtasila*) of the marshlands of lower Mesopotamia who practiced frequent ablutions and washed everything they ate. Their founder was an *al-Ḥasīḥ.* They believed that Jesus was but one of a series of revealers, and they rejected Paul. They rebaptized for the forgiveness of severe sexual transgressions. They prayed toward Jerusalem, and allowed for dissimulation under severe persecution.

The most thorough study of the Elchasaites is that by G. P. Luttikhuizen, who cautions scholars to keep separate the various accounts of the Book of Elxai, and the Elchasaites at various times and places, and not to lump them all together. But he goes too far, in my opinion, when he wishes to suggest that Elchasai and the Greek Alchasaios are just similar sounding names and are not to be identified.

Mani and Manichaeans

Prior to 1970 scholars such as Kurt Rudolph, following Thomas (219) had identified the Mughtasila of an-Nadim's Fihrist as the Mandaeans and dismissed the reference to Elchasai as secondary (Rudolph 1960: 41-42). Geo Widengren had also confidently identified the baptists among whom Mani lived as the Mandaeans. In 1965 he had written:

> Thanks to the conformity which characterizes Mandaean and Manichaean myths, their gnostic outlook as a whole, their rites, and many of their specialized expressions, we may confidently assume that Patik (the father of Mani) joined a Mandaean group in southern Babylonia and that Mani was brought up in this baptist community. (Widengren 25)

Widengren, after identifying many Parthian elements in Mandaeism and in Manichaeism, maintained that this indicated a link to a pre-Christian Iranian Gnosticism. (Widengren 17-19; for a critique of this position see Yamauchi 1983: ch. 5 and pp. 206-10.)

But then in 1970 two German scholars, A. Henrichs (now at Harvard) and L. Koenen (now at Michigan), published a tiny codex in Greek, which contained sensational information about Mani's background (Bianchi). Its pages, which are 4.5 cm. x 3.5 cm. (barely over an inch square), contain an average of 23 lines. It is titled "On the Genesis of His (i.e. Mani's) Body." It is a translation dated to the 4th-5th centuries, which may be based on an Aramaic original by Mani himself. The codex contains 192 pages, which detail Mani's childhood, several revelations, the customs of Elchasaites, and Mani's departure from the sect. The sect's founder was a certain *Alchasaios* (Αλχασαιος) who surely (<u>pace</u> Luttikhuizen) is the same as the figure described in patristic sources as Elchasaios.

The Cologne Mani Codex (Codex Manichaicus Coloniensis = CMC) gives us some invaluable information. It specifies that Mani was born on April 14, 216, that he received his first revelation from his *Syzygos* ("companion" or divine twin) on his 12th birthday on April 1, 228, and his second revelation on his 24th birthday, April 19, 240 (Koenen 1971: 247-50). Mani was four when his father Pattikaios joined the sect. The Elchasaites observed the Jewish Sabbath or "rest of the hands" but also celebrated the Eucharist with unleavened bread and water. They performed regular ablutions on themselves and washed their food. They were ruled by a council of elders.

When Mani cut dates, their blood oozed, and the plants cried out because they were sentient. He concluded from the fact of digestion that the body could never become clean by ablutions, and that the daily baptisms did not effect purification (CMC 91:4-19). He declared:

> Therefore inspect yourself and find out what your purity means. For it is impossible to make your bodies entirely clean. Every day the body is set in motion and (again) stands still, because it discharges the waste of digestion. Accordingly, your rite (sc. baptism) is performed without a commandment of the Savior. Hence, the purification mentioned in the Scriptures is the purification through gnosis, i.e., the separation of Light from Darkness, of Death from Life, of Living Waters from Turbid Waters. (Koenen 1981: 737)

Mani even viewed baptism as a sin against water. To demonstrate that his views were correct and not heretical, Mani cited the authority of Alchasaios himself, claiming that "The water told him that it would be harmed by the dirt; thus he refrained from washing himself." The reactions were violent as the Elchasaites "thrashed" Mani, after trying him before their council. He would have been killed had it not been for the intervention of his father.

Depressed by this reaction, Mani was granted a vision by his Twin, promising him that he would carry his message "to every people, every school, every city, and every place" (CMC 104:14-17). With his father and two other converts, Simeon and Abizachias, he then traveled to Ctesiphon during the spring flood of the Tigris (CMC 106.14-19; 109.14-20).

From other sources in many languages (including Coptic, Uighur, and Chinese) we learn that Mani conducted a far-flung ministry of over thirty years in Mesopotamia, Persia and India (Sundermann 1971, King). Mani converted a number of rulers, most notably Peroz, the governor of northeastern Persia and the brother of the king. He enjoyed the patronage of Shapur I (AD 240-273), the second king of the new Sasanid dynasty, and even accompanied the king on campaigns against the Roman emperor, Valerian (Yamauchi 1998). Shapur's son, Bahram I, however, turned against Mani at the instigation of Karter, a zealous Zoroastrian, who persecuted all other religions.

After being bound in chains for 26 days, Mani died in prison in 276. He was decapitated, and his corpse was buried by his followers at Gundi-shapur in southwestern Persia.

Mani wore flamboyant clothing such as a blue cloak and red and green trousers. He was a gifted painter, who composed the *Ardahang,* a picture book, to propagate his faith among the illiterate. He wrote seven canonical works, which included: 1) the *Shapurakan,* dedicated to Shapur, a work which dealt with cosmology and eschatology. It was the only text written in Middle Persian; his other six works were written in an east Aramaic dialect in a distinctive Syriac script known as Manichaean. 2) *The Living Gospel* proclaimed Mani as the seal of the prophets and the Paraclete foretold by Christ. 3) *The Pragmateia* was a treatise which dealt with ethical matters. 4) *The Book of the Mysteries* contained a refutation of Bardaisan, a famous Syrian heretic (see Drijvers). 5) *Letters of Mani.* 6) *Psalms and Prayers.* 7) *The Book of the Giants.*

Fragments of *The Book of the Giants* from the oasis of Turfan in central Asia were identified in 1943 by W. B. Henning. Then in 1971 J. T. Milik identified this composition with fragments found also at Qumran. So though Mani denounced Jews as "murderers of God" it turns out that one of his canonical scriptures is actually a Jewish work which is a legendary expansion of the "Sons of God" passage in Genesis 6:2. Another Turfan fragment refers to the Burxan (i.e. Buddha) Henoch (i.e. Enoch) according to Klimkeit (1980). This demonstrates according to Reeves (1992, 1996) the importance of Jewish influence, probably mediated through the Elchasaites, upon Mani's early thinking (see also Gruenwald). Mani made the Enochic legend of the Watchers and the Giants a cornerstone of his theological speculations (Reeves 1996: 207). Manichaeanism as a highly syncretistic movement was also influenced by Zoroastrianism and by Gnostic Christianity, perhaps by the Marcionites.

Mani taught that there were two independent realms of Light and Darkness. In the first epoch light and darkness were separate; in the second epoch they were intermingled; and in the final epoch they were to be separated once more. In the first epoch the Great God (Zurvan) lived apart in the realm of light, the prince of darkness (Ahriman) lived in the realm of darkness. Both Zurvan and Ahriman are Zoroastrian terms (Yamauchi 1990: ch. 12).

In the second epoch the Great God created the Mother of Life, who in turn produced the Primal Man (Ohrmizd) as bait for the demons. The Primal Man with his five sons fought the forces of darkness but was defeated and devoured. A second envoy, the Living Spirit, liberated Primal Man but he left behind his sons: Light, Air, Fire, Wind and Water. Primal Man then flayed the demons and made the sky from their skins, the mountains from their bones, and the earth from their excrement. Only the sun and the moon were made of pure light.

When the third envoy appeared in the sun ship with twelve maidens, the male demons viewed them as naked women and the female demons as naked men. The male demons ejaculated and the female demons had abortions. From the ejaculated seed came trees and from the abortions came animals. To try to retain some particles of light the powers of darkness created Adam and Eve. Man's body was therefore but an animal manifestation of the evil archons. Man was unaware that he possessed a particle of light in his soul.

The third envoy called forth Jesus the Splendor and sent him to Adam to redeem the light concentrated in his mind (νουσ), but not his body. The Manichaeans taught a docetic view of Christ (Yamauchi 1982) and emphatically denied that Jesus was born in "a womb unclean." Salvation was mediated through *gnosis* or knowledge of man's divine soul. Perfected Manichaeans had to persevere through ascetic practices until death, which means the liberation of the soul from the body. The particles of light rose up in the Column of Glory in the Milky Way first to the moon, then to the sun, and finally to Paradise.

The Manichaeans were sharply divided between an elite circle known as the *Electi,* and the mass of laymen known as *Auditores* "Hearers." The souls of the auditors at death were reborn as other men by transmigration. The auditors, who lived the lives of ordinary citizens, offered daily gifts of cucumbers and melons, which were believed to possess a great deal of light, to the elect. As L. Koenen (1990: 18) describes the process, "The stomachs of the elect, who as New Men live in abstinence and fasting and do not violate the divine soul captured in this world, liberate the particles of Light contained in vegetarian food and send them, under prayer, through their mouth to heaven."

At the end of the world all evil will be burned in a final conflagration, which will set free most but not all the particles of light. The damned and the demons and some unredeemed particles of light were to be encased in a great prison lump (Greek *bolus,* Latin *globus*).

The Manichaeans were zealous missionaries who enjoyed great success both in the West and in the East (Lieu). As is well known from his writings, Augustine was a Manichaean auditor for nine years (Koenen 1978). His anti-Manichaean writings did much to stem the Manichaean advance in the West, though Manichaean-like doctrines continued to surface in the Middle Ages among the Paulicians, Bogomils, and Cathars/ Albigenses (Ries).

In the East the Manichaeans along with Nestorian Christians utilized the Silk Route to penetrate into China, adapting their message to their Buddhist audiences (Yamauchi 1966a). For a time Manichaeism became the state religion of the Turkish Uighur kingdom. Many Manichaean documents have been recovered in a variety of dialects including Uighur, Persian, and Chinese from the Turfan oasis (Klimkeit 1993).

The Mandaeans

The Mandaeans of southern Iraq and southwestern Iran are the sole Gnostic community to survive from antiquity (Drower, Rudolph 1978, Lupieri). Though many of the scholars of Mandaeanism in the past and present such as E. S. Drower, R. Macuch, and K. Rudolph have assumed a pre-Christian date for their Gnosticism, I have argued that this movement cannot be dated earlier than the second century AD (Yamauchi 1970).

Their earliest texts are magical incantations inscribed on lead amulets or on terra cotta bowls (Yamauchi 1967, idem 1996b, idem 2000). None of these can be dated before the second century. The bowls have been dated to the late Sasanian era or the early Islamic period. The major religious documents, on the other hand, are manuscript copies which are no earlier than the 16th century, though colophons claim much earlier pre-Islamic dates for their composition (Gündüz).

The Mandaic script has affinities with the Nabataean script, the Elymaean script used around Susa, and the Characenian script of Charax Spasinu at the head of the Persian Gulf. Scholars disagree over its derivation. While the Nabataean script may be pre-Christian, both the Elymaean and Characenian scripts date to the 2nd century AD. R. Macuch, who believes in the early western origin of the Mandaeans, asserts that the Mandaic script most closely resembles the Nabataean (Macuch 1971). Other scholars disagree (Coxon, Naveh, Klugkist).

When the major Mandaean manuscripts were first translated by M. Lidzbarski early in the 20th century, scholars of the History-of-Religions school such as W. Bauer seized upon them as evidence of a pre-Christian Gnosticism. They were used in turn by Rudolf Bultmann in interpreting John and Paul. The Mandaean "fever" of the 1920's to 1940's (see Yamauchi 1966) has been eclipsed by the subsequent discovery of the Nag Hammadi Coptic Library in 1945 (Yamauchi 1987) and the Dead Sea Scrolls in 1947.

The 1970 publication of the Cologne Mani Codex was also a turning point in Mandaean studies. Though Kurt Rudolph acknowledged that the Cologne Mani Codex had disproved his earlier belief that the Mughtasilah of an-Nadim were Mandaeans (Rudolph 1974), he still maintains that the Mandaeans, who to this day live in Southern Iraq, also formed part of this baptist sectarian world which surrounded the young Mani. (Rudolph 1987: 329). A close parallel to Mani's distinction between the physical water and the water of gnosis is the contrast between "the living water" which the Mandaean savior *Mandā dHaiyê* "The Gnosis of Life" drew down into the *mia tahmia* "turbid water" according to the *Ginza*. Koenen (1981: 746-47) has suggested that Mandaeans and Mani's baptists have common ancestors. Both of them developed from Jewish baptists.

Several interesting parallels to Mani's denigration of water baptism as polluted or polluting, in contrast to the spiritual baptism of gnosis, are found in such Nag Hammadi tractates as *The Apocalypse of Adam,* and *The Paraphrase of Shem.* Though these tractates have been used to argue for a pre-Christian origin of Gnosticism, I believe that this anti-baptismal polemic was not directed against a pre-Christian Jewish baptismal sect, but against a Jewish-Christian baptismal sect like the Elchasaites of the second or third century (Yamauchi 1997).

The Mandaeans baptize repeatedly (Buckley 1989) in flowing water which they call *iardna* (Drower and Macuch 187). (At the 1999 Harvard conference on the Mandaeans, in which I participated, a Mandaean priest baptized several candidates in the Charles River - See Figure 1). The obvious derivation from the Jordan River was M. Lidzbarski's chief argument for the western origin of the Mandaeans

Figure 1, Photographs of Baptism in the Charles River.

(Lidzbarski 1928 reprinted in Widengren 1982: 385 ff.). On the other hand, H. Lietzmann suggested that the Mandaeans derived the name "Jordan" for the baptismal waters from the Nestorians, who also used the same nomenclature (Lietzmann 1930, reprinted in Widengren 1982: 94).

While other scholars such as Rudolph and Gündüz have attempted to identify in the Mandaean texts western, i.e. Jewish, elements, I am much more impressed by the legacy of ancient Babylonian traditions, especially in their early magical texts (Yamauchi 1970: 83-86; cf. Greenfield 1973 and 1993).

Among the elements which distinguished the Mandaeans from other Gnostic groups have been their positive evaluation of marriage and procreation (Yamauchi 1970), and their overwhelming emphasis on cult and ritual. While some Gnostic texts such as *The Gospel of Philip* hint at Gnostic rites (cf. Buckley 1983: 336), and while the Manichaeans had their rather elaborate ritual, none have had such an overwhelming emphasis upon the meticulous observance of ritual as the Mandaeans. An elaborate ceremony is necessary for the consecration of a Mandaean priest (Buckley 1985).

It is, I believe, their tenacious adherence to the traditional rituals and customs which has enabled the Mandaeans to survive, and not their Gnostic theology. Ironically, it is such unchanging tradition which now threatens their survival as the rapid changes of modernization make it increasingly difficult to find candidates for the priesthood, just as it threatens the similarly traditional and close-knit community of the Parsees (modern Zoroastrians) in India (Yamauchi 1990: 447-48).

REFERENCES

I am indebted to A. Henrichs, L. Koenen, E. Lupieri, and W. Sundermann for their generosity in sharing their publications with me.

Amidon, P. R., tr.
1990   *The Panarion of St. Epiphanius, Bishop of Salamis.* New York: Oxford University Press.
Bianchi, U.
1985   The Contribution of the Cologne Mani Codex to the Religio-Historical

Study of Manicheism. Pp. 15-24 in *Papers in Honour of Professor Mary Boyce,* ed. A. D. H. Bivar and J. Hinnells. Leiden: Brill.

Buckley, J. J.

1983 Mani's Opposition to the Elchasaites: A Question of Ritual. Pp. 323-36 in *Traditions in Contact and Change,* ed.by P. Slater and D. Wiebe. Waterloo, Ontario: Wilfrid Laurier University Press.

1985 The Making of a Mandaean Priest. *Numen* 32: 194-217.

1986 Tools and Tasks: Elchasaite and Manichaean Purification Rituals. *Journal of Religion* 66: 399-411.

1989 Why Once Is Not Enough: Mandaean Baptism (Maṣbuta) as an Example of a Repeated Ritual. *Numen* 29: 23-34.

Cameron, R. and Dewey, A. J., tr.

1979 *The Cologne Mani Codex: (P. Colon. inv. nr. 4780) "Concerning the Origin of His Body."* Missoula: Scholars Press.

Coxon, P. W.

1970 Script Analysis and Mandaean Origins. *Journal of Semitic Studies* 15: 16-30.

Drijvers, H. J. W.

1966 *Bardaiṣan of Edessa.* Assen: Van Gorcum.

Drower, E. S.

1962 *The Mandaeans of Iraq and Iran.* Leiden: Brill.

Drower, E. S. and Macuch, R.

1963 *A Mandaic Dictionary.* Oxford: Clarendon Press.

Fossum, J.

1983 Jewish-Christian Christology and Jewish Mysticism. *Vigiliae Christianae* 37: 260-87.

Giversen, S.

1990 Mani's Apology (CMC 91,19-97,21). Pp. 67-76 in *Codex Mani-chaicus Coloniensis,* ed. L. Cirillo. Cosenza: Marra Editore

Greenfield, J. C.

1973 Notes on Some Aramaic and Mandaic Magic Bowls. *Journal of the Ancient Near East Society* 5:149-56.

1993 "The Babylonian Forerunner of a Mandaic Formula." Pp. 11-14 in **kinattūtu ša dārâti** *Kutscher Memorial Volume*), ed. A. F. Rainey. Tel Aviv: Institute of Archaeology.

Gruenwald, I.

1983 Manichaeism and Judaism in Light of the Cologne Mani Codex. *Zeit schrift für Papyrologie und Epigraphik* 50:29-45.

Gündüz, S.

1994 The Problems of Nature and Date of Mandaean Sources. *Journal for the Study of the New Testament* 53: 87-97.

Henning, W. B.

1943 The Book of the Giants. *Bulletin of the School of Oriental and African Studies* 11:52-74.

Henrichs, A. and Koenen, L.
1970   Ein griechischer Mani-Codex. *Zeitschrift für Papyrologie und Epigraphik* 5: 97-217.
1981   Der Kölner Mani-Kodex . . . Edition der Seiten 99,10-120. *Zeitschrift für Papyrologie und Epigraphik* 44:201-318.

Irmscher, J.
The Book of Elchasai. Pp. 745-50 in *New Testament Apocrypha* (vol. 2), ed. by E. Hennecke and W. Schneemelcher. Philadelphia: Westminster Press.

King, W. H.
1994   The Travels of Mani: A Short Sketch of Mani's Life. *Humanitas* 18.2: 39-47.

Klijn, A. F. J. and Reinink, G. J.
1973   *Patristic Evidence for Jewish-Christian Sects.* Leiden: Brill.
1974   Elchasai and Mani. *Vigiliae Christiane* 28:277-89.

Klimkeit, H. J.
1980   Der Buddha Henoch: Qumran und Turfan. *Zeitschrift für Religions-und - Geistesgeschichte* 32:367-75.
1993   *Gnosis on the Silk Route.* San Francisco: Harper San Francisco.

Klugkist, A.
1986   The Origins of the Mandaic Script. Pp. 111-20 in *Scripta Signa Vocis,* ed. H. L. J. Vanstiphout et al. Groningen: Egbert.

Koenen, L.
1971   Das Datum der Offenbarung und Geburt Manis. *Zeitschrift für Papyrologie und Epigraphik* 8:247-50.
1978   Augustine and Manichaeism in Light of the Cologne Mani Codex. *Illinois Classical Studies* 3:154-95.
1981   From Baptism to the Gnosis of Manichaeism. Pp. 734-56 in *The Rediscovery of Gnosticism* (vol. 2), ed. B. Layton. Leiden: Brill.
1990   How Dualistic Is Mani's Dualism? Pp. 1-34 in *Codex Manichaicus Coloniensis,* ed. L. Cirillo. Cosenza: Marra Editore.

Koenen, L. and Römer, C.
1985   *Der Kölner Mani-Kodex.* Bonn: Habelt.

Lidzbarski, M.
Alter und Heimat der mandäischen Religion. *Zeitschrift fur neutestamentliche Wissenschaft* 27: 321-27.

Lietzmann, H.
1930   Ein Beitrag zur Mandäerfrage. *Sitzungsberichte der Preussischen Akademie der Wissenschaften, phil.-hist. Klasse.* Pp. 596-608.

Lieu, S. N. C.
1985   *Manichaeism in the Later Roman Empire and Medieval China.* Manchester: Manchester University Press.

Lieu, J. M. and S. N. C.
 1991 Mani and the Magians (?) - CMC 137-140. Pp. 203-223 in *Manichaica Selecta,* ed. by A. Van Tongerloo and S. Giversen. Louvain: International Association of Manichaean Studies.

Lupieri, E.
 2001 *The Mandaeans: The Last Gnostics.* Grand Rapids: Eerdsmans.

Luttikhuizen, G. P.
 1985 *The Revelation of Elchasai.* Tübingen: Mohr.

Macuch, R.
 1971 The Origins of the Mandaeans and Their Script. *Journal of Semitic Studies* 16: 174-92.

Merkelbach, R.
 1988 Die Täufer, bei denen Mani aufwuchs. Pp. 105-33 in *Manichaean Studies,* ed. P. Bryder. Lund: University of Lund Press.

Milik, J. T.
 1971 Turfan et Qumran, Livre des Géants juifs et manichéen. Pp.117-27 in *Tradition und Glaube,* ed. by G. Jeremias, H.-W. Kuhn, and H. Stegemann. Göttingen: Vandenhoeck & Ruprecht.
 1976 *The Books of Enoch, Aramaic Fragments of Qumrân Cave 4* Oxford: Oxford University Press.

Mimouni, S. C.
 1998 Les nazoréens recherche étymologique et historique. *Revue Biblique* 105: 208-62.

Naveh, J.
 1970 The Origins of the Mandaic Script. *Bulletin of the American Schools. of Oriental Research.* 198: 32-37.

Pritz, R. A.
 1988 *Nazarene Jewish Christianity.* Jerusalem: Magnes Press; Leiden: Brill.

Reeves, J. C.
 1991 The "Elchasaite" Sanhedrin of the Cologne Mani Codex in the Light of Second Temple Jewish Sectarian Sources." *Journal of Jewish Studies* 42: 68-91.
 1992 *Jewish Lore in Manichaean Cosmogony.* Cincinnati: Hebrew Union College Press.
 1996 *Heralds of That Good Realm.* Leiden: Brill.
 1999 *Manichaica Aramaica?* Adam and the Magical Deliverance of Seth. *Journal of the American Oriental Society* 119.3: 432-39

Ries, J.
 1994 Manichéens, Paulicians, Bogomiles, Cathares. Pp. 154-64 in *Tradition und Translation,* ed. C. Elsas et al. Berlin: W. de Gruyter.

Rudolph, K.
 1960 *Die Mandäer I.* Göttingen: Vandenhoeck and Ruprecht.
 1974 Die Bedeutung des Kölner Mani-Codex für Manichäismusforschung. Pp.

471-86 in *Mélanges d'histoire des religions offerts à Henri-Charles Puech*. Paris: Presses Universitaires de France.

1978 *Mandaeism*. Leiden: Brill.

1987 *Gnosis: The Nature and History of Gnosticism*. San Francisco: Harper.

1988 Jüdische und christliche Täufertraditionen im Spiegel des CMC. Pp.69-80 in *Codex Manichaicus Coloniensis,* ed. L. Cirillo. Cosenza: Marra Editore.

Smith, Robert W.

1994 "Arabia Haeresium Ferax?" A History of Christianity in the Transjordan to 395 C.E. An unpublished Ph.D.dissertation. Oxford, OH: Miami University.

Sundermann, W.

1971 Zur frühen missionarischen Wirksamkeit Manis. *Acta Orientalia Academiae Scientiarum Hungaricae* 24: 79-125.

1986 Mani's Revelations in the Cologne Mani Codex and in Other Sources. Pp. 105-14 in *Codex Manichaicus Coloniensis,* ed. L. Cirillo. Cosenza: Marra Editore.

Wineland, John

2001 *Ancient Abila: An Archaeological History.* Oxford: Archaeopress

Yamauchi, E. M.

1966 The Present Status of Mandaean Studies. *Journal of Near Eastern Studies* 25: 88-96.

1967 *Mandaic Incantation Texts*. New Haven: American Oriental Society.

1970 *Gnostic Ethics and Mandaean Origins*. Cambridge, MA: Harvard University Press.

1982 The Crucifixion and Docetic Christology. *Concordia Theological Quarterly*. 46: 1-20.

1983 *Pre-Christian Gnosticism*. 2nd ed. Grand Rapids: Baker Book House.

1987 The Nag Hammadi Library. *Journal of Library History* 22:425-41.

1990 *Persia and the Bible*. Grand Rapids: Baker Book House.

1991 Christians and the Jewish Revolts against Rome. *Fides et Historia* 23: 11-30.

1996a Adaptation and Assimilation in Asia. *Stulos Theological Journal* 4: 103-26.

1996b Cyrus H. Gordon and the Ubiquity of Magic in the Pre-Modern World. *Biblical Archaeologist* 59:51-55.

1997 The Issue of Pre-Christian Gnosticism Reviewed in the Light of the Nag Hammadi texts. Pp. 72-88 in *The Nag Hammadi Library after Fifty Years,* eds. J. Turner and A. McGuire. Leiden: Brill.

1998 "God and the Shah": Church and State in Sasanid Persia. *Fides et Historia* 30:80-99.

1999-2000 Mandaic Incantations: Lead Rolls and Magic Bowls. *Aram* 11-12: 147-57.

Scythopolis, City of the Scyths?

Keith N. Schoville
University of Wisconsin-Madison

Introduction

Scythopolis, or more exactly Nysa-Scythopolis, was the Hellenistic/Roman/ Byzantine town which was founded on the site of the more ancient Beth-Shean. The city was distinguished by its location at the junction of the Jezreel and Jordan valleys, thus at a natural crossroads of major routes through Syria-Palestine. But even more, it was distinguished as the only city of the Decapolis lying west of the Jordan River. It was both this connection of the site and that of Dr. W. Harold Mare to the Decapolis, the latter through his on-going excavations at Abila of the Decapolis, that has motivated this study. It is my hope that the results will honor him as much as he has honored me with the pleasure of years of association in the Near East Archaeological Society.

From Beth-Shean to Scythopolis

The ancient tell (Tell el-Husn, the mound of the fortress) had a long history prior to the conquests of Alexander the Great, beginning with ceramic evidence from the late Neolithic (Yarmukian) and early Chalcolithic periods (ca. 4500-3300 B.C.). These were discovered above virgin soil in a deep probe on the site by G. M. Fitzgerald during the last two years of the University of Pennsylvania's excavations[1] (Fitzgerald 1930 & 1933: 5-22). The probe, however, was necessarily very limited in the area exposed at the lowest level (Stratum XVIII). But in 1954 Nehemiah Tsori found similar Chalcolithic remains, consisting of pottery and flint implements comparable to Stratum XVIII-XVII on the tell and to Tuleilat Ghassul in the lower Jordan valley. The place in the lower city on the site where he discovered this evidence was 250 m. West of the Roman theater. The early remains were below a large Byzantine insula which he excavated and beneath the Chalcolithic stratum he found virgin soil (Tsori 1954: 265-6).[2]

Subsequently, Y. Yadin and S. Geva excavated atop the tell in 1983 for the Institute of Archaeology of the Hebrew University of Jerusalem, then in 1989 Amichai Mazar, (Mazar 1997: 62-76), on behalf of the Institute of Archaeology and the Tourism Administration of Beth-Shean, resumed work on the mound through 1996[3] (As a result of these excavations, it is clear that Level IV relates to the Iron IIB era)(ca. 800-600 B.C.). Then followed a gap in occupation, although Persian period tombs found to the east of the tell indicate human activity in the vicinity during that period[4] (Mazar 1996-97: *ABD* 1-222).

Level III marks the resettlement of Beth-Shean in the Hellenistic period, in the first half of the third century B.C., possibly during the reign of Ptolemy II Philadelphus[5] (Tsafrir and Foerster 1997: 86). The settlement became a polis within a century after its establishment, likely under the Seleucids, and was renamed Nysa-Scythopolis,[6] although it is possible that the Greek name was given to the city by the Ptolemies[7] (Tsafrir and Foerster 1987-88:42). M. Avi-Yonah has noted that it was uncharacteristic of the Ptolemies to name a town based on an ethnic designation. When changing Semitic names, they either chose dynastic names, such as in the change of Acco to Ptolemais, or Rabbath Ammon to Philadelphia and Elath to Berenice, or they simply gave the Greek equivalent of the Semitic name, as with the change of Sussita to Hippos[8] (Avi-Yonah 1962: 123-4). K. J. Rigsby has argued that the city was named Nysa after the name of the daughter of the Seleucid king Antiochus IV[9] (Avi-Yonah 1980: 238-42), although in the Roman era a local tradition held that the city was founded by the god Dionysus, who named it after his nurse, Nysa, whom he buried there[10] (Tsafrir and Foerster 1980: 86-7). The full name, Nysa-Scythopolis is impressed on some of the coins of the city and is used in official inscriptions, but normally the name was shortened to Scythopolis[11] (Meshorer 1975: 142-3). The earlier Semitic name, however, was never completely lost, as attested by references to the elided form Beshan in Hebrew and Aramaic, in Talmudic references, as well as in Syriac. As Avi-Yonah explained the situation, "The Greek name was used in Hellenized circles; the locals used Beth-Shean or Bîshan.... Thus, if the town was Hellenistic, the district remained inhabited by people speaking a Semitic language" (Avi-Yonah 1962: I:123).

The Semitic name reemerged as the place name with the Arab conquest of the region in the form Beisan. In fact, the Arab victory in A.D. 636 over Byzantine forces in the region was called the Day of Beisan (Mazar NEAEHL 1:214). Thus ended the designation Scythopolis, although the city continued to be inhabited until it was abandoned after the fourteenth century, and only the village of Beisan remained thereafter near the Crusader fort and amphitheater on the southern edge of the site (Foerster NEAEHL 1:223).

Scythopolis and the Decapolis

It appears that Scythopolis was so named prior to the more formal identification of the Decapolis. The earliest author to mention Scythopolis was Polybius (V, 70), in reference to the conquest of Antiochus III in 218 B. C. (Avi-Yonah: 123). The LXX also glosses Beth-Shean with Scythopolis (Βαιθσαν ἥ ἐστιν Σκυθῶν πολιζ) in Judg. 1:27 and Judith 3:10. The New Testament references to the Decapolis are the earliest textual evidence for the term, although Flavius Josephus refers to ten Syrian cities who came to Vespasian with a complaint, and he also mentions that Scythopolis, to the west of the Jordan, was the largest city of the Decapolis (Josephus *Life* 74:410; *J.W.* IX.7.446). These statements of the Jewish historian refer to the time of the First Revolt of the Jews against Rome. Pliny the Elder, a contemporary of Josephus, also refers to the Decapolis, as do other classical writers (Tzafrir, Di Segni and Green

1994: 223-25). Although it was earlier thought that the ten cities comprised a league established under Pompey (Bietenhard 1963: 24-58), S. T. Parker has shown that this was not the reality (Parker 1975). As J-P. Rey-Coquais indicates:

> The 10 cities experienced different destinies during the first part of the Roman domination; they did not form a politically coherent unit. Their unity comes from their Hellenistic character, which distinguished them sharply from neighboring populations. ... The 10 cities were Greek cities not only in origin and institutions but in culture (ABD, II:116).

The designation is more regional and cultural than political. The relationship of the cities to Pompey is due to the view held by their inhabitants and leaders that a new era had dawned for them when the Roman leader intervened in the chaotic situation in the region. The ten cities marked their liberation with Pompeian eras depending on the date of liberation, either in the autumn of 63 B.C. or the autumn of 64 B.C. Scythopolis used the latter era, and this usage continued until the end of the Roman empire (Bietenhard 1963: 24-58).

What remains unclear is when and why the city received the name Scythopolis, although we have suggested above that it occurred when Antiochus IV took control of the region. Y. Tsafrir and G. Foerster incline toward its establishment under Ptolemy II Philadelphus, with the subsequent attainment of polis status under the Seleucids (Tsfrir and Foerster 1997: 86-141). It is, of course, a well-known fact that Alexander established many cities during the course of his meteoric conquests (Amos and Lang 1992: 190), as did his successors following his early death and the fragmentation of his empire (Amos and Lang 1992: 195). To Alexander have been attributed the establishment of Macedonian colonies at Samaria, at Scythopolis, and at Neapolis, near the site of ancient Shechem (Bentwich 1919: 45). Whether this tradition is based on fact is open to question. As noted above, Ptolemy II Philadelphus transformed ancient Rabbath-Ammon into a Greek city named after himself, Philadelphia, and he could have established Scythopolis as well. But all of these possibilities reveal the underlying question of when and how the city came to be associated with the Scythians.

Eusebius and Syncellus in the Byzantine era connected the name of the city with the Scythian foray through the region all the way to the borders of Egypt in the days of King Josiah. [This invasion is based on Herodotus (I, 103-105), rather than on biblical data.] They thought that some of the Scythians settled in Beth-Shean and thus gave the city their name. (Chronikon: II, 88; 1892, Syncellus: I, 45). Though this view long held sway among scholars, V. Tscherikower effectively demolished it in 1927 (Tscherikower 1927: 71-2). Other Greek and Latin authors sought the origin of the name in mythology; their explanations are mere fables, although the connection with Dionysus was at least as old as the Hellenistic era (Avi-Yonah 1962: 126)

Others connect the assumed Scythian invasion to references to the *umman-manda* in the Babylonian Chronicle from the time of Nabopolassar (625-605 B.C.) They identify this group with the Scythians and believe that they appeared on the scene before the fall of Nineveh and the demise of the Assyrian empire. The view is that they became allies of the Medes rather than their enemies, and they joined the Medes and Chaldeans against the Assyrians and the Egyptians, including the siege of Nineveh, which ended with its fall in 612 B.C. They then joined in the siege of Harran for another two years, and it is assumed that they then took advantage of unsettled conditions in Syro-Palestine to invade the region in the spring of 609 B.C. Within a few months they reached the borders of Egypt and were bought off, likely by Pharaoh Psamtik (664-609 B.C.)(Avi-Yonah 1962: 126). This approach means that the Scythians did not control the region for an extended period, but simply made a raid lasting but a few months. If this was the valid scenario, then the question is: How indeed could a city of foreign horsemen maintain itself in hostile surroundings for three hundred years until the arrival of the Greeks and still keep its identity? (Avi-Yonah 1962: 125). That the Scythians pillaged Palestine may be allowed, following Herodotus, however, any relationship to the re-naming of Beth-Shean in the Hellenistic age seems unlikely.

In the 18th century H. Relandus proposed that the name Scythopolis was a distortion by the Greek language of the biblical word Succoth (Relandis 1714: 992-8). In the 19th century, George Adam Smith proposed an idea that has more recently been advanced by E. Frézouls, that is, that the basis of Scythopolis is ultimately connected with the Semitic name she'an = quiet, which underlies an assumed scyth, derived from the Hebrew sheqe = quietness (Frezouls 1987: 88; Rey-Coquais: *ABD* II:118). If valid, which is questionable to say the least, this solution would eliminate any need to involve the Scyths in the name and would derive it from the older name, Beth-shan. The she'an element of the name is apparently related to the Semitic root Š-'-N "to be at ease or at peace, rest securely" (*BDB*, 983). Apparently the Canaanites had named their city after a deity, She`an, who represented the idea of "peace, security " (little of which the place actually experienced, as testified by the many destruction layers in the tell) and had built a temple to his honor. But in the LXX there is no slippage toward sheqe; the translators simply transliterated into Greek. It is more likely that the Hellenistic name Scythopolis was actually connected with Scythians. Jean-Paul Rey-Coquais has summarized possibilities of Scythian connections as follows:

> According to the 6th century Chronography of John Malalas (5.178) the name recalled a Scythian settlement there from the time of the Trojan War. A Scythian settlement might date from the 7th century according to Herodotus (4.105), or perhaps might have arisen under Ptolemy II (*ANRW* 278, 262-94 and ABD, II: 117-18).

The idea of a settlement related to the Trojan War seems highly unlikely; the other suggestions remain a possibility. But the matter remains unsettled, and it is a fact that no archaeological evidence of Scythians has been found in the pre-Hellenistic strata. But who were the Scyths?

Scythopolis, City of the Scyths?

The Scythians

The Scythians shall forever be associated with the horse and with the development of horse riding (Trippett 1974: 9). Lost in the shadows of prehistory on the steppes that stretch from Hungary to Manchuria is the story of the emergence of the predecessors of the Scythians. Those were the first humans to master mounting and riding the small, sturdy ponies that roamed the steppes, perhaps as early as 1000 B.C.

The story of the symbiotic relationship of the horse to humans is readily available; suffice it to note here that the Cro-Magnons included the horse in their cave paintings. Apparently they were hunted for food, and the paintings were a part of religious exercises to assure successful hunts. Horses were first domesticated in the Neolithic age, and not before the domestication of sheep, goats, and cattle. We can assume that the domestication of horses was at first for the purpose of supplying humans with meat, milk and hides. (Scythians, and likely earlier horse nomads, enjoyed an intoxicating drink made from fermented mare's milk today known as kumiss, just as do modern herdsmen of Central Asia and Mongolia.)

Some of the earliest evidence for domesticated horses comes from the Ukraine, where their bones appear in 4th Millennium B.C. garbage heaps deposited by farmers and early pastoralists (Trippett 1974: 43). By the beginning of the 2nd Millennium B.C., the archaeological record in the Ukraine breaks off, which has been interpreted as evidence that the people had turned to semi-nomadism, presumably due to unknown forces. Their horses were likely used for pack animals or to pull carts, and perhaps occasionally someone would sit on a more docile animal. Meanwhile, in the more developed cultures of Mesopotamia, horses were not used; instead, the ox and the onager served as draft animals. Both could be controlled by a nose ring. The horse was known as 'the ass of the mountain' when it first appeared in Mesopotamia, and it was controlled by a thong or rope over the nose and under the chin. Nose rings were inappropriate for controlling the high-strung horse. The nature of the untrained horse is such that the idea of riding the animal came late in the process of domestication. Further, until selective breeding was practiced, the horses of the steppes were small, just over four feet tall. So they were first used to pull carts and chariots, displacing the onagers for that purpose. This was particularly true with the introduction of the light chariot by the Hittites around 1700 B.C. and its rapid adoption by the major powers in Egypt and Mesopotamia. Connected with this was the development of equipment to control the horse. The earliest proof of a mounted rider is of a wooden figure from an Egyptian tomb dated to ca. 1350 B.C. Interestingly, the first riders mounted horses as they had mules, riding on the rump rather than the back. As riding techniques improved, the position of the rider moved forward to the normal riding location. Not until the 4th Century A.D. was the contoured saddle developed, nor were stirrups invented before the 6th Century.

Evidence from tombs in the Altai Mountains of Siberia indicate that the horsemen of the steppes, such as the Scythians, rode tall and well-kept geldings, mounted on decorated saddle cloths, with the bridles also decorated. The Scyth became both the master of horsemanship and the terror of his world, thus described by Frank Trippett:

65

They were in all respects a passionate people—bearded men with dark, deep-set eyes, weather-cured faces and long, wind-snarled hair. They drank from the skulls of slain enemies and flaunted the scalps of their foes as trophies 37(2 Maccabees 7:4, Herodotus iv, 64). In a time when nations had not yet developed skilled cavalrymen and relied almost entirely on foot soldiers and chariots, the Scythians came riding at a gallop, shooting fusillades of singing arrows from their bows. The arrows were armed with deadly three-edged heads, and as these projectiles rained down on their adversaries, the Scythians would plunge forward as though to engage. Then, in the instant before contact, they would wheel about, launch fresh flights of arrows over the rumps of their retreating horses (the so-called Parthian shot) and, shrieking, thunder away to regroup for a new onslaught, leaving the dust-enveloped enemy in disarray (Trippett 1974: 9).

Mounted on a horse, a man towered over foot-soldiers and could easily outrun his enemies, striking terror to their hearts. It is likely that the first encounter of the Greeks with the Scythians or a similar group sparked the mythology of the Centaur, the creature with the body of a horse and the torso and head of a human being. Symbols of the wild savagery and barbarism of the Centaur first appeared on painted vases and bronzes in the 8th Century B.C. (Devambez 1967: 95). Similarly, another tribe of horsemen from the eastern steppes—the Sarmatians—whose women rode and fought alongside their men seem to have been the basis for the Greek depictions of the legendary Amazons (Trippett 1974: 22; Devambez 1967: 32-3).

The earliest historical mention of the Scythians appears to be Assyrian references to *Ashguzai* in the annals of Esarhaddon (681-668 B.C.). *Ashguzai* is likely related to biblical *ashkenaz* (Gen 10:3; 1 Chr 1:6; Jer 51:27). In the Jeremiah passage *ashkenaz* is associated with the northern regions of Minni and Ararat (Yamauchi 1982: 41) and in a context calling for horses to be sent up (against Babylon) like a swarm of locusts. Other references in Jer 4:29; 5:15-17: 6:22-26; and 50:41-42, referring to cruel and merciless destroyers who sound like the roaring sea as they ride on their horses in battle formation, may also refer to Scythian horsemen; however, once the Assyrians became aware of the savagery of Scythian horsemen in battle and the advantage of mounted warriors, they allied with the Scythians against the Cimmerians. (The latter had been forced south into the northern regions of Assyria by the Scythians.) The leader of the Scythians, King Bartatua, married an Assyrian princess in 674 B.C. By the time of the prophet Jeremiah, the Assyrians were quite familiar with the value of calvary and both adopted the use of mounted horsemen in their armies and employed Scythians as mercenary forces (Trippett 1974: 10-11), so the early references in Jeremiah may have referred only to Assyrian cavalry. The Scythians may be alluded to in the prophecies of Zechariah as well (Malamat 1950: 149-59).

Much of what is known about the Scythians comes from Herodotus, who obtained much of his information while visiting Olbia, a Greek city on the Black Sea, in which

Scythopolis, City of the Scyths?

Scyths and Greeks commingled (Trippett 1974: 11). Herodotus reported Scythian domination of an enigmatic upper Asia for twenty-eight years. This may have been in the region of Azerbaijan but, as E. Yamauchi has pointed out drawing on the work of A. Millard, it likely comprised twenty years of dominance in eastern Turkey (645-625 B.C.) and eight years in Media during the first years of Cyarxes (625-617 B.C.)(Yamauchi 1998: 52). Their dominance, however, was largely that of their normal activities as marauding raiders, nomadic warriors plundering settled folk. Such tactics may have driven the Medes into a confederacy that was to ultimately rise to power as the Persian Empire (Trippett 1974: 11). Whether or not during this time Scythians rampaged down through Syro-Palestine is uncertain although, as noted above, it has been stated that "Apparently they plundered their way through Palestine right to the border of Egypt; the Pharaoh halted their advance by buying them off" (Trippett *1974:* 11; Herodotus 1.105). As it turned out, Cyaxares was able to defeat the Scythians, expelling them from Media. A remnant may have later become mercenaries of the Babylonians and been involved in Nebuchadnezzar's conquest of Jerusalem (Yamauchi 1982: 99).

Combatants of Scythian origin, or natives of the Greek cities of the Bosphoran kingdom, who were also called Scythians, served in the armies of Alexander and his successors, including the Ptolemaic army (Launey 1950: 421-23, 1205). It is possible that Ptolemy II settled Scythian veterans at Beit-Shean. They were not necessarily pure-blooded Scythians, but a mixture of people from varied backgrounds. This would be similar to mixed groups designated Macedonian or Persian in Hellenistic and Roman Egypt, while having little or nothing in common with those nations but the name (Tcherikover and Fuks 1957: 13-15; Tarn and Griffith 1952: 218). So it is possible, as Avi-Yonah ponders, that the Beth-Shean region was an appropriate place for horse-archers, because it had ample grazing grounds for horses, in comparison to the intensively cultivated Nile Valley. He notes, as well, that comparable veterans known as Dahians who fought in the army of Antiochus III at Raphia in 217 B.C. might have included some of the settlers of Scythopolis, who had gone over to the Syrian side. Dahians reappeared in Antiochus III's army at Magnesia in 188 B.C. (Avi-Yonah 1962: 127; Launey. 1950: 568, n.3). Despite these observations, the connection of Scythians to Scythopolis remains hidden behind a veil of possibilities.

Scythian contact with the Assyrians, the Babylonians, the Medes and Persians, and particularly the Greeks in their colonies along the north shore of the Black and Azov Seas in time lost some of their savagery and were attracted to the blandishments of the more sophisticated culture. Over time many of them abandoned the nomadic way of life and settled in cities. For example, the bowmen who served as policemen in Athens were all recruited from Scythia (Devambez 1967: 424). Another group of horse nomads, the Sarmatians, forced the Scythians that remained in the 2nd Century B.C. into the Crimea, where they established a kingdom with a capital at Neapolis. The site of some 40 acres lies adjacent to modern Simferopol, and the ruins exhibit the influence of Greece in architectural and artistic remains (Trippett 1974: 86).

The end of the Scythians is aptly described by Trippett:

This new Crimean kingdom, ruled by urbanized horsemen, was powerful enough to pose a serious threat to Mithradates the Great, King of Pontus in Asia Minor. Alarmed, Mithradates sent an expedition against them and vanquished them in 106 B.C. Soon after their final defeat the Scythians vanished entirely as a distinct people. They would be virtually forgotten for many centuries to come, overshadowed by other hordes of the enduring, ever-fermenting people of the nomadization who rode out to command the attention and to affect the destinies of waxing and waning civilizations all around the steppes (Trippett 1974: 86).

From Scythopolis to Beisan

Hellenistic Period

What can be known about Beth-Shean/Scythopolis from the period of its abandonment until the renewal of settlement in the Hellenistic period is scanty and based largely on archaeological evidence. Some Persian clay figurines found on the tell suggest the possible continuation of cultic activity (Mazar *ABD* 1:222). On the mound later Roman period construction has greatly disturbed Hellenistic remains. The renewed occupation, however, spread around its base. Across the Nahal Harod to the north, excavations at Tel Iztabba in 1992-94 uncovered Hellenistic buildings, and G. Foerster suggests that the initial settlements beyond the tell in the Hellenistic period were first on the crests of nearby hills, rather than in the undefended, low-lying area (Mazar *ABD* 1:223), some of which were to become the city center in the Roman and Byzantine periods. The Tel Iztabba excavations also produced 466 Hellenistic period coins. Fourteen were of Ptolemy II, the rest from the time of a later, unidentified ruler; 270 Seleucid coins of Antiochus III (12); Antiochus IV (33); Demetrius I (2); Alexander I Ballas (19); Demetrius II (25); Antiochus VI (2); Antiochus II (12); Alexander II Zabinas (20); Cleopatra Thea and Antiochus VIII (42); Antiochus VII (13) and Antiochus IX (6)(Mazar and Bar-Nathan. 1998: 30-36). The Tel Iztabba buildings were destroyed by a fierce fire prior to the close of the 2nd Century B.C. (Mazar and Bar-Nathan 1998: 30-36; Avi-Yonah 1962: 130-1). This was likely due to the Hasmonean conquest successfully pursued by John Hyrcanus (106-104 B.C.) (Josephus War I:65-6). The Hasmonean policy offered inhabitants the choice of adopting Judaism or of leaving. The Hellenized inhabitants chose to leave, and their places were taken by Jewish settlers. Pompey and Gabinius restored the city to its pre-Hasmonean status, although Jews still continued in the mixed population of the city and in their villages in the hinterland (Mazar and Bar-Nathan 1998: 17: 35-36). Between 1992-94 at Tel Iztabba six Hasmonean coins were recovered, in addition to several Roman coins from various mints, a number of them Late Roman, and many Byzantine and Umayyad (Mazar and Bar-Nathan 1998: 30-36).

Scythopolis, City of the Scyths?

Roman Period

The designation of the Hellenistic cities in the region as the Decapolis, including Scythopolis, may have occurred during the governorship of Syria by Gabinius (57-55 B.C.)(Tsafrir, Di Segni and Green 1994: 10). The Pennsylvania excavations revealed a monumental Roman temple atop the mound, but Mazar's more recent excavations have produced hardly anything of the period. The interpretation is that the mound remained essentially unoccupied while a large Roman city flourished to the south of the tell (Mazar 1997: 74), reflecting the attitude of peace and security provided by Roman suzerainty.

Much of the early Roman era development seems to have occurred in the 1st century A.D. A civic basilica abutted a street some 12 m. wide, with shops along its sides. An early phase of the theater construction is from the same period, a bathhouse, the first stage of a temple with a round cella, and basalt streets and squares have been exposed; however, much of the early Roman period remains are below the impressive Late Roman and Byzantine city (Tsafrir and Foerster 1997: 89).

The main period during which the town flourished in the Roman era seems to have been during the 2nd or, at the earliest, the late 1st Century A.D. For example, the theater was likely built in the late 2nd or early 3rd Centuries, in the era of the Severans (A. D. 193-235)(Sperber 1998: 168). It is the largest theater yet discovered in Israel and could seat from between six and eight thousand spectators (Applebaum 1978: 77-97). The general plan of the city is attributed to the second half of the 2nd Century A.D., and unlike many Roman-era cities was not orthogonal, due to the dictates of the terrain with the confluence of the valleys of the two streams in the area. In this flourishing period, Scythopolis shared the pattern of other cities, enhancing their surroundings out of local patriotism. Joseph Geiger notes:

> The process of channeling its energies into social and cultural endeavors characterized ancient cities, rather than spending their energies on war, under the pax romana, as noted by Aelius Aristides in the 2nd century, 'As on holiday the whole civilized world lays down the arms which were its ancient burden and has turned to adornment and all glad thoughts with power to realize them. All other rivalries have left the cities, and this one contention holds them all, how each city may appear most beautiful and attractive. All localities are full of gymnasia, fountains, monumental approaches, temples, workshops and schools, and one can say that the civilized world, which had been sick from the beginning, as it were, has been brought by the right knowledge to a state of health (Sperber 1990: 141-150; Schurer, Vermes and Miller 1979: 50).

Scythopolis also enjoyed the titles of "City of Refuge," and "Holy City" (Sperber 1990: 141-150; Star 1991: 575), the latter no doubt due to the Roman temple which succeeded both Canaanite and Hellenistic cultic structures on the mound.

As the city developed, a colonnaded street paved with long, basalt stones laid in herringbone fashion linked the theater with the foot of the tell (Mazar ABD: 223). Evidence of the beginning of a monumental stairway, apparently leading to the temple atop the tell was discerned (Mazar 1997: 74).

In the course of time the city center included the theater, a portico in front of the theater, two bathhouses, a public latrine, the colonnaded street noted above and designated Palladius Street (based on an inscription related to it), three additional colonnaded streets with related shops, a semicircular plaza, an Odeon, a Nymphaeum providing running water in a public place, two temples and additional Roman cult structures, three propylons, a sigma, decorative pools, porticos, monuments and commemorative inscriptions (Tzafrir and Foerster 1997: 51, Fig. D: 1994: 92-99). Valley Street led from the city center to the Nahal Harod which was bridged by two arches and connected with the northeast city gate. A west gate has been exposed on the south side of the Harod valley; the road leads to a single-arched bridge. Following the city streets, the distance between the two gates is about 1.4 km. Literary evidence indicates that Scythopolis had six gates; four remain to be discovered (Tzafrir and Foerster 1997: 93). Outside the city center a hippodrome was constructed in the 2nd century. The latter was estimated to hold some 12,000 spectators.

Byzantine Period

Scythopolis continued to flourish and to expand from the mid-fourth to the mid-sixth centuries, in keeping with the general trends which saw an increase of population to about one million people in western Palestine. The population of Scythopolis likely reached fifteen to eighteen thousand by the end of the third century (Tzafrir and Foerster 1997: 94, 100; Broshi. 1979: 1-10), all this due to the long period of relative peace and stability, interrupted by an occasional natural disaster such as the earthquake of A.D. 363, and ending with the Samaritan revolts of A.D. 529, 536 and a bubonic plague of A.D. 541-2. Excavations and surveys indicate that the city underwent extensive expansion with Byzantine quarters established almost everywhere (Tzafrir and Foerster 1997: 100). This included re-occupation of Tel Iztabah, with its Monastery of the Lady Mary, (Metropolitan) Andreas' Church, and the Church of the Martyr (Tsafrir and Foerster 1997: 104, n.80, 106-7). Atop the ancient mound, a fine residential quarter occupied the entire area, (Mazar 1997: 74) with a circular church (Fitzgerald 1931: 18-30). Since many Jews lived in Scythopolis, along with Christians and pagans, not surprisingly, two synagogues have been excavated, one of which may have been Samaritan (Tsafrir and Foerster 1997: 103-4).

A wall was constructed around Scythopolis at an indeterminate date in this era, incorporating two freestanding monumental gates mentioned above. The renovation of the wall is mentioned in two inscriptions, but they were not found in relation to the actual wall. The suggested date for the reconstruction is near the end of the first quarter of the 6th century, the same period in which Scythopolis reached the zenith of its building activities, during the reigns of Anastasius and Justin I. The construction and renovation of a wall suggests declining security; other cities in the region also built walls at the end of the 3rd century and the beginning of the 4th century (Tzafrir and Foerster 1997: 101).

Indications of the major religious and cultural changes in Scythopolis as Christianity became dominant is evident in the archaeological remains. These include undated but obviously Christian inscriptions, decorated with crosses, evidence of the failure to rebuild damaged temples after the earthquake of A.D. 363, and their abandonment no later than the 5th century. Nevertheless, the essential Hellenic character of monuments and monumental buildings continued to exist in the city, apparently out of citizens' appreciation of their beauty and out of civic pride. Two of the four monolithic columns, with their huge, attractively decorated Corinthian capitals, and some elements of the entablature stood in front of the temple of Scythopolis until the early Islamic period, collapsing in the earthquake of 749 (Tzafrir and Foerster 1997: 111)." Apart from the renovation and alteration of structures over the several centuries of Byzantine occupation before the Arab conquest (ca. A.D. 635/6), an important innovation in the late 4th or early 5th centuries was the mosaic paving of porticoed sidewalks along the streets. All of this points to the general prosperity which the city enjoyed until the mid-6th century, when a decline set in, as noted previously. The factors involved in the decline were likely multifaceted, importantly including a slow reversion from the concept of the ordered Hellenistic and Roman planned city to the organic or spontaneous developments that characterized much earlier Iron Age urban growth. As Tsafrir and Foerster have noted, "In the Byzantine period we find the first signs of a reversion from rigid town planning to the organic or spontaneous style (Tsafrir and Foerster 1997: 140-1)." Characteristics of these changes included the narrowing of streets to lanes, the invasion of private buildings into public squares, the concealment of monumental facades behind private buildings erected against them, older sewage systems no longer maintained with sewage running in the streets, the streets no longer cleaned of dust and waste, and no effort made to re-erect fallen columns and capitals.

Something of the importance of the city before its decline was its designation as the main city of Palaestina Secunda, with the division of the region into three provinces at the beginning of the 5th century A.D. But by the end of the 6th century, the theater ceased to be used for entertainment; in the early Islamic occupation, it was used for a potter's workshop and some flimsy private dwellings.

From the 5th century on the amphitheater declined and lost its role as a center for the entertainment of the masses. Soon after the Islamic conquest, Scythopolis — now Baysan—lost its political significance when the capital of the province of al-Urdunn, the Islamic successor to Palaestina Secunda, was shifted to Tiberias.

Yet the ancient city was renowned for its olives, its bountiful harvests of wheat, and, as a gentile friend of Rabbi Hiyya boasted, everything that was made in the Six Days of Creation (Avi-Yonah 1962: 132). But the city proper was also famed for the fine linen cloth produced there. It became one of the great weaving centers of the Roman Empire, and a Latin author of the 4th century noted Scythopolis as one of the cities which supplied textiles to the entire world (Avi-Yonah 1962: 132). As Avi-Yonah explains:

Beyond the Jordan

The last stage (before the Arab conquest) in the evolution of the urban population of Scythopolis is marked by a movement of the Jewish population and possibly other members of the lower classes out of the town and back to the country. This is the period when the synagogues at [near by] Beth Alpha and Kefar Qarnayim were built. ... The reasons ... [were the effects of empire policies that] made the expert textile workers serfs working in state factories.

While the condition of the city worker worsened gradually, the great estates ... offered him employment and protection. ... Encouraged by such a change in the respective conditions of town and country, there was a corresponding shift of population. The Jews and Samaritans were especially ready to quit the cities which were ruled by hostile governors, supervised by bishops who had the full power of church and state behind them, and swayed on occasion by hostile mobs. Even before the Arab conquest, which sealed the doom of most of the Byzantine cities, the native population had given their judgement 'with their feet' (Avi-Yonah 1962:134).

The mystery of the "Scyth" in Scythopolis remains, but the story of one of the great cities of the Decapolis continues to be revealed through ongoing archaeological and literary research.

NOTES

[1] The University of Pennsylvania excavated the site between 1921-1933.

[2] Y. Meshorer, *IEJ* 25 (1975), 142-3 reports therein the recovery of several coins bearing the head of Dionysos, spikes of grain, and the inscription, "Of the people of Nysa, which is also Scythopolis." The coins were dated between A.D. 51/2 and A.D. 66/7. A gap in coinage then exists until the reign of Antoninus Pius (A.D. 139-61).

[3] For a more detailed exposition of this scenario, see M. Avi-Yonah, "Scythopolis," *IEJ* 12 (1962), 125-6; for additional information see D. J. Wiseman, *Chronicles of Chaldean Kings* (London, 1956), 15-16. Thomas W. Africa, in *The Ancient World* (Boston: Houghton Mifflin, 1969), 48 states, "Pursued by the Scythians, Ashuruballit withdrew his troops to Syria to await Egyptian aid. The Scythians plundered Palestine and returned to the northern steppes from whence they had come."

[4] *2 Macc* 7:4 100-63 B.C., refers to the Scythian method of scalping, in reference to one of seven brothers slain before their mother. Drawing on Herodotus (iv.64), the method is described as "cutting all the way around at the level of the ears and removing the scalp by pulling and shaking."

[5] *2 Macc, AB9*, 41A, 304. Much of what is known about the Scythians, apart from Herodotus' descriptions, is based on the decorative golden art which they used to adorn them-selves and their horses. These were primarily the work of Greek artisans, apparently using themes desired by their Scythian patrons, thus illustrating significant elements of their culture. There are no written records of Scythian origin. For suggested resources for a much more detailed description of Scythian art, consult the bibliography below.

[6] The Scythians occupied a large area to the north of the Black Sea north of the Caucasus beyond which the Kingdom of Urartu (Ararat) lay to the south. The Minni occupied an area south of Lake Urmia, as E. Yamauchi has indicated in *Foes from the Northern Frontier* (Grand Rapids: Baker, 1982) 41. The Scythians joined forces with the Assyrians to destroy Urartu.

[7] Josephus indicates that Antiochus VIII established a mint in Scythopolis (*Ant.*, XII, 277; *War*, I, 65).

[8] The evidence here contravenes the suggestion of M. Avi-Yonah.

[9] The theater was excavated in the late 1950s.

[10] Sperber, *Greece and Rome*, 141-150 "For the Roman Empire as a whole the era from A.D. 14 to 180 . . . was the most peaceful and secure that the ancient Mediterranean world ever experienced."

[11] Tsafrir and Foerster, *DOP* 51, 104, n. 80, 106-7, " . . . where it is suggested that, even though inscriptional evidence for the identity of the martyr has not been found, it may have been St. Procopius, who suffered martyrdom at Caesarea in A. D. 303, a St. Basilius , or Manathas / Ennathas, a woman who also suffered martyrdom at Caesarea in A. D. 309."

REFERENCES

Africa, T. W.
1969   *The Ancient World.* Boston: Houghton Mifflin.
Applebaum, S.
1978   *The Roman Theatre of Scythopolis.* Pp. 77-99 in Scripta Classica Israelica 4, 77-97.
Amos, H. D. and Lang, A. G. P.
1992   *These Were the Greeks.* Chester Springs, Pa.: Dufour Editions, Inc.
Avi-Yonah, M.
1962   Scythopolis. *Israel Exploration Journal* 12: 123-6,127, 132,134.
Bentwich, Norman
1919   *Hellenism* Philadelphia: Jewish Publication Society of America.
Bietenhard, E.
1963   Die Dekapolis van Pompeius bis Traian. *ZDPV* 79, 24-58.
Broshi, M.
1979   The Population of Western Palestine in the Roman Byzantine Period. *BASOR* 236: 1-10.
Brown, Francis; Driver, S. R. and Briggs, Charles A.
1962   *A Hebrew and English Lexicon of the Old Testament.* Oxford: At the Clarendon Press.
Devambez, P.
1967   *The Praeger Encyclopedia of Ancient Greek Civilization.* New York: Frederick A. Praeger.
Fitzgerald, G. M.
1935   The Earliest Pottery of Beth Shan. *Museum Journal* 24:5-22.
1931   Beth Shan. Excavations 1921-1923. III: The Arab and Byzantine Levels. Philadelphia.

Foerster, G. and Tsafrir, Y.
    1987 *Excavations and Surveys in Israel* 6: 42.
    1993 *NEAEHL* I: 223
Frézouls, E.
    1987 Historical Geography of the Holy Land. London, 22nd ed., n .d., Pp. 363-
           364; in *Du village a la ville: Problémes de l'urbanisation dans la Syrie
           hellénistique romaine* Strasbourg, 88.
Jones, A. H. M.
    1971 Cities of the Eastern Roman Provinces, ed., rev. A. Avi-Yonah et al. Oxford,
           Oxford University Press.
Josephus, Flavius
    n.d.   William Whiston, trans. Grand Rapids: Baker.
Launey, M.
    1950 *Recherches sur les armées hellenistiques.* Paris.
Malamat, A.
    1950 *The Historical Setting of Two Biblical Prophecies.* Israel Exploration
           Journal 1 (1950-51), 149-59.
Mazar, A.
    1993 Beth-Shan. *ABD* 1- 693-96.
    1997 *Biblical Archaeologist,* 60:2, 74.
Mazar, G., and Bar-Nathan, R.
    1998 The Beth-She'an Excavation Project - 1992-1994. Pp. 30-36 in
           Excavations and Surveys in Israel 17, 30-36.
Meshorer, Y.
    1975 *Israel Exploration Journal* 25, 142-43. 139-61).
Parker, S. T.
    1975 The Decapolis Reviewed. *Journal of Biblical Languages* 94:437-41.
Relandus, H.
    1714 *Palestina ex monumentis veterbis illustrata,* II. Utrecht.
Rey-Coquais, J.
    1992 "Decapolis." Trans. Stephen Rosoff, from French. ABD II - 116- 119.
Rigsby, K. J.
    1980 Seleucid Notes. *Transactions and Proceedings of the American
           Philological Association* 110: 238-42.
    1892 *Syncellus,* I, ed. W. Dindorf. Bonn.
Schurer, E., Vermes, G. and Miller, F.
    1979 *The History of the Jewish People in the Age of Jesus Christ, 2.* Edinburgh.
Sperber
    1990 *Greece and Rome in Eretz Israel.* Jerusalem: Israel Exploration Society.
    1998 *The City in Roman Palestine.* New York: Oxford University Press.
Starr, C. A.
    1991 *A History of the Ancient World.* New York: Oxford University Press.
Tarn, W. W., and Griffith, G. T.

1952 *Hellenistic Civilization.* London.
Trippett, F.
1974 *The First Horsemen: Emergence of Man.* New York: Time-Life Books.
Tscherikower, A. V.
1927 *Die hellenistischen Städtegründungen.* Leipzig:
Tscherikower, A. V. and Fuks, A.
1957 *Corpus Papyrorum Iudaicarum, I.* Cambridge.
Tsafrir, Y. and Di Segni, L, and Green, J.
1994 *Tabula Imperii Romani, Judaea-Palaestina: Maps and Gazetteer.* Jerusalem: Israel

"And They Raised Over Him a Great Heap of Stones That Stands to This Day"[1]

David Merling
Randall W. Younker

The stoning of an entire family has to be the most sorrowful deaths one could witness: familiar pleas for mercy, heavy stones breaking bones on many, the blended weeping of young and old, and, finally, the somber desertion of former friends from the place of judgment. The ethos of such an event is one of the reasons the story of Achan and the execution of his family is a compelling Old Testament story: one man, one sin and a family dead.[2] Surprisingly, the 1999 Tall Jalul Excavations, sponsored by Andrews University, have discovered what could be evidence of the execution of an entire family.[3]

At the end of the Tall Jalul 1996 season the supervisors of Field C, Paul Ray and Dick Dorsett, discovered the opening of what looked like a cave/cistern. Since the crevice was discovered during the last week of excavation, it was decided to reseal the entrance until the next expedition season. The excavation team then anxiously awaited the 1999 season for the opportunity to unlock the mysteries waiting to be found.

Even though we have now fully emptied the cave, we are still not sure that what we have found is a cave. Because of its location inside a Persian building, it looks to be a cistern, and many ancient buildings had cisterns as integral parts of their building complex. On the other hand, most cisterns were plastered to help the local porous limestone hold water. In this case, our cave (?) showed no signs of plaster. Our best guess is that this facility was a storage facility, not a cistern.[4]

In the 1999 season the supervisors of Field C were Connie Gane and, again, Dick Dorsett. One of their first duties was the opening of the mystery cave. As they began to excavate, it became obvious that what they had uncovered was more than a usual find, for within the cave the skeletal remains of 14 individuals were discovered: adults, several children, and one infant. There are three reasons that have caused us to conclude that these individuals may have been executed.

First, the size of the debris that covered each body was unusually large. Commonly, in burials, even when found in caves, one finds dirt covering the skeletons. In some late periods, a row of stones covers the dirt. In the case of those who were buried in the Field C cave, the stones that covered the dead were massive. There was

76

no attempt to bury the individuals with dirt. Each individual appears to have been "tossed" into the cave and smothered with huge boulders. To give the reader an idea of the size of the boulders, to complete the excavation process, we had to hire a crane to remove the boulders. No matter how many workmen worked together, they could not budge some of those stones.

Secondly, most who are buried in ancient and modern times are placed in a dignified position. In ancient times many were laid in the fetal position. Since Islamic times, it has been common to find burials with a person facing south toward Mecca. At Tall Jalul in Field A, we have uncovered over 100 burials dated to the 19th century. Every evidence of their burials showed they were most likely poor: shallow graves and few treasures were included in the burials. Yet, in each case the individuals were carefully buried in individual graves facing toward Mecca. Contrary to the usual carefulness, those found in the Field C cave were literally on their heads, with none of their skeletal remains in any natural position. They all gave the appearance of being tossed into a pit, then crushed by giant boulders.

In addition, it appears that all of the dead were buried at the same time. Careful excavation can usually discover surface layers between burials. In this case, no stratigraphic separations could be found. It appeared as though an individual was thrown into the cave, then several boulders were dumped on him/her, then another individual was cast into the cave, and more boulders were rolled on top and so on, until these fourteen individuals were executed, then the entire cave was sealed. Some skeletons had boulders directly on their bones.

Some have suggested that those buried may have been buried due to earthquake activity. The problem with this explanation is that the seismic activity would have had to last too long in order to allow the dozens of multi-ton boulders to have worked their way to the cave entrance and tumble in. At the same time, while the boulders were being shaken toward the cave entrance, like balls in a pin-ball machine, the walls of the Persian building that surrounded the cave remained unaffected. An earthquake explanation is not very likely. With the information we have, the best explanation is that the boulders were purposely pushed on to the individuals in the cave.

The building over the cave was dated to the late Iron II—that is, the 7th-6th centuries BC, so it seems likely that the skeletons found in the cave were from this same general time period (the time of Isaiah—7th century BC or Jeremiah—6th century BC). This dating was supported by the overwhelming amount of ceramic evidence found with them in the cave (which dated to the 7th/6th centuries). Even a 7th century seal was found near the cave. The pottery, the seal and some clay figurines found in the cave with the skeletons were Ammonite in style, which would strongly suggest that the victims were Ammonites. The intriguing mysteries that remain are, who was this family, why were they killed, and who killed them. Certainly the 7th-6th centuries BC were turbulent times for Transjordan, according to the Bible and extra-biblical texts. Hopefully, future excavation will shed more light on this puzzle.

NOTES

[1] Josh 7:26.

[2] Of course, much more was involved in the Achan story. Cf. E. G. White.

[3] The Tall Jalul Excavations are part of the Madaba Plains Project, loosely affiliated schools currently including La Sierra University, Canadian University College, and Walla Walla College excavating at Tall Jalul, Tall Hisban, and Tall al-Umaryi.

[4] In recent times the Jordanian Department of Antiquities has designated a formal transliteration system for ancient archaeological site names. One of the more noticeable changes is the transliteration of "tall" for the more commonly used "tell," for Jordanian mounds of ancient cities.

Tell Jalul Rock Buried Skeleton.

The Cities are Great and Walled Up To Heaven: Canaanite Fortifications in the Late Bronze I Period

A Paper Delivered to the Near East Archaeological Society
at the 52nd Annual Meeting of the Evangelical Theological Society
November 16,2000 Nashville, Tennessee
Colonel David G. Hansen, Ph.D. (USA, Ret.)
Associates for Biblical Research

Introduction

One of the most vociferously attacked historical accounts in the Bible is the Old Testament description of the Israelite Conquest of Canaan as recorded in the book of Joshua. According to many critics, the archaeological evidence does not support either the Biblical version or date of the Conquest events. In a recent analysis of the status of archaeology in contemporary Israel, the Israeli archaeologist Ze'ev Herzog said:

> This is what archaeologists have learned from their excavations in the Land of Israel: the Israelites were never in Egypt, did not wander in the desert, did not conquer the land in a military campaign and did not pass it on to the 12 tribes of Israel (Watzman 2000).

Christian evangelical scholars seem to agree and many have conceded that the biblical account of the Conquest is less than accurate and, as a result, are reinterpreting events so that they come into agreement with the supposed "assured" results of archaeological research. One notable example of this trend is an article authored by Daniel C. Browning Jr. (Ph.D. in Biblical Backgrounds and Archaeology, Southwestern Baptist Theological Seminary), in the conservative theological journal, *Southwestern Journal of Theology* (Browning 1998). Browning's article, "The Hill Country is Not Enough For Us: Recent Archaeology and the Book of Joshua," was reviewed by Dr. Bryant Wood (1999a, 1) who quoted the following from Browning's article:

> In order to defend—in a credible way—a military invasion [of Canaan], the conservative interpreter must be willing to concede that the book of Joshua is a glorified account of relatively small military encounters with an occasional

victory. The interpreter must further accept the possibility of etiological elements and editorial expansion of the story and the likelihood that some elements which composed Israel had their origin with the land itself.

Dr. Wood rhetorically asks, "is the problem with Scripture, or is it with scholars' interpretations of archaeological science?' This intriguing question prompted the development of this paper, which is intended to examine one of the problems confronting scholars as they try to correlate the biblical Conquest narratives with archaeological evidence: the presence or absence of fortified cities in Canaan during the Late Bronze Age IA/B period.

Background

The Date of the Conquest

To gain an appreciation of the difficulties facing scholars as they try to harmonize biblical stories and archaeological evidence, it is necessary to address the way archaeologists affix dates to their finds. Archaeological research operates within the framework of historical timelines. The Conquest narratives occurred in a time broadly referred to by most Near Eastern archaeologists as the Late Bronze Age. Archaeologists believe that the entire Bronze Age covered about two millennia, ca. 3100 - 1200 B.C., and have separated the Bronze Age into three sub-periods: Early (EB), Middle (MB) and Late (LB). The Bronze Age is sometimes referred to as the "Canaanite period"; but, for purposes of this paper, it will be designated as the Bronze Age.

A typical method for dating the sub-periods of the Bronze Age, and the transition into the subsequent Iron Age, is shown in Table 1. This paper's focus will be on the shaded years in Table 1, LB IA/B and IIA, which is the time of the Exodus and Conquest in the Bible.

It is well known that during the past 100 years or so there has developed a sizable body of scholarship that argues that the Old Testament Conquest accounts are, for the most part, an "editorial expansion" of the original story or, even worse, outright fabrications. In tandem with these theories is another proposition that archaeological evidence is lacking for the Conquest occurring in the 15th century BC, the date derived by a literal reading of the Bible. As a result, recent Bible commentaries and books addressing the Conquest have usually reported that the event happened in the 13th or, even later, in the 12th century BC.

To illustrate this point, Browning concluded his article with the statement that "nearly all participants in this discussion now place the emergence [not Conquest!] of Israel represented by the hill country villages—in the late 13th or early 12th century B.C.E."(Browning 1988: 26) This date (not to mention the means) blatantly contradicts the Bible. Even the editors of the evangelical journal *Christianity Today* do not appear to subscribe to the 15th century date. In a cover story, "Did the Exodus Never Happen?", the author (Miller 1998) approvingly places the Exodus and Conquest in the 13th century BC. Miller's article is based on the views of J. Hoffmeier. Hoffmeier, a respected Egyptologist formerly at Wheaton College and now at Trinity International University, summarized the prevalent situation in a recent book: "if there is a prevailing view among historians, biblical scholars, and archaeologists, an exodus in the Ramesside era (1279-1213 B.C.) [13th century] is still favored" (1997: 126).

Placing the Exodus and Conquest in the 15th century BC, a time known as the "early" date in some literature, is grounded on at least two biblical texts, I Kings 6:1 and Judges 11:26. I Kings 6:1 is the most direct statement in the Bible about the date of the Exodus. It places the event 480 years before Solomon's fourth regnal year, a time that can be dated with some certainty to 967/6 BC. Knowing this, the date of the Exodus can be mathematically determined as ca. 1447/6 BC (967/6 + 480 = 1447/6). According to the Bible, the Israelite military invasion into the land of Canaan began 40 years after they left Egypt, or ca. 1407/6 BC (1447/6 - 40 = 1407/6), which places the Conquest in the late 15th century BC and squarely in the first part of the Late Bronze Age, or the LB IB archaeological period.

The second Scripture from which a date for the Conquest can be determined is Judges 11:26. This verse records a seminal historical detail recounted by Jephthah during his negotiations with the king of Ammon (Judg 11). The Old Testament records that the Israelites occupied the contested Transjordanian and Ammonite territory just prior to their crossing of the Jordan River (Deut 2:26 ff.). In Judges 11:26 the Ammonite king laid claim to the Israelite land east of the Jordan River because the land had been forcibly, and therefore illegally, taken 300 years before by the Israelites during the Conquest. Judge Jephthah's rebuttal was that Israel had lived there for the past "three hundred years, [so] why did you [the king] not recover them [the lands] within that time?" (Judg 11:26b NASB). Biblical historians who accept that Jephthah was an actual person believe he lived around 1100 BC (for example, Malamat 1976: 76-7). Adding 300 years to the time of Jephthah (300 + 1100) results in a date for the Conquest of ca. 1400 BC—well in the Late Bronze Age and in general agreement with the date extrapolated from a literal reading of I Kings 6: 1.

LB I Fortified Cities

Regardless of whether a scholar subscribes to a date for the Exodus and Conquest in the "early" 15th century, or the "late" 13th/12th century, there is another problem. The books of Numbers, Deuteronomy and Joshua describe Canaanite cities as fortified and walled (e.g., Num 13:28; Deut 1:28; 3:5; 28:52; Josh 2:15; 6:5; 6:20; 7:5; 8:29, etc.). In fact, the Hebrew word, עִיר most often translated as "city" in English Bibles (1099 times in the Old Testament), always refers to a permanent settlement surrounded by a wall (Birdsall 1997; Frick 1977: 39; and Schultz 1980: 664). In the few instances when עִיר was used to identify an unwalled location (e.g., Deut 3:5; Esth 9:19) it was modified with the adjective פְּרָזָה, which means an "open region," or the word חָצֵר meaning an unwalled settlement. The Old Testament made a distinction between a fortified place (עִיר, קִרְיָה, קִרְיָה) and unfortified, dependent towns and/or villages (בְּנֹת, חֲצֵרִים) (Wood 1999b: 23).

The English word "city" masks how the Old Testament Hebrew intended to differentiate between permanent walled cities and unfortified and unwalled settlements. For example, in Numbers 13:19 Moses gave specific instructions to the twelve Israelites who had been selected to explore Canaan prior to the Conquest. The NASB translation of this verse makes it clear that Moses wanted strategic intelligence as to which of the settlements were walled cities (עיר) and which were unprotected camps (מחנים). However, Moses also wanted to know which of the cities were fortified (מבצר). The implication is that in addition to walled cities, Moses asked the men to determine what other type of fortification the Israelites might encounter and he used the adjective, מבצר, in conjunction with city, עיר, to convey that meaning. The root word of מבצר is בצר, and of the 73 occurrences of מבצר and its derivatives in the Old Testament, all but eight have to do with fortifications. Of the eight exceptions, seven refer to the grape harvest. Thus, for practically all of the Old Testament, the term "fortified" when used in conjunction with the term "city" designated the largest and most important sites, that is, walled cities that were "fortified" (Oswalt 1980).

The 12 scouts returned and verified that Canaan had walled and fortified locations: the "cities (עיר) are fortified (מבצר) and very large" (Num 13:28). On several other occasions Moses reiterated that the Israelites would find fortified cities in the land they were to occupy. For example, in Deuteronomy 1:28 Moses reminded the people of the report given by the twelve explorers. He repeated that "... the cities are large and fortified (מבצר) to heaven..." (NASB). Later, as the Israelites prepared to invade Canaan, Moses warned them, "You are crossing over the Jordan today to go in and dispossess nations greater and mightier than you, great cities fortified (מבצר) to heaven, ..." (Deut 9:1, NASB). Moses also recalled that the places they had occupied east of the Jordan had been cities "fortified (מבצר) with high walls, gates, and bars, besides a great many unwalled towns" (Deut 3:3-5, NASB).

The Consequences

In spite of clear biblical statements that Canaanite cities were walled, and many locations named in Joshua are described as fortified, most archaeologists believe the excavated evidence has revealed few, or no, fortified cities in Canaan during the period of the Late Bronze Age (ca. 1480-1175 BC). If this interpretation of the archaeological record is correct, it means that regardless of whether one holds to the 12th/13th ("late") or 15th century ("early") BC Conquest scenarios, Canaanite cities were, for the most part, unfortified and the biblical descriptions are incorrect. With this as background, it is easy to understand why secular historians and some archaeologists can conclude that the biblical description of the Conquest is flawed. The respected archaeologist, A. Mazar (1990: 243), has bluntly stated what many scholars believe and teach today:

> one of the most amazing features of the Late Bronze Age is the almost <u>total lack of fortifications</u>. At most sites excavated, none have been found, although at some sites the mighty Bronze Age defenses may have continued in use during the Late Bronze period [emphasis added].

The Cities are Great and Walled Up to Heaven

Although LB Egyptian reliefs do show Canaanite cities with crenelated walls, R. Gonen (1992: 246) suggests the reliefs were "artistic conventions rather than true representations" since the "archaeological evidence shows that few towns were encircled by walls" [emphasis added] in the Late Bronze Age. Here is a case of a respected archaeologist dismissing the factuality of artifacts because of a dubious archeological theory that "archaeological evidence shows that few towns were encircled by walls." N. Na'aman (1994: 233) slightly modified this view and, more in keeping with Mazar, declared that "in the Late Bronze Age, . . cities were either unfortified or the fortification was no more than a renovation of the Middle Bronze defense system [emphasis added]." Paul and Dever (1974: 84) introduced a chapter on "Fortifications" in their textbook *Biblical Archaeology* by asserting that the "Late Bronze [Age] appears to be a period of highly developed cultural life with uninteresting remains of fortifications or none at all" [emphasis added].

The alleged absence of archaeological evidence for fortifications at Canaanite Late Bronze I sites clearly contradicts the Bible. It has caused scholars and students, who might otherwise be disposed to accept the biblical description of an Israelite military invasion of Canaan, to question the historicity of the entire Exodus and Conquest episode. Gary Byers (1999: 2) has eloquently summarized where this has led:

Unfortunately, as the majority opinion of modern scholarship, this perspective regularly finds its way into the textbooks used by many conservative Christian colleges and seminaries. . . [and] many sincere Bible students, desiring to be intellectually honest with the historical and archaeological evidence, find themselves beginning to question the authenticity of all these stories. While not rejecting the accounts themselves, they unfortunately pass along their doubts about the Biblical stories to their students and congregations.

For some people who have ideological reasons not to accept the historicity of the Bible, it is understandable that the seeming inability of archaeologists to establish evidence for the existence of fortified Canaanite cities at the time of the Conquest can be construed as proof that the Bible story never occurred. However, for those who want to believe the Bible and the history it represents, the possible lack of archaeological evidence for fortified cities in Canaan has caused many to question the historicity of the Conquest. Certainly, the theory that Canaanite cities have no, or little, archaeological evidence for walls and fortifications has complicated attempts by scholars to harmonize the biblical account and the archaeological record.

Investigation of LB I Locations in Palestine

Research Methodology
In order to provide a factual basis for testing the archaeological record of fortified Canaanite cities at the time of the Conquest against biblical history, I examined Palestinian Late Bronze Age IA/B (ca. 1480-1390 BC) archeological evidence (Hansen

2000). I did so to determine what Late Bronze Age I defensive architecture, if any, had actually been found by archaeologists at Palestinian sites with evidence of LB I occupation. To limit the scope of the study, I selected geographic parameters similar to those referred to in Numbers 13. In verses 21-22 and 29 of that chapter, the 12 leaders scouted the land from Zin in the south to Rehob in the north (a location near the source of the Jordan River) (Mitchell 1997: 1006) for 40 days. The territory encompassed the Negev, hill country, Hebron and Jebus regions. The east and west limits of their investigation were the Mediterranean coast and the banks of the Jordan.

I then examined the literature for every archaeological site that had produced evidence of Late Bronze Age occupation within the previously described geographical tract. These locations were identified by using the *New Encyclopedia of Archaeological Excavations in the Holy Land* (NEAEHL) (Stern 1993). That initial list was supplemented and updated using *The Oxford Encyclopedia of Archaeology in the Near East* (OEANE) (Myers 1997). Data for a few other sites, too recent to have been included in the NEAEHL or OEANE (e.g., Khirbet el-Muqatir, Khirbet Nisya), were collected from professional journals and/or published and unpublished excavation reports.

Every effort was made to consult all the relevant published excavation reports for each site. In many instances the best source, and the one with the most current and complete data was, in fact, the discussions in either the NEAEHL or OEANE. On the other hand, many excavators and excavation teams have produced multiple volumes about a single site, chronicling several seasons of excavations and/or analysis of artifacts. In a few instances only cursory reports have been published. Other excavators have published the results of their labor in professional journals and, of course, those were consulted as appropriate. A total of 51 sites met the criteria for the study.

Summary of the Research

Table II summarizes the results of the research. To provide a geographic dimension to the analysis, each site was subjectively placed in one of six geographic "zones." Based on the research the sites were classified as *fortified, not fortified, or uncertain* and, if appropriate, the table provides a general indication of what type of fortification was found. The *uncertain designation* was used when architectural remnants of fortifications or walls that could possibly be interpreted as LB I were present at a site but the stratigraphic evidence was unclear and the walls or fortifications could, just as well, have been from a different archaeological period. Map I displays the sites and the status of their fortifications as found in the archaeological record.

The research revealed that 27 of the 51 excavated sites (53%) had architectural evidence for fortifications and/or walls in the Late Bronze Age period. Some of the fortifications were impressive, others were modest and represented small fortresses, or walled residences for Egyptian governors. Some of the smaller fortresses, as well as Egyptian sites whose walls were an interconnection of homes, were built on high mounds or hills. These would have given a traveler, like the Israelite spies who came upon them in the course of their reconnaissance of Canaan (Num. 13), the impression they were places "fortified to heaven" (Deut 9: 1).

The Data and the Biblical Description of Canaan in LB I

As reported above, 27 of the 51 sites (53%) were found to have evidence of having been "fortified" in LB 1. Of the 33 other ("not fortified") locations, six had evidence of fortifications that could have been dated to the Late Bronze Age. However, for reasons ranging from incomplete excavation reports to serious site erosion that complicated stratigraphic determinations, it could not be stated with certainty that the site was, in fact, fortified in LB 1. Therefore, the six were labeled "uncertain."

Four "not fortified" locations (Aphek, Tel Kitan, Tel Mevorakh, Shiloh) had evidence of being cultic centers in the Late Bronze IB period. Shiloh, for example, agrees with the biblical portrayal of it as a religious site (Josh 18:1, 8-1 0; 19:5 1; etc.). Although archaeologists found an impressive Middle Bronze Age defensive wall at Shiloh, the site was not defended by that wall in LB. This, too, agrees with the biblical description of Shiloh as a "camp" (Josh 18:9, NASB, NIV), not a walled location or "city" (עִיר). Another three "not fortified" sites (Tel 'Ein Zippori, Khirbet Nisya, and Tell el-Wawiyat) were unwalled LB IB rural villages, completely in accord with the biblical description of Canaanite cities having a "great many unwalled towns" (Deut 3:5, NASB).

Three other "not fortified" sites presented an unusual problem. These three, Beth Shean, Lachish, and Jokneam are described as "cities" (עִיר) in Joshua. Each was under Egyptian control and each had unusual characteristics that could have made it appear to be a walled city "fortified to heaven" to an outsider. Tell Beth Shean is on an unusually high mound and the LB I level has produced no evidence of walls or fortifications (Mullins 1999). Beth-Shean's citizens relied on the sheer height of the mound and its steep slope to dissuade attackers. In addition, it has been found that the outer walls of buildings on the crest may have presented the appearance of a defensive wall.

Lachish, also on a high hill, was a cultic worship center during LB IA/B. David Ussishkin (1993: 899; 1997: 318) believes that the LB I houses on the summit were joined to form a continuous belt of walls which served as a line of fortifications. This arrangement, coupled with the tell's height, would have presented a menacing appearance to potential aggressors, or to the Israelite spies. The third location, Jokneam, had no evidence of exterior city walls but did have LB I structures on the high, steep slopes of a mound, similar to those at Beth-Shean and Lachish. Tell Jokneam's height, coupled with the walls of buildings built into the crest, could have presented a formidable appearing obstacle to a potential aggressor. Each of these three sites have similar unique physical settings which might have resembled "cities [that were] fortified and very large" (Num 13:28).

The above discussion, summarized in Table 111, suggests that 10 of the 18 "not fortified" locations fit the biblical description of what the Israelites were to find once they entered Canaan. Combining the 27 "fortified" locations with the three agricultural, four cultic, and three Egyptian sites suggests that of the 51 locations known to have been occupied in the Late Bronze Age, 37 (72.5%) of them accord with the biblical description of the land of Canaan at the time the Bible says the Conquest occurred. Adding the six "uncertain" sites (those with fortifications which could possibly be LB 1) increases the number to 43 (84.3%).

Application of Research to the Biblical Period of the Conquest and Conclusions

This study was initiated to investigate the proposition that during the Late Bronze Age IA/B period (ca. 1480-1390 BC), Canaanite cities were generally unwalled and unfortified. To investigate the question, Table IV was constructed to help analyze the data. Table IV lists 30 sites from the study which have been identified by archaeologists as a place (actual or assumed) in the book of Joshua. Table IV summarizes how the Bible identified the location: either as a "city" which would imply it was a walled location, or by other reference. Seventeen of the 30 sites (56%) have evidence of LB I walls and/or fortifications. There is general agreement that 22 of the 30 sites (73%) are, in fact locations mentioned in Joshua; another eight have been tentatively identified. This leads to the following findings:

I.   **Of the 22 LB I sites unquestionably identified as locations in the Book of Joshua,**
   A.   The Book of Joshua, and in one instance Deuteronomy, identify 14 of the 22 as walled (i.e., "city") and/or fortified. LB I walls and/or fortifications have been located at all 14.
   B.   Six sites do not have evidence of LB I fortifications or walls.
      (1) Of these six, the Book of Joshua states three were a "city" (i.e., walled): Beth Shean, Jokneam, Lachish. All three have unique topographic characteristics that could have made them appear as large cities "with walls up to the sky" (Deut 9:1 NIV).
      (2) The Book of Joshua is silent regarding the defenses at the three remaining sites (Aphek, Ashkelon, Shiloh), although Shiloh is depicted as a "camp" (Josh 18:9). Thus, the lack of excavated evidence for LB I walls/fortifications corresponds to the Biblical depiction of the three.
   C.   Evidence for LB I fortifications/walls is uncertain at the two remaining LB I Canaanite sites. Of these two, one (Tel Sera'—Ziklag) is reported to have been a "city" (i.e., walled) but the Book of Joshua is silent regarding the other, Jaffa.

II. **Eight of the 30 LB I Canaanite sites have been tentatively identified as places in the Book of Joshua. Assuming the identifications are correct, the following observations are appropriate to this study:**
   A.   Three of the sites have evidence of LB I fortifications and all three (Beitin=Bethel? or Beth Aven?, Muqatir=Ai?, Abu Hawam=Shibor-libnah? or Achshaph?) are described in Joshua as fortified and/or walled.
   B.   Four other sites have not produced evidence for LB I walls and/or fortifications. The Book of Joshua described three (Halif—Rimmon? or

Hormah?, Qashish=Dabbesheth?, Wawiyat=Neah?) as a "city" (i.e., walled) but is silent regarding the architectural defenses of the other (Hefer=Hepher?).

C. At the remaining site, Tel Keisan=Achshaph?, walls or fortification evidence is <u>uncertain</u>. The Book of Joshua is silent regarding Achshaph's LB I defenses. Finally, a comment about the inclusion of Tel Halif and Tel Sera', in the list of 30. Tel Halif's biblical identification is extremely questionable, and it most probably was an Egyptian trading post in LB IB (Seger 1997). At Tel Sera' (= Ziklag), walls and fortifications have been found that might well be LB I but the stratigraphy is very unclear. Ziklag is mentioned twice in Joshua as a "city." Including Ziklag (=Tel Sera') in the final analysis would strengthen the study's correlation between the mention of "cities" in Joshua and their extant LB I remains. But, pending more conclusive evidence for either the small fortress at Tel Sera', or confirmation of Tel Halif's identification, those sites were not included in the list of 22 "known" LB I sites from the Book of Joshua.

Summary

This study examined the proposition that during the Late Bronze Age, Palestinian cities are considered to have been unwalled and/or unfortified. In accepting that proposition as truth, many archaeologists and Bible historians have argued that if the Israelites invaded Canaan in the LB 1, they would not have had to contend with walled and/or fortified cities. However, the depiction of Canaanite cities as unwalled or unfortified contradicts the biblical picture of urban settlements at the time of the Conquest. Moses cautioned the Israelites that they would confront cities during the Conquest which were "large and fortified to heaven" (Deut 1:28; 9: 1) which is supported by the account of the 12 spies in Numbers 13. This study has found archaeological evidence establishing the fact that LB I Canaan was similar to the biblical description with both walled and fortified cities, cultic sites, and unwalled villages. Of the 51 Palestinian archaeological sites with evidence of LB I occupation, 27 (53%) were "fortified" with city walls and/or other fortifications.

Deeper analysis of the data revealed that 30 of the sites are locations described in the Book of Joshua and 22 of those have been positively correlated with places in Joshua. The Bible describes 14 of those 22 locations as walled or fortified and, in fact, walls and/or fortifications have been found at all 14. The Bible ascribes walls to three more sites. These three are situated on high tells and were Egyptian administrative centers in LB I; however, they could have appeared to have been cities with "walls up to the sky" (Deut 9: 1, NIV). The Bible is silent regarding walls/fortifications at the other four and, in fact, LB I walls or fortifications have not been found at those locations.

Therefore, archaeological evidence fully supports the biblical description of Canaan as having walled and/or fortified cities at the time of the Conquest along with a number of unfortified villages and cultic locations. This study should support evangelical scholars who agree with the biblical description of Canaan at the time of the Conquest and provide a response to theories and neo-historical accounts that seek to alter the Scriptural record.

TABLES

Table I: Commonly Accepted Dates for Palestinian Archaeological Periods
Adapted from P. J. Ray (1996:6)

Date (all are B.C.)	Archaeological Period
3250 - 2900	Early Bronze Age I (EB I)
2900 - 2650	Early Bronze Age II (EB II)
2650 - 2250	Early Bronze Age III (EB III)
2300 - 1950	Early Bronze Age IV or Middle Bronze Age I
1950 - 1720	Middle Bronze Age IIA (MB IIA)
1720 - 1600	Middle Bronze Age IIB (MB IIB)
1600 - 1480	Middle Bronze Age IIC (MB IIC)
1480 - 1440	Late Bronze Age IA (LB IA)
1440 - 1390	Late Bronze Age IB (LB IB)
1390 - 1295	Late Bronze Age IIA (LB IIA)
1295 - 1175	Late Bronze Age IIB (LB IIB)
1175 - 587	Iron Age

Table III: Summary of Sites that Conform to the LB I Biblical Description
37 of 51 Agree with the Biblical Description of LB I Canaan

Classification	Comment	Number	Sites
Fortified	LB I	27	See Table I: LB Fortifications and/or walls
Not Fortified	Rural Village	3	Tel 'Ein Zippori, Khirbet Nisya, Tell el-Wawiyat
Not Fortified	Egyptian Center	3	Beth Shean, Lachish, and Jokneam ("great cities walled up to the sky" Deut 9:1, NIV)
Not Fortified	Cultic Location	4	Aphek, Tel Kitan, Tel Mevorakh, Shiloh
Sub-Total		37	
Uncertain dating of Fortification	LB I City?	6	Fortifications and/or walls are present; date unclear
Other Not Fortified	Unclear	8	Excavator not certain of purpose of LB occupation
Total		51	

Table IV: Canaanite Archaeological Sites Occupied During the Late Bronze Age

Site Name	Location[1]	Zone[2]	Status[3]	Walls	Gates	Glacis/Rampart	Other
Abu Hawam, Tell	1521.2452	C	F	X		Rampart	X
Acco, Tel	1585.2585	C	F	X		Rampart	X
Achzib	1598.2727	C	F	X		Rampart and Glacis	X
'Ajjul, Tell el-	0934.0976	C	F	X		Rampart and Fosse	X
Aphek	143.168	C	N				
Ashdod	1180.1290	C	F	X	X	Fosse	X
Ashkelon	107.119	C	N				
Batash, Tel	1410.1320	S	F	X			
Beit Mirsim, Tell	1415.0960	H	F	X			X
Beitin	172.148	H	F	X	X	Rampart	
Beth-Shean	1977.2124	J	N				
Beth Shemesh	1477.1286	S	F	X	X		
Beth Zur	1590.1108	H	F	X			
Dan	2112.2949	G	F	X	X	Rampart	X
Dothan	173.202	H	F	X			
Far'ah, Tell el- (N)	1823.1882	H	F	X	X	Glacis and Fosse	
Gerisa, Tel	1319.1665	C	F	X		Glacis	
Gezer	1425.1407	C	F	X	X		
Hadar, Tell	2112.2507	G	F	X	X		X
Halif, Tell	1373.0879	N	N				
Haror, Tel	0879.1125	N	N				
Hazor	2023.2691	G	F	X	X	Fosse	
Hefer, Tel	1976.1415	C	N				
Hesi, Tel el-	1240.1060	S	U	X			X
Jaffa	162.127	C	U	X			
Jemmeh, Tel	097.088	N	U	X			
Jericho	1925.1420	J	F	X		Rampart and Glacis	
Jokneam, Tel	1604.2289	H	N				
Keisan, Tell	164.235	C	U	X			
Kitan, Tel	2043.2270	J	N				
Lachish	1357.1083	C	N				
Megiddo	1675.2212	H	F	X	X	Glacis	
Mevorakh, Tel	1441.2156	C	N				
Michal, Tel	131.174	C	F	X	X	Rampart	X
Miqne, Tel	1356.1315	C	F				X
Maqatir, Kh. El-	1738.1469	H	F	X	X		
Mor, Tel	1175.1368	C	U	X			X
Nagila, Tel	127.101	C	N				
Nisya, Khirbet	1718.1449	H	N				
Qashish, Tel	160.232	C	N				
Rabud, Khirbet	1515.0933	H	F	X			
Regev, Tel	158.241	C	F	X			
Sera', Tel	119.088	N	U	X			
Shechem	177.179	H	F	X	X		
Shiloh	1775.1626	H	N				
Shiqmona	1462.2478	C	N				
Taanach	171.214	H	F	X			
Wawiyat, Tell el-	178.244	G	N				
Yavneh- Yam	1212.1479	C	F		X	Rampart and Glacis	X
Zeror, Tel	1476.2038	C	N				
'Ein Zippori, Tel	1761.2374	G	N				

Note: 1 = *Location*: Survey of Israel identification
   2 = *Zone*: C (Coastal); S (Shephelah); H (Hill Country); G (Galilee Region);
      J (Jordan Valley); N (Sinai/Negev)
   3 = *Status*: F (Fortified); U (Uncertain); N (Not Fortified)

REFERENCES

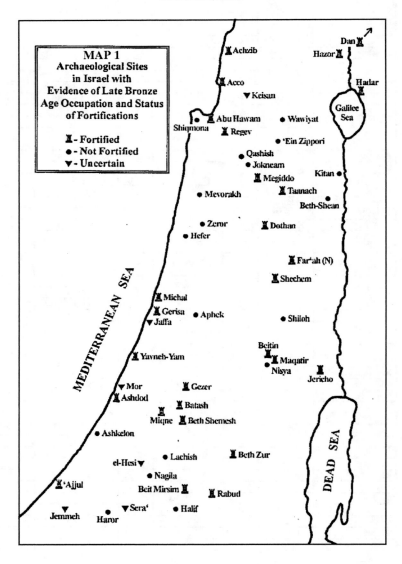

MAP 1
Archaeological Sites
in Israel with
Evidence of Late Bronze
Age Occupation and Status
of Fortifications

▉ - Fortified
● - Not Fortified
▼ - Uncertain

Birdsall, J.
   1997   City. In *New Bible Dictionary,* 3rd ed., eds. A. Marshall, A. Millard, J. Packer and D. Wiseman. Downers Grove: InterVarsity

Browning, D. C.
   1998   The Hill Country is not Enough for Us: Recent Archaeology and the Book of Joshua. *Southwestern Journal of Theology* 41, 1: 25-43.

Byers, G. A.
   1999   The Prince of Egypt: What Archaeology Tells Us About Moses. *ABR Newsletter* 30, 2:1-3.

Frick, F. S.
   1977   *The City in Ancient Israel.* Missoula MT: Scholars.

Gonen, R.
   1992   The Late Bronze Age. Pp. 211-257 in *The Archaeology of Ancient Israel,* ed. A. Ben-Tor. Trans. C. Greenberg, from Hebrew. New Haven: Yale University.

Hansen, D. G.
   2000   Evidence for Fortifications at Late Bronze I and IIA Locations in Palestine. Unpublished Ph.D. Dissertation, Trinity College and Theological Seminary (Newburgh, IN).

Hoffmeier, J. K.
   1997   *Israel in Egypt: The Evidence for the Authenticity of the Exodus Tradition.* New York: Oxford University.

Kochavi, M.
   1994   The Land of Geshur Project, 1993. *Israel Exploration Journal* 44,136-141.

Malamat, A.
   1976   Origins of the Formative Period. Pp. 3-87 in *A History of the Jewish People* ed. H. H. Ben-Sasson. Cambridge MA: Harvard University.

Mazar, A.
   1990   *Archaeology in the Land of the Bible 10,000 - 586 B.C.E.* New York: Doubleday.

Miller, K. D.
   1998   Did the Exodus Never Happen? *Christianity Today,* September 7: 44-51

Mitchell, C. M.
   1997   Rehob. P. 1006 in *New Bible Dictionary,* 3d ed., eds. A. Marshall, A. Millard, J. Packer and D. J. Wiseman. Downers Grove: InterVarsity.

Mullins, R.
   1999   Beth Shean Level IX Revisited. Paper presented at the annual meeting of the Near East Archaeological Society, Boston.

Myers, E. M. ed.
   1997   *The Oxford Encyclopedia of Archaeology in the Near East*, 5 vols. New York: Oxford University

Na'aman, N.
1994 The Conquest of Canaan. Pp. 218-281 in *From Nomadism to Monarchy: Archaeology and Historical Aspects of Early Israel,* eds. I. Finkelstein and N. Na'aman. Washington: Biblical Archaeological Society.

Oswalt, J. N.
1980 270 g. Fortification. Pp. 1: 123 in *Theological Wordbook of the Old Testament,* eds. R. Harris, G. Archer and B. Waltke. Chicago: Moody.

Paul, S. M. and W. G. Dever
1974 *Biblical Archaeology.* New York: Quadrangle/The New York Times Book Co.

Ray, P. J., Jr.
1997 Problems of Middle and Late Bronze Age Chronology: Toward a Solution. *Near East Archaeological Society Bulletin* 42: 1-13.

Schultz, C.
1980 1615, City. Pp. 1:664-5 in *Theological Wordbook of the Old Testament,* eds. R. Harris, G. Archer and B. Waltke. Chicago: Moody.

Seger, J. D.
1997 Lahav, Tel. Pp. 553-5 in *The Oxford Encyclopedia of Archaeology in the Near East,* ed. E. Myers, vol. 3. New York: Oxford University.

Stern, E., ed.
1993 *The New Encyclopedia of Archaeological Excavations in the Holy Land,* 4 vols. Jerusalem: Hebrew University of Jerusalem.

Ussishkin, D.
1993 Lachish. Pp. 313-323. *The New Encyclopedia of Archaeological Excavations in the Holy Land,* ed. E. Stern, vol. 3. New York: Simon & Schuster.
1997 Lachish. Pp. 313-323 in *The Oxford Encyclopedia of Archaeology in the Near East,* E. Meyers, vol. 3. New York: Oxford University.

Watzman, H.
2000 A Reluctant Israeli Public Grapples with what Scholarship Reveals about the Old Testament's Version of History. *The Chronicle of Higher Education* 21 January, A 19.

Wood, B. G.
1999a Beneath the Surface: An Editorial Comment. *Bible and Spade* 12: 1-3.
1999b The Search for Joshua's Ai: Excavations at Khirbet. El-Muqatir. *Bible and Spade* 21-30.
1999c Beth Aven: A Scholarly Conundrum. *Bible and Spade* 12: 101-108.
2000 News and Notes: Khirbet el-Muqatir. 1995-1998. *Israel Exploration Journal* 50: 123-30.

Another Look at the Period of the Judges

Paul J. Ray, Jr.
Andrews University
Berrien Springs, Mi

Any chronology of the Joshua-Judges period is, at best, only a tentative chronology, due to several gaps in our knowledge. However, it is possible to put together a plausible reconstruction on the basis of related biblical data which narrow these gaps considerably.

The history of the interpretation of the chronological data of the Book of Judges has been dominated by various views concerning the meaning of the numbers. Whatever the exact basis which the compiler of this book used, from at least the time of Josephus,[1] the total number of years have been arrived at by a simple adding of the given figures. This results in an apparent irreconcilable difference with another set of biblical data in 1 Kgs 6:1. Some interpreters have therefore arbitrarily omitted some of the figures (Moore 1895: xlii; Nödelke, 1869:173-98) or judges (Garstang 1931: 65, 345) in order to bring the two sets of data into agreement. The opposite tendency has been to view the numerical data of Judges in terms of round numbers representing the approximate period (Bertheau 1883: xii-xvii; Wellhausen 1885: 229; Driver 1972: 161; and Boling 1975: 23). Washburn (1990: 417) believes that the book contains so many blank chronological spaces that only a relative time line can be reconstructed.

Chronological Restraints

There are three texts outside of the numeration within the book which have a bearing on the total, or in one case a large portion of time represented therein, and therefore, help to define the perimeter of actual time which this period represents.

1 Kings 6:1

This passage presents a total of 480 years between the Exodus and the year Solomon began to build the temple. For those who see it as an authentic representation of the actual period, this places the Exodus around 1450 B.C. and the building of the temple about 970 B.C.[2] (Shea 1982: 230-38; Ray 1986: 231-48). There are others who view this verse as giving either an approximate (Bimson 1978: 96, 102) or schematic (Wright 1962: 84-85; Finegan 1959: 121) representation of the actual time period, a view which is partially perpetuated by the LXX (MSS ABMN d-hjm-qstv-a$_2$)[3] which arrive at only 440 years.

The proposed schematization of this period is based on a hypothetical 12 units of 40, that number theoretically representing a generation or a round number referring to an unspecified (Garstang 1931: 56-57; Albright 1966: 33, 39; Cogan 1992: 1005) or even symbolical (Harrison 1969: 1163) period of time. Its use here is thought to equal a corresponding period of time from the building of the first temple to that of the second. This is based on the succession of high priests in 1 Chr 6:3-15 extending from Aaron to the first temple, and from there to the second temple, each section consisting of 12 generations at what is thought to be 40 years each (Burney 1903: 59; Driver 1972: 161, n.; Cundall 1968: 31-32, n.1).

This view is strained however, in that the high-priestly genealogy is incomplete.[4] A look at the text itself reveals fourteen names for the first part and only nine names for the second period. Therefore, Joshua, who was high priest at the time of the second temple, but who is not represented in this list, is added, and by transferring the data on Solomon's temple from vs. 10 to vs. 9 to include two more names (Bimson 1978: 84), two sets of 12 are arrived at.

Another way of arriving at 480 years for this period, and thus, support for a corresponding 480 years for the first period, is to add up the lengths of the reigns of Judah's kings from the fourth year of Solomon to Zedekiah by dead-reckoning and add 50 years for the Exile (Bimson 1978: 82-83). However, the actual length of the kingdom of Judah, from the building of the temple to 586 B.C., was 384 years.[5] This would give a total of 454 years, not 480.

The theory that the author of 1 Kgs 6:1 used the figure of 480 years to correspond to a later one would require that he was unaware of the actual number of priests and years involved. The alternative view is to assume that the number is authentic. The fact that the year and month of Solomon's reign is given, would also lend support to this.

The Number 40 and the Judges

The number 40 and its multiples are often viewed as mere round numbers. There are five 40-year periods and one twice that length (80 years) during the period of the Judges, and therefore, these figures have likewise been seen as round numbers. This leaves the period we are dealing with open to a variety of speculation as to its actual length. Indeed, many figures involving the number 40 or its multiples are found in chronological statements in the Scriptures. If this view is to be taken as normative, then chronologists in general, and biblical chronologists in specific, will be hard pressed when dealing with much of their data.

An alternative is to view this number from a theological standpoint. The number 40 and its multiples frequently occur in conjunction with probationary[6] and judgment[7] periods. Viewed in this way, the three 40-year periods of rest in connection with Othniel, Deborah, and Gideon and the 80-year period of rest connected with Ehud might have been considered probationary periods for God to see how long Israel would remain faithful. The 40-year oppression by the Philistines might be considered as a judgment against Israel for their lack of faith. Finally, the 40-year judgeship and high priesthood of Eli may also be seen in terms of a probation on the priestly line of

Ithamar.[8] Since, in the book of Judges, there is a continuous alternation between oppressions and times of peace, this scenario of probations and judgments would fit the context at least as good, if not better, than the view of unspecifiable round numbers

Judges 11:26

The context of this passage is a verbal exchange between Jephthah and the Ammonite invaders. Jephthah indicated that Israel had dwelt in Heshbon and its nearby towns for 300 years. This statement is not of the chronicled variety, like the other numerical data of the book. It is doubtful that Jephthah stopped to check the records on the exact date and should therefore be considered a round number, rather than an exact expression of reality.

Acts 13:19-20

This passage, according to MSS D, E, P and ψ (KJV), has caused the problem of attributing 450 years to the period of the Judges. It disagrees with the 480 years between the Exodus and the building of the temple (1 Kgs 6:1). There are at least two possibilities for reconciliation, without resorting to emendation or disregarding one or the other text as unauthentic. Since Josephus (*Life* 1.2), who was both a priest and a Pharisee, reckons the period of the Judges at 450 years, it is also possible that Paul, who was also a Pharisee (Acts 23:6; 26;5; Phil 3:5), would reckon them with the same number, if it was common to that school (Keil and Delitzsch 1981: 277-78, n. 1). An alternate explanation follows MSS א, A, B, C and p[74]. These MSS allow a different arrangement with the 450 years before the time of the Judges. The text from this arrangement indicates a period of about 450 years, which include 400 years of bondage in Egypt, 40 years in the wilderness, and seven years conquest of Canaan. This would add up to 447 years or about 450 years (Bruce 1951: 264; Marshall 1980: 223). It would seem, then, that a straightforward reading of 1 Kgs 6:1 is quite reasonable in terms of a time frame in which to deal with the period of the Judges,[9] and that the intermediate numbers should be taken at face value. Once 40 years for the wilderness wanderings, about seven years[10] for the initial conquest under Joshua, and 40 years of David's reign are deducted, this leaves 394 years or ca. 1404-1010 B.C. for the period under discussion.

Primary Areas of Consideration

There are four areas within the above-mentioned time frame, of which the text either does not provide an exact chronological reference, or lack a complete set of data. These areas must be narrowed down in order to provide a reasonable reconstruction for this period. In addition, there are some periods of overlap which must be taken into consideration.

The Death of Joshua

The death of Joshua occurred when he was 110 years old (Josh 24:29; Judg 2:8), but the text does not synchronize this with any other datable point. However, we may arrive at an approximate date because of the relative age to that of Caleb, his contemporary. Joshua and Caleb, along with ten other individuals were sent into the land of Canaan as spies in the second year after the Exodus (Num 10:11; 13:6, 8, or 1449 B.C.). Caleb was 40 years old at that time (Josh 14:7). In 1404 B.C., or 45 years later, Caleb would have been 85 years old and according to the biblical text still in good health (Josh 14:10). However, Joshua was already an old man and come into years (Josh 13:1), an expression which denotes advanced age approaching death (Keil and Delitzsch 1981: 134). It was at this time that God asked him to divide the land, even though there was much yet to possess (Josh 13:1-7). Since Joshua was now evidently too old to lead them any longer, the individual tribes were left to take what was yet unconquered (Josh 13:1-17:18; 18:2-21:41).

If we take the suggestion that a generation is approximately 25 years[11] (Harrison 1969: 317; Bright 1976: 121; LaSor, Hubbard and Bush 1996: 767, n.14), and note that Joshua's grand-father, Elishama, was the tribal leader (נשיא) of Ephraim (Num 7:48) in the same year that theland was spied out (1449 B.C.), then we may approximate Joshua's age at that time. Since Caleb was 40 years old (Josh 14:7) and Elishama was about 50 (25 x 2) years older than Joshua, it is possible that Elishama was about 105 years old; Nun, the father of Joshua, about 80; and Joshua himself about 55 at that time.

If these figures are reasonably correct, Joshua would have been about 100 years old when Caleb was 85, after the end of the initial conquest of Canaan. This would leave him about 16 or 17 years of life after the 40 years in the wilderness (Keil and Delitzsch 1981: 134; Wood 1975: 409). Accordingly, Joshua would have died ca.1394 B.C.

The Duration of the Elders

After the death of Joshua, the people served Yahweh all the days of the elders (הזקנים) who outlived him (Judg 2:7). This was before Israel's first apostasy and following oppression. Again, the text is silent as to the exact length of this period. That whole generation (דור), which had seen the great work that Yahweh had done for Israel during the Exodus and conquest, had died (Judg 2:7, 10) before the first oppression. This was the same generation which was under 20 years old in 1449 B.C., survived the 40 years in the wilderness, and came into the land of Canaan with Joshua (Num 14:29-33; 32:11 cf. Deut 2:14, Num 1:3). The earliest any of this generation could have been born is, therefore, 1469 B.C. They can probably be seen as having died off by 100 years later or ca. 1369 B.C., or about 25 years after the death of Joshua.

Overlapping Judgeships

There are certain sections in the narrative of the book of Judges which seem to indicate overlaps (Jack 1925: 214; Oswalt 1979: 679; Fensham 1982: 1158). It has been noticed that the Judges only had control over restricted geographical regions. A look at a map of the territory under Israelite control at this time reveals three major areas of occupation, namely parts of Transjordan to the east, the central hill country in the west, and a section to the north of Jezreel Valley, west of the Sea of Chinnereth (Galilee) (Aharoni and Avi-Yonah 1977: 50, map 68; Aharoni 1979: 213). Therefore, it is possible at various times to have an oppression in one of these areas without it affecting the others (LaSor, Hubbard and Bush 1996: 160). However, this possibility is open to abuse without some constraints. Therefore, we have postulated it only in places where the text itself would seem to indicate an overlap. There are only two.

The first place in the account which indicates an overlap is in Judges 4:1. The Moabites had oppressed the Israelites on both sides of the Jordan River for 18 years. Ehud had come on the scene and the Lord delivered Israel through him. The period of rest is related as 80 years (Judg 3:30). Israel began another period of apostasy after Ehud was dead. Since Ehud could not have participated as a man of war before the age of 20 (Num 1:3) and, since the possibility exists that he was even older than that at this time, it is therefore probable that he did not live throughout the full extent of the 80 years of rest.

The apostasy of Israel is in close connection with his death[12] (Keil and Delitzsch 1981: 280, 300; Goslinga 1986: 228-29), which could have happened at least 20 or so years before the 80 years were expired, giving him a minimum of about 80 years of life, possibly more. If this was the case, then the 20-year oppression by the Canaanites on the northern tribes of Israel, which were separated from the central hill country by the Jezreel Valley of which they did not control (cf. Aharoni and Avi-Yonah 1977: 50, map 68), should be seen as overlapping with the last 22 years of the 80 years rest in connection with Ehud, and the following periods reckoned accordingly (Table 1).

The other period of overlap is even more explicit. This consists of an oppression by the Ammonites against the Transjordan tribes[13] and the Philistines against the tribes of the central hill country (Judg 10:7). Both oppressions began at the same time in 1090 B.C. (Table 1), the former lasting 18 years, the latter lasting 40 years (Oswalt 1979: 679; Block 1999:61-62; Shea 2000: 247).

The Ammonite oppression ended with the judgeship of Jephthah. He is followed by Ibzan, Elon, and Abdon. This chronological series is not resumed, but the contemporaries, Eli and Samson, are continued in a line which follows the Philistine oppression. This ended with the battle of Ebenezer[14] in 1050 B.C. (1 Sam 7:13), when Samuel became the last judge.[15]

The Reign of Saul and Samuel's Judgeship

The length of Saul's reign is not given in the extant text of the Old Testament. Paul reckons the figure of 40 in Acts 13:21, but this seems way too high when compared to other information in the Old Testament. Josephus attributes 20 years to Saul in one place (Ant 10.8.4), but 40 in another (*Ant* 6.14.9). This second figure is followed by many (Harrison 1969: 713; Wood 1975: 401; Archer 1974: 497). However, this assumes that Saul was 20 or 30 years old at his accession to the throne, on the basis that he was a young man (בחור)[16] at the time (1 Sam 9:2). The text reveals instead that his son Jonathan was of military age and commanded a division of the army very early in Saul's reign (1 Sam 13:2-3). Therefore, Jonathan must have been at least 20, if not older, and Saul at least 40 at this time (Keil and Delitzsch 1981: 123; Bimson 1978: 101). It seems that בחור should be taken then as chosen one, from the *Qal* passive particle of בחר a term reflecting military parlance (Harris, Archer and Waltke 1980: 101; Bimson 1978: 260-61, n. 8).

The text of 1 Samuel 13:1 is of the type which is commonly found in date formulas (2 Sam 2:10; 1 Kgs 14:21, 22:42). However, the extant text is incomplete. The first number of the formula is completely missing, as well as one element of the second. The text as it now reads is: "Saul was one year old when he began to reign, and he ruled over Israel two years."

The lacunae of this verse are older than the LXX, so it is of no help. The verse is missing completely in LXX[B].[17] The reading, "Saul was thirty years old when he began to reign" appears in LXX[b, mg] goe$_2$ (all but MS $_g$ being Lucianic or Proto-Lucianic), but this reading, as we have seen, would still make him too young, since Jonathan was at least 20 years old at the time.

Since it is widely recognized that this is a remnant of a date formula (Keil and Delitzsch 1981: 122-23), the question remains as to which numbers belong there. David was a young man (נער) when he first came into contact with Saul (1 Sam 17:58). He was probably close to 20 years old, in that he had fought and killed wild animals while protecting his father's sheep (1 Sam 17:34-36). It also seems likely, from the narrative, that David and Jonathan were close in age.[18] If Saul came to the throne when he was about 40 years old which, as we have seen, seems to be the case, and reigned 40 years, as with Paul and Josephus, he would have died on the battlefield of Mount Gilboa at the age of 80 (Jack 1925: 212). This seems rather improbable since David, who was partially contemporary, died as an old man of 70 (2 Sam 5:4, 1 Kgs 1:1, 2:11).[19] A reign of 30 years would make Saul 70 years old at this time, which is still rather high for someone to die in battle at this point in history. Therefore, a number closer to 20 seems to be more likely. Since the text of 1 Sam 13:1 has the number 2 for the last element of the regnal years, a round number such as 40, which is indicated by Paul, would seem unlikely. The addition of 2 to the number 20, already arrived at, would provide a total of 22 years for Saul's reign (Keil and Delitzsch 1981: 283; Bimson 1978: 98; Shea 2000: 247), which he began, it would seem, at age 40. Thus, he died at 62 on the battlefield. If this is the case, then the reconstructed text of 1 Sam 13:1 should read, Saul was [forty] years old when he began to reign, and he ruled over Israel [twenty]-two years.

What then are the possibilities for Acts 13:21 if our reconstruction of 1 Sam 13:1 is correct? A round number such as 40 does not seem to fit well with a number whose second element is two, as we have seen. Therefore, as with Acts 13:19-20 (see above), the same possibilities exist. Either the figure 40 represents the figure arrived at in the Jewish Schools (Josephus, *Ant* 6.14.9; Keil and Delitzsch 1981: 283; Bimson 1978: 98), or it represents the years of Samuel's judgeship and Saul's reign combined together[20] (Bengel 1877: 628), i.e., 18 years for Samuel and 22 for Saul.

As indicated above, Samuel became judge in 1050 B.C., when he became the instrument for ending the Philistine oppression at the Battle of Ebenezer. However, there is no indication as to how long his judgeship lasted and, in connection with it, the beginning of Saul's reign.[21] On the basis of the date which has been reconstructed from Saul's reign above, we tentatively arrive at the figure of 18 years for his judgeship, from the battle of Ebenezer unto the coronation of King Saul. If he was a youth of about 12 years of age at the battle of Aphek in 1070 B.C., when Shiloh was destroyed (1 Sam 4:1-22; Ps 78:60; Jer 7:12, 14; 26:9), and died within a few years before the death of Saul (1 Sam 25:1), then he must have lived to be about 70 years old.

Overview of the Judges

The following table summarizes the reconstruction of the chronology suggested by the above analysis.

Table 1. Israelite Judgeships

1450	Exodus
1411/10-1404	Conquest of Canaan
1394	Joshua dies
1394-1369	Period of the Elders
1369-1361	Oppression of Aram-naharaim
1361-1321	40 years Rest—Othniel
1321-1303	Moabite Oppression
1245-1225	Canaanite Oppression
1303-1223	80 years Rest—Ehud
1225-1185	40 years Rest—Deborah
1185-1178	Midianite Oppression
1178-1138	40 years Rest—Gideon
1138-1135	Abimelek's Rulership
1135-1112	Tola
1110-1070	Eli's Judgeship
1112-1090	Jair
1090-1050	Philistine Oppression
1090-1072	Ammonite Oppression
1072-1066	Jephthah
1070 B.C.	Battle of Aphek
1070-1050	Samson's Judgeship
1066-1059	Ibzan
1059-1049	Elon
1050 B.C.	Battle of Ebenezer
1050-1032	Samuel's Judgeship
1049-1041	Abdon
1032-1010	Saul's Kingship
1010-970	David's Kingship
974/3-931/30	Solomon's Kingship

Conclusion

The argument that the period of the Judges is internally irreconcilable since its numbers are only approximations and cannot be fitted into the 480 years of 1 Kings 6:1 in that its total exceeds that number, seems unwarranted. It has been possible to reconstruct a plausible chronology of the period while treating the numbers of the Masoretic Text at face value and without arbitrarily leaving figures out. Areas where information in the text is lacking have been treated by appealing to related biblical data.

NOTES

[1] Josephus, *Ant* 20.10.1; *AgAp* 2.2, reckons a total of 612 years for the time between the Exodus and the building of the temple; 450 years for the judges (i.e., 410 + 40 years for Eli's judgeship); 40 years wilderness wanderings; 25 years for Joshua (*Ant* 5.1.29); 12 years for Samuel before the election of Saul (*Ant* 6.13.5); 40 years for Saul; 40 1/2 years for David; and 4 years of Solomon. However, in *Ant* 8:3:1, cf. 10.8.5, he reckons 592 years, evidently counting the 20 years of Samson as part of the 40-year Philistine oppression.

[2] This model assumes a four year coregency between David and Solomon. Thus, according to the official count of his reign in the records of the kingdom (1 Kgs 11:41-42; 2 Chr 9:29-30), 970 B.C.. was Solomon's accession year. However, it was also in part the fourth year of his co-regency with his father. Therefore, 1 Kgs 6:1, 37-38 would seem to reflect another reckoning with the co-regency inclusive. Similar dates, but which do not consider a co-regency include 1446 B.C. (Wood 1970: 31, 88; Aling 1981: 78, 96); 1445 B.C. (Archer 1974: 223); and 1440 B.C. (Jack 1925: 200).

[3] Aquila and Symmachus, as well as LXX MSS Z bic$_2$e$_2$ indicate 480 years as does the MT. MSS bic$_2$e$_2$ are Lucianic or perhaps proto-Lucianic, depending on which side of the debate one aligns himself (cf. Cross 1964: 292-297; Barthélemy 1972: 16-89, and Tov 1972: 101-113).

[4] Johoiada (2 Kgs 11:15, 12:2), Zechariah (2 Chr 24:20), and Urijah (2 Kgs 16:11, 15-16) are known to have existed, but are not in this genealogy. The priests of the house of Ithamar, of whom Eli was the first, are not mentioned either (1 Sam 1:3-4, 18, 14:3, 21:1, 22:20, 23:9, cf. Josephus, *Ant* 5.11.5). Block 1999: 63 (cf. his chart on p. 60) has suggested that the connection between the literary structure in the book of Judges with other biblical texts is strengthened by the fact that the number of judges/rulers in/over Israel is exactly twelve. He arrives at this by the inclusion of Abimelek as a judge. However, Abimelek is not said to have been a judge (as were Othniel, Deborah, Tola, Jair, Jephthah, Ibzan, Elon, Abdon, and Samson), nor are the other formulas of the book such as God raised up for them/gave them a deliverer or the like (as with Othniel, Ehud, Deborah, Gideon Tola and Samson), the land had rest/peace x number of years (Othniel, Deborah, Deborah and Gideon) or the Spirit of the Lord came upon him (Gideon and Samson) used. Far from being appointed by Yahweh as a judge as the others are, either directly stated or assumed to have been, Abimelek appropriated his position (9:22) by fratricide. Some add Shamgar as a twelfth judge, but likewise he is not designated as a judge, none of the other formulas are used with him and his name suggests that he was not even an Israelite. It seems more likely that he was a foreigner used by Yahweh to relieve his people.

[5] On the various views concerning the meaning of the 70 years (cf. Winkle 1987: 201-214).

[6] Examples include the 120 years probation before the judgment of the Flood (Gen 6:3); 400 years of Israelite sojourn in Egypt in connection with the probation of the Amorites (Gen 15:13, 16); two periods of 40 days when Moses was on Mt. Sinai in order for God's people to show their faithfulness (Exod 24:18, 34:28); the probation on Nineveh (Jonah 3:4); and Jesus' lengthy probation against the devil's temptations (Luke 4:2).

[7] The 40 days and nights of the Flood (Gen 7:4, 17); 40 years of wandering in the wilderness (Num 14:34); and the judgment against Egypt (Ezek 29:12).

[8] God had ordained that the *high* priestly line was to go through Eleazar (cf. Num 3:32, 20:25-28, 25:12-13). Eli was the first of five high priests from the line of Ithamar which, for some reason, interrupted the legitimate line of Eleazar. Toward the end of Eli's judgeship, God let him know that he was not pleased with him or his house (1 Sam 2:27-36), and would destroy them (fulfilled in 1 Sam 4:11-22; 22:11-21). During the time of David, there was one priest from each line (cf. 1 Chr 24:3).

[9] This title is used loosely to indicate a period extending from the end of the initial conquest under Joshua unto the beginning of the reign of David. For two other studies, which treat the biblical data within the confines of the time-frame of 1 Kings 6:1, but with which I differ at several points (cf. Payne 1954:. 78-91 and Wood 1975: 10-17, 409-11).

[10] These seven years should be seen as inclusive of the last year (40th) of the wilderness wanderings, in that the Transjordan territory was conquered at that time.

[11] This figure, which is probably correct for this period of history, would not be for earlier points in time.

[12] Deborah was a judge, unlike others in the book, before a decisive battle (Judg 4:4), and she was located in the southern part of the hill country of Ephraim or, more specifically, in the same area as Ehud had judged, in Benjamin, i.e., between Ramah and Bethel (Judg 4:5). It seems unlikely that the two were judges in the exact same area, at the same time. Therefore, it is possible that Ehud was already dead by the time Deborah began to judge.

[13] The Ammonites also crossed the Jordan River into the tribes of Judah, Benjamin, and Ephraim, cf. Judg 10:9.

[14] Samson only began to deliver Israel, cf. Judg 13:5.

[15] Elon's judgeship was contemporaneous with Samuel for one year and with Abdon's for eight years, cf. Table 1.

[16] i.e., young man, still unmarried, cf. Holladay 1971: 36.

[17] The later LXX minuscules b[txt] ef m (sub ✕) xzc$_2$ (the last one being Lucianic), follow the Masoretic Text in their translations of this text.

[18] If Jonathan was 20 years old in 1032 B.C. at the battle of Michmash, then David, who was born in 1040 B.C. (2 Sam 5:4), would have been eight at that time. There, thus, would have been 12 years between them.

[19] This seems to be the high point of age for natural death at this time. The figures on the later kings of Judah, where they apply, are all less (cf. Thiele 1983: 218).

[20] Perhaps an ως has fallen out of the text at this point.

[21] Samuel's judgeship is usually seen as ending with the coronation of Saul, although 1 Sam 7:15 indicates that he was considered a judge until his death.

REFERENCES

Aharoni, Y., and Avi-Yonah, M.
1977 *Macmillan Bible Atlas*. New York: MacMillian.

Aharoni, Y.
1979 *The Land of the Bible: A Historical Geography*. Trans. A. F. Rainey. Philadelphia: Westminster.

Albright, W. F.
1966 Syria, the Philistines and Phoenicians. Pp. 56-57 in *The Cambridge Ancient History*, ed. I. E. S. Edwards, C. J. Gadd, and N. G. L. Hammond; Cambridge: Cambridge University.

Aling, C. F.
1981 *Egypt and Bible History: From Earliest Times to 1000 B. C.*, Grand Rapids, MI: Baker.

Archer, G. L.
1974 *A Survey of Old Testament Introduction*. Chicago: Moody.

Barthélemy, D.
1972 Les Problèmes Textuels de 2 Sam 11, 2-1, Rois 2, 11, Reconsiderés à la Lumière de Certaines Critiques de Devanciers d'Aquila. *Septuagint and Cognate Studies* 2: 16-89.

Bengel, J. A.
1877 *Gnomon of the New Testament*. Edinburgh: T and T Clark.

Bertheau, E.
1883 *Kurgefasstes Exegetisches Handbook zum Alten Testament*. Leipzig: S. Hirzel.

Bimson, J. J.
1978 *Redating the Exodus and Conquest*. Sheffield: Almond.

Block, D. I.
1999 *Judges, Ruth*. Nashville, TN: Broadman and Holman.

Boling, R. G.
1975 *Judges*. Garden City, NY: Doubleday.

Bright, J.
1976 *A History of Israel*, 2nd ed. Philadelphia: Westminster.

Bruce, F. F.
1980 *The Acts of the Apostles*. London: Tyndale.

Burney, C. F.
1903 *Notes on the Hebrew Text of the Book of Kings*. Oxford: Clarendon.

Cogan, M.
1992 Chronology. Pp. 1002-11 in *Anchor Bible Dictionary*, vol. 1, ed. D.N. Freedman. New York: Doubleday.

Cross, F. M.
1954 History of the Biblical Text in Light of Discoveries in the Judean Desert. *Harvard Theological Review* 57: 292-97.

Cundall, A.
    1968   *Judges.* Downers Grove, IL: Inter Varsity.
Driver, S. R.
    1972   *An Introduction to the Literature of the Old Testament.* Gloucester, MA;
           Peter Smith.
Fensham, F. C.
    1982   Judges, Book of. Pp. 1157-59 in *International Standard Bible
           Encyclopedia,* vol. 2, ed. G. W. Bromley. Grand Rapids, MI: Eerdmans.
Finegan, J.
    1959   *Light from the Ancient Past,* 2nd ed. Princeton: Westminster.
Garstang, J.
    1931   *The Foundations of Biblical History: Joshua-Judges.* Grand Rapids, MI:
           Kregel.
Goslinga, C. J.
    1986   *Joshua, Judges, Ruth.* Trans. R. Togtman. Grand Rapids, MI: Zondervan.
Harris, R. L.; Archer, G. L.; and Waltke, B. K.
    1980   Bāḥar, P. 101 in *Theological Word Book of the Old Testament,* vol. 1.
           Chicago: Moody.
Harrison, R. K.
    1969   *Introduction to the Old Testament.* Grand Rapids, MI, Eerdmans.
Holladay, W. L.
    1971   *A Concise Hebrew and Aramaic Lexicon of the Old Testament.* Grand
           Rapids, MI: Eerdmans.
Jack, J. W.
    1925   *The Date of Exodus.* Edinburgh: T and T Clark.
Keil, C. F., and Delitzsch, F.
    1981   Joshua, Judges, *Ruth and I and II Samuel.* Grand Rapids, MI: Eerdmans.
LaSor, W. S; Hubbard, D. A.; and Bush, F. W.
    1996   *Old Testament Survey: The Message, Form and Background of the Old
           Testa ment.* Grand Rapids, MI: Eerdmans.
Marshall, I. H.
    1980   *Acts.* Grand Rapids, MI: Eerdmans.
Moore, G. F.
    1895   *A Critical and Exegetical Commentary on Judges.* Edinburgh: T and T
           Clark.
Nödelke, T.
    1869   *Untersuchungen zur kritik des Alten Testaments.* Kiel.
Oswalt, J. N.
    1979   Chronology of the Old Testament. Pp. 673-85 in *International Standard
           Bible Encyclopedia,* vol. 1, ed. G. W. Bromley. Grand Rapids, MI:
           Eerdmans.
Payne, J. B.
    1954   *An Outline of Hebrew History.* Grand Rapids, MI: Baker.

Ray, P. J.
    1986   The Duration of the Israelite Sojourn in Egypt. *Andrews University Seminary Studies* 24: 231-48).

Shea, W. H.
    1982   Exodus, Date of the. Pp. 230-38 in *International Standard Bible Encyclopedia,* vol. 2, ed. G. W. Bromley. Grand Rapids, MI: Eerdmans.
    2000   Chronology of the Old Testament. Pp. 244-48 in *Eerdmans Dictionary of the Bible,* ed. D. N. Freedman. Grand Rapids, MI: Eerdmans.

Thiele, E. R.
    1983   *The Mysterious Numbers of the Hebrew Kings,* 3rd ed. Grand Rapids, MI: Zondervan.

Tov, E.
    1972   Lucian and Proto-Lucian. *Revue Biblique* 79: 101-13.

Washburn, D. L.
    1990   The Chronology of the Judges: Another Look. *Bibliotheca Sacra* 147: 414-25.

Wellhausen, J.
    1885   *Prolegomena to the History of Israel.* Edinburgh: A. C. Black.

Winkle, R. E.
    1987   Jeremiah's Seventy Years for Babylon: A Reassessment of, Part I: The Scriptural Data. *Andrews University Seminary Studies* 25: 201-14.

Terqa, Dagan, and the Amorites in the Late Bronze Age

Dr. Mark Chavalas
University of Wisconsin-LaCrosse

Dagan (biblical Dagon), one of the primary gods of the Philistines known from Scripture, is well attested from extra-biblical sources from the third and second millennia BC in Syria and Mesopotamia. Moreover, the Amorites, known for their belligerent behavior against the Israelites, are also well documented from these regions in the same period. The city of Terqa on the Euphrates River in the Syrian portion of Mesopotamia was a major Amorite center in the second millennium BC as well as one of the centers of the worship of Dagan. Thus, the relationship of Terqa, Dagan, and the Amorites affords insight into the cultural milieu of northern Mesopotamia, the homeland of the patriarchs, the ancestors of the Israelites (Chavalas 1996: 90-103).

For a variety of reasons archaeological research in Syria has flourished only in the past generation (Chavalas and Hayes 1992: 1-3). Although the finds from Ugarit, Mari, and Ebla are well known, there are other important sites that have revealed Syria's cultural importance in the third and second millennia BC. Recent work in Syria east of the Euphrates River has revolutionized our perception of ancient Southwest Asia. Syria is an area which must now be considered as the western half of the cultural continuum known as Mesopotamia (Bucellati and Kelly-Buccellati 1977a: 1-43). One of the most important sites in this region of Syria is the aforementioned Terqa (modern Tell Ashara) (Rouault et al 1997: 73-103). Terqa's geographic position is strategic as it stands halfway between the coastal sites of the Mediterranean and Mesopotamia proper. It can thus be considered an important bridge between the two. The site featured a massive defensive system at the onset of the third millennium BC, revealing its prominence in understanding the origins of urbanization. Moreover, Terqa was likely the capital of the Khana kingdom, a successor state to Mari after it fell to Babylon about 1760 BC. The excavations at the site have furnished a great deal of valuable data which has brought light to this period, once considered a veritable 'dark age', at least in terms of our knowledge of Syro-Mesopotamian history.

Terqa had relations with Mari in the Shakkanakku period when Mari was a province of the Ur III dynasty, about 2100-2000 BC (Durand 1985: 147-72 and Rouault in Tunca and Deheselle 1996: 105-9). Area F at Terqa has shown evidence of administrative and scribal activity in this period, including delivery notes, personnel and agricultural lists, round school tablets, and many clay door sealings (Rouault "Terqa" 1991: 728). The oldest documents found to date at Terqa are in this area in an administrative complex, and several tablet fragments have been found under wall foundations, as well as one text found on the surface (G. Buccellati and M. Kelley-Buccellati 1977b: 44-89). Many of the texts are lists of persons and contracts (Rouault 1992: 248). In the succeeding Old Babylonian period (c. 2000-1595 BC), Terqa apparently had a subordinate relationship with nearby Mari until the period of Shamshi-Adad I and Zimri-Lim (1815-1760 BC). Terqa's political fate after the fall of Mari is not clear; it was either under the control of Babylon or the capital of the independent Khana state (1760-1595 BC). A number of important structural remains from this period have been found at the site, including an administrative center, a series of private residences, and a temple dedicated to Ninkarrak, Mesopotamian goddess of healing.

Until recently it was thought that Terqa was occupied until c. 1600 BC. Because there appeared to be no extant stratigraphic material from after this period, it has been stated that there was a period of abandonment and hence a political vacuum in the region (Buccellati 1996: 231 cf. Rouault 1991: 729). However, recent published texts and the last few seasons of work have caused a reevaluation of the history of the Khana kingdom (Rouault 1993-94: 285-9).

The history of the Khana period between the Babylonian conquest of Mari and the Middle Assyrian empire can be reconstructed as follows: shortly after the reign of Hammurapi of Babylon a series of minor kings ruled the region with Terqa as the capital (Podany 1991-93: 60-62). Most of the personal names in these texts have close parallels with those at Mari. Furthermore, Mari administrative terms were also preserved at Terqa (Buccellati 1988: 45-9). It has thus been postulated that the Mari dynasty may have relocated here after the fall of Mari. However, after the defeat of Yadikh-Abu of Khana by Samsu-iluna of Babylon (1721 BC), the land was probably dominated by Babylon; the next kings (Kashtiliashu and Shunuhru-ammu) were likely Babylonian vassals. Some of the recent texts at Terqa show Ammisaduqa and Samsuditana of Babylon (c. 1650-1595 BC) in control of the Middle Euphrates region (Rouault 1991: 728-9 and 1992: 253). This may be why the Khana kingdom was not mentioned in either Hittite or Babylonian records of this period, since it was not an independent region (Podany 1991-93: 60.). The Khana kings were then in a mediator role in the restoration of the Marduk statue to Babylon.

The Khana kingdom may have reached its zenith after the fall of Babylon (1595 BC). It apparently ruled much of the middle Euphrates from Qattunan to Dura-Europas. However, the center of this kingdom may not have been Terqa, but on the Khabur River where there were three cities mentioned in texts, Saggaratum, Iggid-lim, and Qattunan (Podany 1991-93: 60). Also, Ishar-Lim built a palace at Bidah (site unknown). We know little of the political activity of the Khana kings as no royal inscriptions have been uncovered (except for what is on the royal seals). The royal succession apparently succeeded from father to son.

It is highly probable that the Khana state influenced the Kassite kingdom of Babylonia (c. 1600-1155 BC). Some have argued that there are intimate similarities between Khana and Kassite seal impressions, as well as Khana real estate transaction texts and Kassite kudurrus (boundary stones) (Podany 1997: 419-27; Sommerfield 1995: 917-30.).

The Khana state was then conquered by Mitanni and later ruled by the Middle Assyrian empire. This is evidenced by a group of thirty texts found in two jars in Area E of Terqa that are contemporary with Paratanna and Shaushatar of Mitanni (Rouault 1991: 728-9 and 1992: 253). They are dated to several local kings bearing Hurrian names. Furthermore, a Khana legal text has been found that is contemporary with Tukulti-Ninurta I of Assyria in the 13th century BC (Kummel 1989: 191-200). The collapse of the Hittite and Assyrian powers (c. 1200 BC) fostered a possible resurgence of Khana rule (Podany 1991-93: 62.). Two Khana kings are mentioned from this period, Ilu-Iqisha and Tukulti-Mer, and are dated to the 11th century BC (Pinches 1885: 351-3 and Weidner 1935: 22-4). In sum, the list of Khana kings at present stands at fifteen without mentioning those who were fathers and sons of kings and those subordinate to the external interference of Babylon or Mitanni. The excavations at Terqa continue to provide important material for the Middle and Late Bronze Ages.

Because of the limitations caused by the unique geographic environment in the Middle Euphrates/Lower Khabur region, it has been suggested that there was a contrast in the socio-political structure between that area and southern Mesopotamia (Buccellati 1992: 83-103 and Buccellati 1990: 98-102.). The peasants in the region appear to have been induced to create a system of wells to draw from the resources of the agrarian rural landscape. This rural class (also known from the Mari texts) slowly became autonomous from local urban political rule, causing a 'nomadization' of these peasants, who became agro-pastoralists. Furthermore, they developed into a political power, eventually resulting in the establishment of the Amorite dynasties (Buccellati 1992: 87), with their notion of tribal identity (Charpin and Durand: 1986: 157-74). Buccellati postulates that the term Amorites generally refers to this rural class of peasants who developed a specific ethnic/tribal identification because of unique circumstances (Buccellati 1992: 87-8.). This can be demonstrated in part by the large number of Amorite personal names in the Terqa and Mari texts (Podany: 1988: 103-6, 227-238). These agro-pastoralists were able to create a sense of identity since the central state did little to control the steppe. Thus, the Amorites (known as the Khaneans, Suteans, and Yaminites in the Mari texts) were not outside intruders but an internal development from the Khana rural class.

One of the major Amorite groups in the Middle Euphrates region were the Benjaminites (or Yaminites), who do not appear to be connected with the biblical Benjaminites. They are, however, the most widely studied West Semitic tribe mentioned in the Mari archives (Luke 1965: 60ff.). The geographical range of the Yaminites was indeed large (Kupper 1982: 47-9 and *Archives royales de Mari: transcriptions et traductions* II: 83:18-20). Though they were concentrated along the

Beyond the Jordan

Middle Euphrates in the Khabur region, (Kupper 1982: 47, *Archives royales de Mari: transcriptions et traductions* II. 83:18-20, 90.7-8, 92.5ff; III.16.5-6, 21.5ff, 38.15ff, 58.5-10, 70.4ff; Dossin, 1938: 178, Lines 8-15), they were also found north along the Euphrates near Harran and northwest in the area of Yamkhad, Qatna, and Amurru along the Syrian coast (Luke 1965: 70.). The tribal organization was very large, and several sub-tribal groups of Yaminites are known (Ubrabum, Iahrurum, Amnanum, Iarihum, and possibly the Rabbianum). The economy of the Yaminites was a combination of sheep-pastoralism and village agriculture. They were pastoralists by nature, migrating with their flocks north of Mari, and west near Yamkhad, Qatna, and the area of Amurru, not unlike the patriarchal migrations. They did, however, possess villages, especially in the Euphrates Valley in the vicinity of Terqa and northward (Dossin, 1938: 174-86.). Since the Yaminites and Suteans (another Amorite tribal group) lived on the borders of a prosperous kingdom, they are often depicted as sheep raiders (*ARMT* XV.259.). However, Kibri-Dagan, governor of Terqa during Zimri-Lim's reign (c. 1780-1760 BC) complains to the king that the Yaminites refused to send men for corvée work (*ARMT* III.38.). He claims that they were a constant source of trouble during the harvest. Thus, the Yaminites appear to have been semi-nomadic pastoralists, with an economy based on sheep raising, with seasonal alternation between villages on the Middle Euphrates and nearby regions, and pastures in the north (Luke 1965:78-9.). Their agricultural phase consisted of raising grain in the fields near the villages, and they often were weavers and garment makers. At any rate, the villages and pasturelands of the Yaminites were located in regions that were contested politically in the Mari period (Luke, 1965: 84). The territory of the Khana kingdom was thus physically larger than other sovereign urban polities, although there were few urban centers in this large region (Bucellati: 1988: 56.). The Khana kings appeared to control an area north to the Khabur triangle and no further south than Haradum on the Euphrates, a border outpost of the Old Babylonian kings which may have been a city planned in response to Khana presence in the area (Buccellati: 1988: 47.). The Khana kings also controlled the western trade routes leading to Tadmor in the Syrian steppe.

The history of Terqa is also intertwined with the cult of Dagan (Schmokel 1928: Montalbano 1951: 381-97; Wyatt 1980: 375-9; Holter 1989: 142-7; and L. Feliu and W. Watson, 2003) Dagan is attested as having been the patron deity of the Middle Euphrates of Syria around Emar (Fleming, 1992: 241-52), Tuttul, Mari, and especially Terqa, from the third millennium B.C. onwards (Roberts, 197218; Pettinato and Waetzoldt 1984; 239-48; Wyatt 1980: 375.; and *ANET* 1968: 268.). There is evidence of a third millennium temple to Dagan at Mari. The name of the god is also found in the Ebla texts and in the inscriptions of Sargon of Akkad (c. 2334-2279 BC). Pettinato & Waetzoldt 1984: 234; Wyatt 1980: 375; *ANET* p. 268.). Sargon worshipped Dagan at Tuttul, south of Mari, and both he and his grandson Naram-Sin attributed their success to him, since they had conquered his territory. Proper names with the Dagan element are common in Mesopotamia by the mid-third millenium (Roberts 1972: 18.). Puzur-Ishtar, a governor during the Ur III period, dedicated a statue to Dagan

108

(Revue d'Assyriologie et d'Archeologie orientale 1947: 150). Like Sargon, Hammurapi of Babylon claimed to have conquered the Middle Euphrates region with Dagan's help (*ANET*: 165.).

The etymology of Dagan is uncertain. The name probably has Semitic origins, since it is attested in Akkadian, Ugaritic, and Hebrew, but not in Sumerian. Dagan is either connected with the Semitic root *dgn*, cloudy, rainy (Albright 1920: 319 n. 27), or *dgn*, grain (Roberts 1972: 76, n. 104). He is often identified as the northwest Mesopotamian equivalent to Enlil, the active head of the Mesopotamian pantheon, (Lambert 1967: 131, n.14 and Goetze 1965: 132-8) and has paternal ties with the storm god Hadad and ties to the underworld (Roberts 1972: 75, n. 98). The Dagan cult is also found in Palestine by the second half of the second millennium at Ugarit and in the Amarna letters. He is the recipient of sacrifices to the dead at both Mari (*Archives royales de Mari II*. 90 and III. 40) and Ugarit (Dussaud 1935, pp. 177-80), and often called, 'lord of the sacrifices to the dead' (*Archives royales de Mari* X. 63:15). Ba`al is Dagan's son in Ugaritic texts (*Mission de Ras Shamra* X. 6 i 51-2 (krt) pp. 77-8).

Shamshi-Adad I of Assyria (ruled 1814-1781 BC) built and dedicated the temple of Ekisiga (or Bit kispum, a temple in which offerings were given to the dead and royal ancestors) to Dagan at Terqa (Grayson 1972: 24-5). He writes in a letter to his son Yasmah-Adad that he would be in Terqa on the 'day of kispum' (*Archives Royales de Mari* I. 65). Zimri-Lim made sacrifices to his deceased father and also spoke of the Dagan temple at Terqa, presumably the same structure constructed by Shamshi-Adad a generation earlier (Kupper 1947: 151). Dagan is mentioned at Terqa in many legal contracts from Zimri-Lim's time and later. Not honoring a contract is likened to eating the consecrated property of the god Dagan (*Archives royales de Mari* XIII. 16ff.). Zimri-Lim states that Terqa was the city that Dagan loved. Kibri-Dagan, governor of Terqa during Zimri-Lim's reign, claimed that Terqa was at the center of the god's cult (Kupper 1947: 173-4). Dagan continued to have prestige after the fall of Mari (c. 1760 B.C.E.). There are many personal names containing the element Dagan in the Khana kingdom (Kupper 1947: 152.).

It is apparent from the Mari letters that Dagan spoke to his worshippers by way of dreams, ecstatic possession, and by oral command. He gave messages to both male and female prophets, as well as commoners.

Among the large corpus of feminine correspondence from Mari, there is one letter concerning an oracle from Dagan during the reign of Zimri-Lim (*Archives royales de Mari* 9. 122-3, no. 80). Inibsina writes to an unidentified 'star' and makes an allusion to an oracle from Dagan to a certain Shelibum, a prophetess in the service of Dagan. She has come to give a revelation concerning the 'man of Eshnunna' (a major polity northeast of Babylon). The prophetess claims that he is a hypocrite and Dagan will destroy his city. Furthermore, Zimri-Lim should not enter into his city until he receives the oracle. The letter shows the intensified political influence that prophecy had at Mari. For the most part, prophetic oracles are relegated to a mundane plain, placing divine demands (usually of a very material nature) before the king or his advisors. They are often concerned with the king's well-being (Malamat 1984: 79).

Commoners could also address the king. A certain woman named Yanana writes to the king directly with no evidence of a third party (*Archives royals de Mari* X. 100.). She addressed Zimri-Lim in the name of Dagan concerning a young woman who was abducted while the two of them were on a journey. Dagan came to her in a dream saying that only Zimri-Lim could save and return the girl.

Last is a text which is an odd example of military intelligence from the Mari archives (Dossin 1948: 125-34). The letter is to Zimri-Lim from one of his high officials, Itur-Asdu, governor of Nahur in northern Mesopotamia. Although officially subordinate to the Mari kings, the Yaminites were causing problems along the Euphrates between Mari and Terqa. Zimri-Lim, however, was away because of another military campaign. Because of the problem, Dagan decided to intervene.

A certain Malik-Dagan of Shakka had visited Terqa and went to the Dagan temple, where Dagan spoke to him in a dream:

> I entered the temple of Dagan and I prostrated myself before Dagan. During my prostration, Dagan opened his mouth and said: 'Is there peace between the Yaminite kings with their troops and the troops of Zimri-Lim which have gone upstream?" I answered, 'There is no peace:' (Dossin 1948: 120, lines 14-22; English Translation from Luke 1965: 81.).

Dagan responded by asking why the messengers of Zimri-Lim did not regularly come before him with this affair, since he was prepared to deliver the sheiks of the Yaminites into the hands of Zimri-Lim. He thus commanded Malik-Dagan to go to Zimri-Lim and speak thus,

> Send me your messenger and put the affair before me, then I will lead the sheiks of the Yaminites away with hooks in their noses (Dossin 1948: 129, lines 37-8,English Translation from Luke: 81.).

This letter shows the political nature of Mari prophecy, the importance of Dagan worship along the Middle Euphrates, as well as the turbulence of the semi-nomadic groups that had connecting spheres of influence with local sedentary governments.

It is apparent that the Middle Euphrates region provides abundant information for a better comprehension of the patriarchal narratives in Genesis, and for understanding the context of the patriarchs in northern Mesopotamia.

NOTES

[1] Tell Qraya was a small Uruk Period site about six kilometers north of Terqa along the Euphrates River. For the excavations at Tell Qraya , consult K. Simpson, 1988.

===
CHART 1: CHRONOLOGICAL OUTLINE OF TERQA
(Chavalas 1996)

	Date	Period	Description
1.	3200-3000	Protoliterate	Village life at Tell Qrayal
2-3.	3000-2100	Early Dynastic/ Sargonic Wall built	Settlelment at Terqa, City
4.	2100-1760 (2100-2000)	Ur III/Early Sargonic	Shakkanakku period Terqa 2:8 Province of Mari
5.	1760-1720	Khana I	Independent kingdom
6.	1760-1595	Late Old Babylonian	Vassals of Babylon
7.	1595-1500	Khana II	Independent kingdom
8.	1500-1200	Mitanni/ Middle Assyrian	Domination by foreign powers, abandonment of Terqa?
9.	1200-1000	Khana III	Later Khana Kingdom (not centered at Terqa?)

===

CHART 2: RULERS OF KHANA
(Buccellati 1988, Rouault 1992, Podany 1991-93,
Charpin, 1995, Podany 1997)

King   Date

I. Independent Khana Kings
    1. Yapah-Sum[u-?]   c. 1750
    2. Isi-sumu-Abu   c. 1735
    3. Yadikh-Abu   c. 1725

II. Vassals of Babylon?
    4. Zimri-Lim
    5. Kasap-ili
    6. Kuwari
    7. Kashtiliashu   c. 1700
    8. Hanaya
    9. Shunuhru-Ammu   c. 1675
   10. Ammi-Madar   c. 1650

III. Direct control by Babylon
    a. Ammi-Saduqa   c. 1650-1625
    b. Samsuditana   c. 1625-1595

IV. Independent Khana Kings
   11. Iddin-Kakka   c. 1595[2]
   12. Ishar-Lim   c. 1585
   13. Iggid-Lim   c. 1575
   14. Isih-Dagan   c. 1560

Gap of one or two generations

V. Control by Mitanni
    a. Parattarna   c. 1500
    b. Shaushatar   c. 1475
    - Qish-Addu, vassal of Mitanni kings

VI. Independent Khana (?)
    15. Hammurapih

VII. Assyrian Control
    a. Tukulti-Ninurta I   c. 1225

VIII. A New Khana Kingdom?
    16. Ilu-Iqisha   c. 1100
    17. Tukulti-Mer   c. 1100

[2] For information about the royal inscriptions of Ishar Lim, Iggid Lim, Ish-Dagan, and Ham-murapi, consult Frayne's work on the early part of the royal inscriptions of Mesopotamia. (1990: 730-4).

[3] For an overview of the Kassite period, see the survey of Kassite history in Sommerfield. (1995: 917-30).

REFERENCES

The abbreviations used in this paper are found in the *Anchor Bible Dictionary,* vol. I, ed., D. N. Freedman (New York: Doubleday, 1992) lii-lxxviii.

Albright, W. F.
    1920   Gilgamesh, Engidu, Mesopotamian Genii of Fecundity, *Journal of the American Oriental Society* 40: 319 n. 27.

Anonymous
    1967   *Archives Royales de Mari* X:100.

Birot, M.
    1960   Textes administratifs de la salle 5 du palais. *Archives Royal de Mari* IX.

Buccellati, G. and Kelly-Buccellati, M.
    1977a Terqa Preliminary Reports 1. *Introduction and Stratigraphic Record.* SMS 1/3, 1-43.
    1977b Terqa Preliminary Reports 2. *A Cuneiform Tablet of the Second Season.* SMS 1/4 44-89.

Buccellati, G.
    1988   The Kingdom and Period of Khana. *Bulletin of the American Schools of Oriental Research* 270: 45-56, 52.
    1990   River Bank, High Country and Pasture Land in *The Growth of Nomadism on the Middle Euphrates and the Khabur.* Pp. 98-102 in Eds. S. Eichler et al. *Tall al-Hamidiya* 2: Freiberg: Schweiz Universitatsverlag.
    1992   Ebla and the Amorites. Pp. 83-103 in *Eblaitica* 3, eds. C.Gordon and G. Rendsburg. Winona Lake: Eisenbrauns.

1996 From Khana to Laqe: The End of Syro-Mesopotamia, pp. 229-38. ed. O. Tunca, *De la Babylonie a La Syrie en passant par Mari = J-R Kupper Festschrift,* Liege: Universite de Liege).

Charpin, D. and Durand, J. M.

1986 Fils de Sim'al: les origins tribales des rois de Mari. *Archives Royales de Mari* 80:157-74.

1995 A propos des rois de Hana. *Nouvelles Assyriologiques Breves et Utilitaires* 1: 120.

Chavalas, M. and Hayes, J.

1992 Ancient Syria: A Historical Sketch. Pp. 1-20 in *New Horizons in the Study of Ancient Syria,* eds. M. Chavalas and J. Hayes. Malibu: Undena = Bibliotheca Mesopotamica 25.

Chavalas, M.

1996 Terqa and the Kingdom of Khana. *Bulletin of the American Schools of Research* 59: 90-103.

Dossin, G.

1938 Signaux luminex au pays de Mari. *Revue d'assyriologie et d'archeolgie orientale* 35:174-86.

1948 Une revelation du dieu Dagan a Terqa. *Revue d'assyriologie et d'archeologie orientale* 42:125-34.

1950 Correspondence de Shamsi-Adad, Archives *Royales de Mari* I.

1967 Correspondence Feminine. *Archives Royales de Mari* X. Dossin, G., et al.

1967 Textes Diverses. *Mission de Ras Shamra* X.

1967 Textes Diverses. *Archives Royales de Mari* XIII: 16ff. Durand, J.-M.

1985 La situation historique des Sakanakku: nouvelle approche. *Mari Annales Recher- ches Interdisciplinaires* 4: 147-72.

Dussaud, R.

1935 Deux Steles de Ras Shamra portant und dedicace au dieu Dagan. *Syria* 16: 177- 80.

Feliu, L. and Watson, W.

2003 *The God Dagan in Bronze Age Syria.* Leiden: Brill.

Fleming, D.

1992 *The Installation of Baal's High Priestess at Emar: A Window on Syrian Religion.* Atlanta: Scholars Press = Harvard Semitic Studies 42.

Frayne, D.

1990 *Old Babylonian Period (2003-1595 B. C) The Royal Inscriptions of Mesopota mia: The Early Periods,* Vol. 4. Toronto: University of Toronto Press.

Goetze, A.

1965 An Inscription of Simber-Shihu. *Journal of Cuneiform Studies* 19: 132-8.

Grayson, A.

1972 *Assyrian Royal Inscriptions,* vol. 1. Wiesbaden: Otto Harrassowitz.

Holter, R.

1989 Was Philistine Dagan a Fish God?, *JSOT* 1:142-7.

Jean, C.
1950 Letters Diverses. *Archives Royales de Mari* II.
Kummel, H.
1989 Ein Kaufvertrag aus Hana mit mittelassyricher Limu-Datierung. *Zeitschrift fur Assyriologie* 49 83-149.
Kupper, J.
1947 Une gouvernement provincial dans le royaume de Mari. *Revue d'Assyriologie et d'archeologie orientale* 49: 51, 150-2, 173-4.
1982 *Les Nomades en Mesopotamie au temps des rois de Mari.* Paris: Les Belles Lettres, 3rd Edition.
Lambert, W.
1967 Enmeduranki and Related Matters. *Journal of Cuneiform Studies* 21:131.
Luke, T.
1965 Pastoralism and Politics in the Mari Period: A Re-examination of the Character and Political Significance of the Major West Semitic Tribal Groups on the Middle Euphrates, ca. 1828-1758 B.C. Unpublished Ph. D. dissertation, University of Michigan.
Malamat, A.
1984 *Mari and the Early Israelite Experience.* Oxford: Oxford University Press.
Montalbano, F.
1951 Canaanite Dagon: Origin, Nature. *Catholic Biblical Quarterly* 13:381-97.
Pettinato, G. and Waetzoldt, H.
1984 Dagan in Ebla und Mesopotamien nach den Texten aus dem 3. jahrtausand. *Orientalia* 54: 234-48
Pinches, T.
1885 Babylonian Art, Illustrated by Mr. H. Rassam's Latest Discoveries. *Transactions of the Society of Biblical Archaeology* 8: 351-3.
Podany, A.
1989 The Chronology and History of the Hana Period. Unpublished Ph.D. Dissertation, University of California at Los Angelos.
1991-3 A Middle Babylonian Date for the Hana Kingdom. *Journal of Cuneiform Studies* 43-5: 53-62.
1997 Some Shared Traditions between Hana and the Kassites. Pp. 417-32 in *Crossing Boundaries and Linking Horizons: Studies in Honor of Michael C. Astour on the Occasion of His Eightieth Birthday.* Eds. G. Young, M. Chavalas and R. Averbeck. Bethesda: CDL Press.
Pritchard, J. B.
1969 *Ancient Near Eastern Texts,* 3rd ed. with Supplement. Princeton: Princeton University Press.
Roberts, J.
1972 *The Earliest Semitic Pantheon.* Baltimore: The Johns Hopkins University Press.

Beyond the Jordan

Rouault, O.
1991 Terqa. *American Journal of Archaeology* 95: 728-9.
1992 Cultures locales et influences extereures. *SMEA* 30: 247-256.
1993-4 Tel Asara/Terqa. *AFO* XL/XLI: 285-9.
1996 Terqa et l'epoque des Sakkanakku. Pp.105-9 in *Tablettes et images aux pays de Sumer et d'Akkad: Melanges offerts a Monsieur H. Limet,* eds. O. Tunca and D. Deshelle. Liege: Universite de Liege.
Rouault, O., et al
1997 Terqa rapport preliminaire (1987-1989). *Mari Annales de Recherches Interdisciplinaires* 8:73-103.
Schmokel, H.
1928 *Der Gott Dagon. Ursprung, Verbreitung und Wesen seines Kultes.* Leipzig: Universitatsverlag.
Simpson, K.
1988 *Qraya Modular Reports I: The Early Soundings.* Malibu: Undena.
Sommerfeld, W.
1995 The Kassites of Ancient Mesopotamia: Origin, Politics, and Culture Pp. 917-30 in Civilizations of the Ancient Near East, Vol. 2. New York: Scribners.
Weidner, E.
1935 Tukulti-Mer. *Analectia Orientalia* 12: 22-4.
Wyatt, N.
1980 The Relationship of the Deities Dagan and Hadad. *UF* 12: 375-9.

Othniel, Cushan-Rishathaim, and the Date of the Exodus

By Clyde E. Billington
Northwestern College

Introduction

Judges 3:7-11 reports that the Israelite Judge Othniel defeated a ruler by the name of Cushan-Rishathaim who was the "king of Aram-Naharaim." While King Cushan is not mentioned in other extant historical sources, his people, the Rishathaim, are referred to in a number of ancient texts. As will be seen below, the Rishathaim are to be identified with an ancient people better known to historians today as the Mitanni. If the Rishathaim are to be identified with the Mitanni, or more properly with the Indo-European ethnic group that ruled the multi-ethnic Kingdom of Mitanni, then there are highly significant conclusions to be drawn on the dating of both the Exodus and the period of the Judges.

Identifying the Rishathaim and the area that they ruled is important not only because it supports the historical accuracy of the Bible but also because it provides a time frame for the period of the Judges, and consequently also for dating the Exodus. As will be seen below, this time frame strongly supports the Early Date Theory for the Exodus—1446 BC—and destroys any possibility that the Late Date Theory — ca. 1270 BC—is correct.

Cushan-Rishathaim and His Kingdom

The story of Othniel's defeat of King Cushan-Rishathaim is found in Judges 3:7-11 which reads as follows:

> 7. The Israelites did evil in the eyes of the Lord; they forgot the Lord their God and served the Baals and the Asherahs. 8. The anger of the Lord burned against them so that he sold them into the hands of Cushan-Rishathaim king of Aram-Naharaim, to whom the Israelites were subject for eight years. 9. But when they cried out to the Lord, he raised up for them a deliverer, Othniel son of Kenaz, Caleb's younger brother, who saved them. 10. The Spirit of the Lord came upon him, so that he became Israel's judge and went to war. The Lord gave Cushan-Rishathaim king of Aram into the hands of Othniel, who overpowered him. 11. So the land had peace for forty years, until Othniel son of Kenaz died. [NIV]

The name translated in the NIV as "Cushan-Rishathaim" is better translated as "Cushan of the Rishathaim." In other words, Cushan was the king of a people known as the Rishathaim. As will be seen, the Rishathaim were a well-known people in the ancient world and are mentioned in a number of ancient texts.

Judges 3:8 also states that Cushan was "king of Aram-Naharaim." Aram-Naharaim is better translated as "Aram between the Two Rivers," the two rivers being the Tigris and Euphrates. In other words "Naharaim," which means "between the two rivers," is a Semitic equivalent of the later Greek term "Mesopotamia." The Greek term Mesopotamia also translates as "between the two rivers." In some English translations of the Bible, Naharaim is even translated by the Greek term "Mesopotamia."

The "Aram" part of Aram-Naharaim is the name of an ancient people known as the Arameans. The Arameans were a Semitic people originally from the northern area of Mesopotamia, an area where Abraham and his family once lived. Haran, the city where Abraham lived until his father died, was located in Aram-Naharaim. It is possible, but not likely, that the city of Haran itself was named after Haran, the brother of Abraham and the father of Lot.[1]

According to Genesis 23—24, the Arameans were relatives of the Israelites. Abraham, when he sent his servant to find a wife for his son Isaac, sent this servant to the family of another one of his—Abraham's—brothers named Nahor, who is said to have lived in "Aram-Naharaim," see Genesis 24:10 (O'Callaghan 1948: 25-6).

Judges 3:7-11 does not say that Cushan was an Aramean. What it says is that Cushan ruled the area where the Arameans then lived.[2] Cushan himself is said to have been a member of a people named the Rishathaim. As will be seen in this study, the Rishathaim were a military minority that invaded Aram-Naharaim from the north. As will also be seen, Rishathaim peoples also invaded northern India at about the same time that they invaded Aram-Naharaim.

It will be argued in this study that the Rishathaim people of Aram-Naharaim are to be identified with an Indo-European people who once ruled the ancient Kingdom of Mitanni. The ancient Kingdom of Mitanni is known—from a variety of ancient sources—to have ruled the area of Aram-Naharaim from about 1550-1340 BC.[3]

The Indo-European rulers of the Kingdom of Mitanni seem to have first invaded Mesopotamia in large numbers after 1700 BC and then eventually defeated, ruled, and merged with the Hurrians (O'Callaghan 1948: 146). While large numbers of Indo-Europeans seem to have first invaded northern Mesopotamia sometime after 1700 BC, there is evidence that smaller groups of Indo-Europeans were in Mesopotamia even earlier.

Besides the Hurrians, some of the other peoples in northern Mesopotamia who were ruled or dominated by the Mitanni during this period were the Arameans and the Assyrians. The Hurrians seem to have been the largest ethnic group in the multi-ethnic Kingdom of Mitanni.

The Kingdom of Mitanni was at various times the mortal enemy of both the Hittites and the Egyptians. Ancient Egyptian records clearly demonstrate that the Mitanni tried repeatedly to expand south into the areas that are today Syria, Lebanon, and Israel. Early 18th Dynasty pharaohs felt so threatened by Mitanni incursions into Palestine that they undertook a series of military campaigns against them. Mitanni attempts to expand south into Palestine in the 15th Century BC fit very well with what is reported about Cushan and the Rishathaim in Judges 3:7-11. As will be seen, there is clear evidence that there were Indo-Aryans and Hurrians expanding into Palestine at least as early as the 15th Century BC.

The Rishathaim in Ancient Texts

The Rishathaim are mentioned in a variety of ancient sources. There is an inscription from the reign of Hatshepsut [ruled ca. 1518-1482 B C] that mentions the "Country of Reshet" (Breasted II 1906: 135, listing no. 321). The inhabitants of the Country of Reshet are almost certainly to be identified with the Rishathaim mentioned in Judges 3:7-11. The "-im" ending on the name Rishathaim is the Hebrew plural and in this instance indicates an ethnic group of people. Removing the "-im" ending leaves "Rishatha" which even in English transliteration looks much like the Reshet mentioned by the Egyptians.

The similarity between these two names is even more striking when the Hebrew text is used.[4] The unpointed Hebrew version of the name Rishathaim can be transliterated into English as "Rishatim." Again, removing the "-im" ending leaves "Rishat," which is nearly identical to the Egyptian "Reshet."

The context of Hatshepsut's inscription suggests that the Land of Rishet was located somewhere to the far north of Egypt. This same inscription mentions the land of Punt to the south. It was a rather common Egyptian convention during the New Kingdom period for a pharaoh to claim to rule from north to south, and two nations, one north and one south, would be named.

The "Land of Reshet" should also probably be identified with the "Land of Reshu" which is also mentioned in Egyptian inscriptions. Another inscription by Hatshepsut states:

> My fame makes the great ones of the countries to bow down while the uraeus [cobra] is upon my forehead...(lacunae)...all lands. The Land of Reshu and the Land of Yu, they cannot hide from my majesty: Punt is mine...(Breasted II 1906: 123-24, listing no. 299).[5]

Variations of the name Reshu also appear in the writings of other ancient peoples. Ugaritic texts dating before ca. 1200 BC mention a people called the "Rishim" and a city called "Rish." (Virolleaud in ed. Schaffer: 1965: 40, 78 and Gondahls: 1967: 178). The exact location of Rish is not known. Both the Rishim and the city of Rish were also located not far from, but to the north of, the ancient city of Ugarit in northwestern Syria (O'Callaghan 1948: 23 and Bryce 1999: 77).[6] It is also likely that the city of Rish in the Ugaritic texts is to be identified with the city of Ursu/Urshu in Assyrian texts, and also with the city of "Warsuwa" in Akkadian texts.[7]

Ancient tablets from the city of Ebla also refer to a city named "Urshu" which was also located somewhere in northern Mesopotamia (Weiss 1985: 191). It is likely that the city of Urshu in the Eblaite texts is also to be identified with the city of Rish mentioned in the Ugaritic texts.

The city of Urshu is also mentioned in Hittite texts which say that it was attacked and conquered by the Hittite kings Hattushili I and Mutsili I in the 17th century BC (Gurney 1966: 191). [8] The fact that the mysterious and as-of-yet, undiscovered city of "Urshu" was attacked by the Hittites is particularly interesting, since the Hittites later were the mortal enemies of the Kingdom of Mitanni. Hittite sources seem to locate Rish/Ursu/Warsuwa in the area near Carchemish. The city of Carchemish for a long period of time was a part of the Mitanni Empire. While there is no certain proof, it seems likely that the city of Rish was a Mitanni city.

India and the Mitanni People

The Rishim people can be connected to the Kingdom of Mitanni in a rather strange way. There was an ancient people called the "Rsi" who conquered northern India sometime before ca. 1200 BC. The exact date for the invasion of the Rsi people into India is not known. However, it is known that the great Indus Civilization began to disappear in the 17th Century BC, and it is also known that an "Indo-Aryan" race replaced the native peoples of the Indus Civilization in the Indus Valley. Indo-Aryans are a branch of the Indo-European peoples.

The Rsi invaders of India were clearly an "Indo-Aryan" people and were related to, if not identical to, the people who came to control the Indus Valley. [9] It therefore appears that the Rsi began to invade India from the north and west through the Indus Valley at about the same time as the Indo-Aryan rulers of the Kingdom of Mitanni began to invade Aram-Naharaim from the north, in other words in the 17th Century BC.

The modern Indian historian and ethnologist Ramaprasad Chanda, in his book *The Indo-Aryan Races*, writes that the Rsi people were a "fair-haired" people who invaded India "from the far north"[10] (Chandra 1969: 180). The Rsi people who invaded northern India can be closely linked to Indo-Europeans who were the ruling military class of the ancient Kingdom of Mitanni. Ramaprasad Chanda writes of the connection between the Rsi of India and Indo-European rulers of the Kingdom of Mitanni:

> Among the gods invoked by the Mitannian king occur the well-known Vedic names Mitra, Varuna, Indra, and Nasatyas (Chandra 1969: 17).

Besides worshiping many of the same deities, the Rsi invaders of India and the Indo-European rulers of the Kingdom of Mitanni shared many of the same personal names. Chester Starr in his *A History of the Ancient World* writes:

> ...the rulers of the Mitanni had names akin to those of the Indo-European invaders of India, as did such of their major gods such as Indra and Varuna (Starr 1965: 86).

While the official language of the Kingdom of Mitanni was Hurrian, the ruling Rishim military class originally spoke a language closely related to Indian Sanscrit. Sanscrit is an Indo-European language that is related to Greek, Latin, German, English, etc. However, the Indo-European language of the Rishim was not used as the official language of the Kingdom of Mitanni. It does, however, occur as one of the languages used in the Hittite archives found at Hattusa (Gurney 1966: 103-4). Hurrian, however, was clearly the official language of the Mitanni Empire.

The Hurrians seem to have been the largest group of people in the multi-ethnic Kingdom of Mitanni, but their language was not an Indo-European language. It is likely that the Rishim people used the Hurrian language as their official language because, when they conquered northern Mesopotamia, they were an illiterate, military minority ruling over the more sophisticated, literate Hurrians.

The Rishim needed a written language for the administration of their kingdom, and the Hurrian language and Hurrian scribes were available. As will be argued below, it is likely that the Rishim of the Kingdom of Mitanni in time stopped speaking their own native Indo-European language and adopted Hurrian as their spoken language. It is also possible that other nations and peoples came in time to see these Rishim as Hurrians.

At present it is not known from the very rare Mitanni inscriptions what ethnic name the military rulers of the Kingdom of Mitanni used for themselves. However, other ancient sources strongly suggest that they called themselves something like the "Rish" or by variants of that name such as "Teresh" and "Reshet." It is nearly certain that these Rish people did not originally call themselves Mitannians. The name Mitanni is almost certainly not Indo-European, and it probably comes from the Hurrian language. Roger O'Callaghan in his *Aram Naharaim* states that the name Mitanni was:

.... primarily a political term, for the state covered not only the land Mitanni of northern Mesopotamia, ...but also extended eastward to embrace the kingdom of Arrapkha, and in the west, that of Mukish in northern Syria as vassal states (O'Callaghan 1948: 78-9).

In other words, the name Mitanni was not used as an ethnic designation but rather as a political term.

Aram-Naharaim and the Kingdom of Mitanni

Ancient Egyptian sources further strengthen the connection between King Cushan of the Rishathaim mentioned in Judges 3:7-11 and the Kingdom of Mitanni. As was stated above, in Judges 3:7-11 Cushan of the Rishathaim people is called "king of Aram-Naharaim."

In early New Kingdom sources in Egypt, the Kingdom of Mitanni is frequently called simply "Naharin." Naharin is an Egyptian version of the Semitic/Hebrew

"Naharaim." In time, Naharin gave way in official Egyptian texts to the name Mitanni. Naharaim may have been the Semitic name for the Kingdom of Mitanni, while Mitanni may have been the Hurrian name for the Kingdom of Mitanni. At first the Egyptians called the Kingdom of Mitanni "Naharin" and then later switched to "Mitanni." This switch seems to have taken place during the reign of Amenhotep III since the name "Mitanni" first appears in Egypt in a letter written to him in the Amarna letters (Bush 1964: 2).

However, about fifty years earlier, Amenhotep II in his "Memphis Stela" boasts that: "His mace has struck Naharin, and his bow has trampled the Nubians (Der Manuelian 1987: 222.)." It should be noted that Naharin is here being contrasted with the Nubians. The Nubians lived south of Egypt, and Naharin was located north of Egypt. Amenhotep is here stating that he dominated all peoples in both directions. This is very similar to the way that Hatshepsut earlier used the name Rishet in contrast to Punt.

By the way, Punt seems to have been located further south than Nubia, apparently along the central coastal area of East Africa. The Egyptians generally had little contact with the people of Punt, but Hatshepsut herself had earlier led a trading expedition to this distant land, and this may be why she used Punt and not Nubia in contrast to Rishet.

In another inscription named the Karnak Stela [ca. 1450 B.C.], Amenhotep II, the grand-nephew of Hatshepsut, makes it clear that the Kingdom of Naharin is to be identified with the Kingdom of Mitanni. While campaigning on the Plain of Sharon in Palestine, Amenhotep II states that he captured an envoy of an unnamed king of Naharin:

Now his Majesty went southwards in the plain of Sharon. He found a messenger of the chief of Naharin (who was) carrying a letter of clay about his neck. He brought him back as a prisoner at the side of his chariot (Der Manuelian 1987: 229.).

Peter Der Manuelian, in his *Studies in the Reign of Amenophis II,* writes of this incident:

At this point Amenophis captured an envoy of the chief of Naharin with correspondence tied around his neck. Was the envoy enroute to various Palestinian chiefs who were conspiring with the Mitannian king to eliminate the Egyptian presence in Retenu? If so, this capture would significantly indicate how far south the anti-Egyptian "alliance" or "conspiracy" had penetrated. The Plain of Sharon, the coastal area of Palestine between Joppa and Caesarea, was far removed from the Mitanni kingdom in the north (Der Manuelian 1987: 67-68).

The Karnak Stela is therefore highly significant for studying Judges 3:7-11 for three reasons. First it proves that the term Naharin/ Naharaim was used by the

Egyptians as an early name for the Kingdom of Mitanni, and since Cushan is called the "king of Aram-Naharaim" in the Bible, it strongly suggests that Cushan was a Mitanni king. Second, the Karnak Stela indicates that the Kingdom of Mitanni was trying to control Palestine just prior to the time that Cushan came to control Palestine for eight years during the period of the Judges. And third, it shows that the story of Othniel in the Book of Judges fits the historical period in which the Bible places it.

Therefore the historical evidence provides strong support for the identification of "Cushan-Rishathaim king of Aram-Naharaim" as a Mitannian king. If this identification is true, as it almost certainly is, then there are some very important ramifications for dating both the Exodus and the period of the Judges. In Egyptian texts the name "Naharin" was replaced by the name "Mitanni" sometime shortly after 1400 B.C. This fact argues strongly for dating Othniel's defeat of Cushan of the Rishathaim to the early part of the 14th century BC.

Before leaving this discussion it must be noted that the Kingdom of Mitanni was at times called by another name, besides the names Mitanni and Naharin. Egyptian, Hittite, Babylonian, and Assyrian sources sometimes refer to the Kingdom of Mitanni as "Hanigalbat." The name Hanigalbat was originally a geographical term first used as a name for an area of Mesopotamia to the north of Aram Naharaim (O'Callaghan 1948:79).

The name Hanigalbat did not at first include the area of Aram Naharaim, but during the period of time that the Kingdom of Mitanni existed, the name Hanigalbat was used at times as a synonym for the Kingdom of Mitanni. It is likely that the area of Hanigalbat was seen in the ancient world as the original homeland for the Hurrians and/or the Indo-Europeans who ruled the Kingdom of Mitanni.

After the demise of the Kingdom of Mitanni, the name Hanigalbat once again assumed its original geographical meaning and was not used for the area of Aram Naharaim (O'Callaghan 1948: 79). The area of Hanigalbat was later absorbed into what was called Armenia during the Greek and Roman periods. The original Armenians—not to be confused with the Semitic Arameans—were Indo-Europeans who invaded Hanigalbat sometime after 1200 BC. Once there, they seem to have merged with the Hurrian peoples who still lived there. It was probably this invasion by the Armenians that led to the eventual disappearance of Hurrian as a spoken language in Mesopotamia

Cushan-Rishathaim and the Dating of the Exodus

As was seen earlier, Judges 3:7-11 states that Othniel, the first Israelite Judge, delivered the Israelites from the rule of Cushan of the Rishathaim who was the king of Aram-Naharaim. If Cushan was a king of the Mitanni as seems almost certain, then Othniel must have defeated him sometime before ca. 1340 BC, because in ca. 1340 BC Suppiluliuma I [ruled 1344-1322], king of the Hittites, crushed the Kingdom of Mitanni (Bryce 1999: 174). After 1340 BC, the Kingdom of Mitanni was incapable of mounting a military campaign in Palestine.

The Kingdom of Mitanni became a client state of the Hittites in 1340 and without the area of Aram-Naharaim was called Hanigalbat. Eventually Hanigalbat fell to the Assyrians in ca. 1270 BC. In ca.1250 BC, the Assyrian client state of Hanigalbat disappeared when King Shalmaneser I destroyed it and ended the reign of its rebellious client King Sattuara (Bryce 1999: 303-4). Shalmaneser I boasts that he drove the fleeing armies of Sattuara to the west into Asia Minor. This may account for the presence of Rishim people there at the time of the fall of the Hittite Empire. Incidentally, the Hittites sent troops to help Sattuara fight against Shalmaneser I, and it is likely that it was the Hittites in the west to whom Sattuara and his army fled for protection after their defeat by the Assyrian army.

Therefore, if Othniel defeated a Mitanni king who ruled over Aram Naharaim, he had to have done so before 1340 BC, because after 1340 BC the Kingdom of Mitanni/Hanigalbat was a client state first of the Hittites and then of the Assyrians. After 1340 BC the Kingdom of Mitanni did not control the area of Aram Naharaim and also could not have launched a military attack against the Israelites. If Othniel defeated a Mitanni king sometime before 1340 BC, then the Late Date Theory for the Exodus becomes an impossibility.

The Late Date Theory dates the Exodus at ca. 1270 BC. According to the Late Date Theory, the Israelites were not even in the Land of Israel during the period of time that the Kingdom of Mitanni existed as an independent state.

By way of contrast, the Early Date of the Exodus does allow Othniel to have fought against a Mitanni king. The Early Date Theory of the Exodus has the Israelites leaving Egypt in ca. 1446 BC and arriving in the Land of Canaan in ca. 1406 BC.

The Book of Judges states that Othniel was the son of Caleb. This suggests that Othniel was one of the early judges, and that he probably defeated Cushan in ca. 1370 BC. Othniel's defeat of Cushan may even have helped cause the fall of the Kingdom of Mitanni to the Hittites in ca. 1340 BC.

Rishathaim Peoples After the Time of Othniel
The Rishathaim people—along with their former subjects the Hurrians, Arameans, and Assyrians—survived the collapse of the Kingdom of Mitanni in ca. 1340 BC. Some Rishathaim peoples continued to live in northern Mesopotamia —probably in Urartu— for centuries afterwards, but they never regained the power that they once enjoyed. As was seen above and as will be seen below, some of the Rishathaim also appear to have migrated to various areas of Asia Minor and northern Mesopotamia, and one group even migrated on to northwest Italy.

The Rishim people are almost certainly to be identified with the Taruisha people of central Asia Minor, who are mentioned in Hittite texts after the destruction of the Kingdom of Mitanni. After the defeat of the Kingdom of Mitanni, there were bands of Rishim people located in various places. There was one band in south central Asia Minor. Another band seems to have moved to northwest Asia Minor. One large band seems to have later conquered and ruled the Kingdom of Urartu. Another band seems to have migrated to the Zagros Mountains north of Elam, and one group appears to have remained in the area of northern Mesopotamia (Billington 1988).[11]

124

The Hittites' protection of Mitanni/Hanigalbat troops after their defeat at the hands of King Shalmaneser I of Assyria may have backfired on the Hittites. It appears that bands of Rishim immigrants in Asia Minor formed an anti-Hittite military alliance there with the infamous Philistines and other tribal groups like the Lukka and Achaean Greeks. The Lukka/Lycians and the Achaean Greeks are known to have been the mortal enemies of the Hittites at the time of the collapse of the Hittite Empire in the late 13th century BC. In other words, it appears that the Rishim peoples of Asia Minor joined the Sea Peoples coalition in ca. 1200 BC. This coalition may even have originally been formed as an anti-Hittite military league. Certainly the Hittite Empire was a major military target of the Sea Peoples coalition.

As will be argued below, the Rishim were known as the "Teresh" in the Sea Peoples coalition. Rish and Teresh are almost certainly only linguistic variations of the same name. Nancy Sanders in her book on the Sea Peoples connects the Taruisha people mentioned in late Hittite inscriptions with the Teresh people who were members of the Sea Peoples coalition (Sanders 1978: 112).

It should be noted that the Philistines, who were leaders in the Sea Peoples coalition, seem to have originally come from Caria in southwest Asia Minor. As was seen above, one band of the Rishim people settled in south central Asia Minor where it appears that they came in contact with the Philistines of Caria who lived just to their west and who at that time probably spoke a Greek dialect.

If the Rishim are to be identified with the Teresh, and they almost certainly should be, then remnants of the Rishim people survived the collapse of the Kingdom of Mitanni and joined the Sea Peoples coalition to fight both the Hittites and the Egyptians. And if the Teresh are to be identified with the Rishim survivors of the fallen Kingdom of Mitanni, then the Rishim were eventually able to avenge themselves on the Hittites for the destruction of the Kingdom of Mitanni 1340 BC.

The famous Sea Peoples coalition, with the help from the Tubal and Meshech peoples, destroyed the Hittite Empire in ca. 1200 BC and then a few years later destroyed the great city of Ugarit. The Sea Peoples coalition shortly afterwards went on to launch at least two major attacks against Egypt. Egypt narrowly survived these attacks in the early years of the 12 Century BC. After their defeat in Egypt, several tribes of the Sea Peoples coalition settled in Israel where the Israelites seem to have called them all "Philistines."

The Taruisha/Teresh people of the Sea Peoples coalition are also almost certainly to be identified with the ancient Etruscans who later moved by sea to conquer northwest Italy. (Helck 1979: 173-4). [12] The historian Agnes Carr Vaughn, in her book *Those Mysterious Etruscans,* states that the Etruscans, when they dwelt in Asia Minor, were called by two names, the "Tursha" and the "Rasna" (Vaughn, 1964: 82). "Tursha" is clearly a Greek version of the Hittite "Taruisha" which is itself a version of the name Teresh. Rasna, as will be seen, was just another version of the name Rish. Rasna was the name that the ancient Etruscans used for themselves in their inscriptions (Pallottino 1978: 231).

There is strong historical evidence connecting the Teresh/ Rishim with the ancient

Etruscans.[13] The name of several Etruscan kings in Italy, "Tarquinius," can be traced back to the Mitanni/ Hurrians and to northern Mesopotamia. Pharaoh Ramses II [ruled ca. 1290-1223 BC] states that, at the Battle of Kadesh, which he fought against the Hittites in ca. 1274 BC, he defeated a charioteer of the Hittites named "Tergenenes" (Breasted 1906, Vol.III: 153, Listing 337). The name Tergenenes is to be identified with the name Tarquinius.

The name Tergenenes is almost certainly Hurrian. Since it is likely that the Rishim spoke Hurrian by 1280 BC, Tergenenes may have even been a member of the Rishim people who, after the defeat of the Kingdom of Mitanni in 1340 BC, may have been forced to fight for the Hittites at the Battle of Kadesh in 1274 BC. The ancient city of Ugarit was located less than 70 miles from where the Battle of Kadesh was fought. As was noted above, Ugaritic inscriptions mention Rishim people as dwelling in an area on the northeastern borders of Ugarit.

Interestingly, the Philistines are also said to have fought on the side of the Hittites in the Battle of Kadesh. Less than 100 years after this battle, the Philistines turned on the Hittites, joined the Sea Peoples coalition, and helped destroy not only the Hittite Empire but also the great city of Ugarit.

Fighting along side of the Philistines in the Hittite army at the Battle of Kadesh was a people wearing a strange helmet with two horns on it (O'Callaghan 1948: pl. XXIV). This same strange helmet is worn by one tribe in the Sea Peoples coalition during one of their attacks against Egypt less than a hundred years later (O'Callaghan 1948: pl. XXV). This helmet is very different from the feathered helmet worn by the Philistines. While there is no certain way to connect the tribe who wore these unique helmets with the Teresh people, the very presence of this unique helmet at the Battle of Kadesh proves that other members of the Sea Peoples coalition once served in the Hittite army. However, I do remember reading somewhere—but I cannot find the source—that one of these horned helmets later was discovered by archaeologists excavating in southern Italy.

A version of the name Tarquinius also appears among the "Hurrian" rulers of the ancient Gutian people of the northern Zagros Mountains just to the east of Aram Naharaim. One "Hurrian" king of the Gutians was named Tirigan (CAH 1924-1982: vol. I: 434). It is possible that these Hurrian rulers of the Gutians were themselves Hurrian-speaking Rishim. It should be noted that Roger T. O'Callaghan in his *Aram Naharaim* argues that there was some sort of connection between the Gutians and the Indo-European rulers of the Kingdom of Mitanni (O'Callaghan 1948: 47-8).

Tirigan and Tergenenes are almost certainly the same name, and both names are to be identified with the name Tarquinius. The names Tarquinius, Tergenenes, and Tirigan are all theophoric names based on that of an ancient god named "Tarhu."

The name of the god Tarhu may also be reflected in the name of an ancient city along the Euphrates river in Aram Naharaim. This city was called "Tirqa.". Tirqa was the site of a temple dedicated to the worship of Dagon (O'Callaghan 1948: 33). As is well-known from the Old Testament, Dagon was also worshipped by the Philistines, who, as was stated above, were also members of the Sea Peoples coalition along with the Teresh.

There was also an ancient king of "Arzawa"—an area in southeast Asia Minor—who was named after the god Tarhu. In the Amarna Letters from Egypt in the 14th Century BC, this king's name is given as "Tarhundaraba." Samuel Mercer, in a footnote in his translation of the Amarna Letters, writes of this name:

> The first element in the name of Tarhundaraba is Tarhu, the name of a god. The same deity appears among the Kassites under the name of Turgu as a storm-god. The Etruscans called him Tarqu. The name Tarhu is now held to be Hittite, Mitannian, or Hurrian (Mercer 1939: vol. I, Letter 31, 183).

Clearly there was some sort of a connection between the Etruscans and Hurrians. This is not to say that the Etruscans were ethnic Hurrians. To the contrary, as is argued above, the Etruscans seem to have been the descendents of the Rishim rulers of the Kingdom of Mitanni. But the Rishim did rule the Hurrians for several hundred years. Since the Rishim were a military minority and since they used the Hurrian language for administrative purposes to run the Kingdom of Mitanni, it seems likely that the Rishim eventually became speakers of Hurrian.

If the Etruscans were the descendents of the Rishim people of the ancient Kingdom of Mitanni, and if the Rishim had earlier dropped their Indo-European language and adopted Hurrian as their spoken language, then it is very likely that the mystical Etruscan language is simply the Hurrian language written in a version of the Greek alphabet.

The Names Rishathaim, Reshet, Teresh, Rasna, and Etruscan

It has been argued above that the names Rishathaim/Reshet, Teresh/Taruisha, Rasna, and Etruscan are all versions of the same name, Rish. As was also argued above it is likely that the Etruscan language is derived from Hurrian. If this assumption is true, then the Etruscan language should provide some clues to explain these various versions of the name Rish. While the Etruscan language is not fully understood, enough is known to provide good explanations for each of these variations of the name Rish.

As was argued above, the name Rish appears to have been the original name of the Indo-European rulers of the Kingdom of Mitanni. If this is true, then the question arises: From where did the variations of the name Rish—Teresh and Rishet—come?

Pallottino, in his book *The Etruscans*, states that in the Etruscan language the word "ta," when used as a prefix attached to the front of a noun, functioned as a "demonstrative adjective or pronoun" (Pallottino 1978: 232). When suffixed to the back of a noun, "-ta" served as a "determinative article." To summarize Pallotino, when used as demonstrative adjective, "ta" was prefixed to the front of a noun and means "this." When used as a definite article and suffixed to back of the noun, "-ta" means "the." However, if Etruscan is a later version of the Hurrian language, as I believe that it is, then the "-ta/tha" suffix in Etruscan is almost certainly "the pluralizing suffix" of Hurrian (Bush 1964: 208). It is likely that Rishathaim and Reshet are only versions of the name Rish with a suffix "-ta" attached. It is also likely that Teresh and Taruisha are only versions of the name Rish with a "-ta" prefixed to it.

Rasna is probably the purest version of the name Rish. As was stated above, this is the version of the name Rish used by the Etruscans for themselves in their inscriptions. The "-na" on Rasna is almost certainly the suffix used in Hurrian to designate the plural definite article (Bush 1964: 157-162). In other words Rasna should be translated as "the Rasnians." The name Etruscan itself may simply be ta+rus+na with an "e" prefix and a "k" added for phonetic reasons. It is very likely that the name "teresh" is derived from the Rish's own original language with the "te" prefix being the "t/d" definite article which is common in Indo-European languages.

It is therefore likely that the names Rishathaim/Reshet, Teresh/Taruisha, and Rasna are all linguistic versions of the original name used by the Indo-European rulers of the Kingdom of Mitanni who called themselves the Rish.

Conclusion

The historical and archaeological evidence strongly suggests that Othniel fought against and defeated a king of the ancient Kingdom of Mitanni named Cushan. The historical and textual evidence also suggests that the Indo-Aryan ethnic group that founded and ruled the Kingdom of Mitanni called themselves originally by a name that sounded something like "Rish." This name is reflected in Judges 3:7-11, where Cushan is said to have been from an ethnic group called the "Rishathaim."

The connection between Cushan and the Kingdom of Mitanni is further strengthened by the term Aram-Naharaim which is used in Judges 3:7-11. As was seen above, "Naharin" was a name used by the Egyptians early in the New Kingdom period for the Kingdom of Mitanni. Since the evidence strongly suggests that Othniel fought against the Kingdom of Mitanni and since the Kingdom of Mitanni is known to have ceased to exist as a military power after ca. 1340 BC, then the Late Date Theory of the Exodus in ca. 1270 BC cannot be true. On the other hand, the story of Othniel's defeat of King Cushan of the Kingdom of Mitanni lends very strong support for the Early Date Theory of the Exodus in ca. 1446 BC.

As was noted above, after their defeat by the Assyrians, some of the Rishim people seem to have split into migratory groups. At least one of these groups, the Teresh, appears to have joined the Sea Peoples coalition and to have helped destroy the great Hittite Empire in ca. 1200. Later, some members of the Teresh/ Rishim migrated to Italy where they came to be called the Etruscans and spoke the Hurrian language; today that language is called Etruscan. Eventually the Etruscans adopted the Greek alphabet to write their Hurrian language and even later adopted Latin as their spoken language.

When Othniel defeated Cushan-Rishathaim, he may have not only helped cause the collapse of the Kingdom of Mitanni but he also may have indirectly helped cause the migration of some Rishim people to northwest Italy where they came to be called the Etruscans. As strange as it may seem, when he fought against Cushan and the

Rishathaim, Othniel seems to have fought against the ancestors of the Etruscans.

By any means, if the story of Othniel is true, and the historical evidence strongly suggests that it is, and if the Rishathaim are to be identified with the Indo-Aryan military minority that ruled the Kingdom of the Mitanni, then the Late Date Theory for the Exodus is an impossibility. This leaves only two alternatives, no Exodus or an early-date Exodus before ca. 1340 BC (Aling 1981: 80-81).

Critical Biblical scholars, who argue that there was no Exodus and that the Book of Judges is historical fiction, have the same problem as those scholars who argue for the late date of the Exodus; they must explain away the fact that Othniel's defeat of Cushan fits perfectly with the political situation which existed in the early 14th century BC in the Middle East. They must also explain away the historically accurate use of the names Rishathaim and Naharaim in the Book of Judges.

The historical accuracy of the story of Othniel and Cushan argues strongly for the historical accuracy of Judges and for the Bible's placement of the Exodus from Egypt in the 15th century BC. The best biblical date for the Exodus and the date that seems to best fit the historical and biblical evidence is the Early Date in ca. 1446 BC (Aling 1981).

NOTES

[1] Haran, the brother of Abraham, had died earlier in the city of Ur before his father Terah moved the family to the area of Haran in northern Mesopotamia. It is possible, but not likely, that the city of Haran was named after Terah's son Haran. If Terah did name Haran after his dead son, then Terah either founded the city of Haran or else he conquered a preexisting city and renamed it after his son.

[2] Genesis 22:20 even suggests—but does not state—that the name Aram was derived from "Aram," one of the grandsons of Nahor who was one of Abraham's brothers. Even if the Arameans were not named after Abraham's grandnephew, Aram, the presence of someone named Aram in the family of Abraham clearly shows an ethnic connection between the Arameans and the Israelites. Nahor was also the name of a city in the area near ancient Haran. O'Callaghan notes that the migration of Abraham from Ur to Haran "Fits in perfectly with the migrations of nomadic and semi-nomadic peoples of the entire first half of the second millennium B.C." p. 26. It is clear that the Book of Genesis is very well acquainted with the geography and history of ancient *Aram Naharaim.*

[3] The Arameans will later expand out of Aram-Naharaim into the areas of western Syria and eastern Lebanon. By the period of the divided monarchy, the Arameans had captured the city of Damascus and made it their capital. It was from the city of Damascus that the Arameans threatened both Judah and the Ten Northern Tribes of Israel, as the Old Testament so clearly records. Consult O'Callaghan, *Aram Naharayim:* 146.

[4] Ancient Hebrew has no true vowels. Some time after ca. 600 AD, Jewish scholars added vowel points and pronunciation marks to the biblical text to aid Jews in reading the Bible. These points are considered useful but not inspired by conservative Bible scholars.

[5] Consult Breasted, *Ancient Records of Egypt,* vol. II: 123-124, listing no. 299, and 135, listing no. 321 as well as vol. III: 153, listing 337.

[6] On the Rishim as a people known to the people of Ugarit, see the works of Freuke Gondahls, p. 178.

[7] On the identification of Urshu/Ursu with Warsuwa in Akkadian texts, see Trevor Bryce: 77.

[8] These "Rishim" people are almost certainly the remnants of the Indo-Aryan rulers of the Kingdom of Mitanni after their kingdom was destroyed by the Hittites in ca. 1340 BC. On the city of Urshu in the Assyrian texts see O'Callaghan, *Aram Naharaim:* 23.

[9] Some fairhaired Indo-Aryans traveled even beyond India to the borders of China. Consult Sergei Rudenko and Otto Maenchen-Helfen. Rudenko reports finding the frozen bodies of blonds in eastern Siberia, and Maenchen-Helfen argues that there were blond Indo-Europeans on the borders of China and Korea in the late ancient and early medieval periods.

[10] The suggestion that the Mitanni rulers were a fairhaired people may surprise some classicists and ancient historians who have for years maintained that blonds were unknown to the peoples of the ancient Near East. However, there are a number of tomb paintings in Egypt from the Mitanni period that clearly show blond slaves working in Egypt. It appears that conquering pharaohs such as Thutmosis I and Thutmosis III brought back captives to Egypt from their battles with the Mitanni. I have even seen a painting from the reign of Akhenaton which shows beautiful, captive, black and blond girls holding hands in full color. cf. Robert Redford, *Akhenaton the Heretic King.*

[11] Clyde E. Billington, *"Gog and Magog in History and Prophecy."* I argue in this work that the Rosh people mentioned in Ezekiel 38-39 are to be identified with the Rishim. Most English translations of the Bible mistranslate the name Rosh in Ezekiel 38:2-3 and 39:1 as "chief." Ezekiel 38:3b should be translated: "I am against you O Gog, prince of Rosh, Meshech, and Tubal." The Septuagint properly translates Ezekiel 38-39 and has the "Ros" as one of three ethnic groups allied with Gog. On the proper translation of Rosh as the name of an ancient people and on their identification with the Rishim see James Price, "Rosh: An Ancient Land Known to Ezekiel." All three peoples—Rosh, Meshech and Tubal—are mentioned in Assyrian texts which date to ca. 700 B.C. See Leroy Waterman, *Royal Correspondence of the Assyrian Empire,* where all three peoples are mentioned in the same text. For another example, see vol. II listing 92, p. 46.

[12] On the identification of the Teresh people with the Etruscans and their eventual migration to and conquest of northwest Italy, see Wolfgang Helck, *Die Beziehungen Agyptens und Vorder-asiens zur Agaus bis ins 7. Jahrhundert v. Chr.,"* See also Sanders, *Sea Peoples,* p. 118.

[13] There are Rishim people who are mentioned in Assyrian texts of the 8th and 7th Centuries BC; so not all Rishim people migrated to Italy. For a number of Assyrian references to the Rishim people, see Waterman's *Royal Correspondence of the Assyrian Empire.*

REFERENCES

Aling, C.
    1981 *Egypt and Bible History.* Grand Rapids: Baker Books.
Billington, C. E.
    1988 "Gog and Magog in History and Prophecy," Unpublished.
Breasted, J. H.
    1906 *The Ancient Records of Egypt,* ed. J. H. Breasted. New York: Russell & Russell, vol. II.

Bryce, T.
1999 *The Kingdom of the Hittites,* Oxford: Oxford University Press.
Bush, F.
1964 *A Grammar of the Hurrian Language,* Ann Arbor: UMI Dissertation Services.
Chanda, R.
1969 *The Indo-Aryan Races.* Calcutta: R.K.Maitra, 1969 reprint of 1916 edition.
Der Manuelian, P.
1987 *Studies in the Reign of Amenophis II* (Hildesheim: Gerstenberg Verlag.
Gondahls, Freuke
1967 *Die Personennamen Der Texte Aus Ugarit.* Rome: Pontificium Institutem Biblicum.
Gurney, O. R.
1966 *The Hittites.* Baltimore: Penguin Books.
Helck, W.
1979 *Die Beziehungen Agyptens und Vorderasiens zur Agaus bis ins 7. Jahrhundert v. Chr.* Band 120 in *Ertrage Der Forshung,* Darmstadt: Wissenschaftliche Buchgesellschaft.
Maenchen-Helfen, O.
1951 *The World of the Huns.* Berkeley: University of California Press.
Mercer, S. A.B. trans.
1939 *The Tell-El-Amarna Tablets.* Toronto: Macmillian Co. 1939.
O'Callaghan, R. T.
1948 *Aram Naharaim, Analecta Orientalia* 26. Rome: Pontificum Institutum Biblicum.
Pallottino, M.
1978 *The Etruscans.* New York: Penguin Books.
Price, J.
1985 "Rosh: An Ancient Land Known to Ezekiel." *The Grace Theological Journal,* 6.1: pp. 74-88.
Redford, R.
1984 *Akhenaton the Heretic King,* Princeton: Princeton University Press.
Rudenko, S.
1970 *The Frozen Tombs of Siberia: The Pazyryk Burials of Iron Age Horsemen.* Trans. by M. W. Thompson, from Russian. Berkeley: University of California Press.
Sanders, N. K.
1978 *The Sea Peoples: Warriors of the Ancient Mediterranean 1250-1150 B.C.* London: Thames and Hudson.
Starr, C. G.
1965 *A History of the Ancient World.* New York: Oxford University Press.
Vaughn, A. C.
1964 *Those Mysterious Etruscans.* Garden City, NJ: Doubleday and Co.

Virolleaud, C.
 1965 *Textes en Cuneiformes Alphabeteques Des Archives Su, Su-Oestet du Petit Palais.* Volume II in Le Palais Royal d'Ugarit, ed. Claude F. A. Schaffer. Paris: Imprimerie Nationale.

Waterman, L.
 1930 *Royal Correspondence of the Assyrian Empire.* Ann Arbor: University of Michigan Press.

Weiss, H.
 1985 "Conflict and Conquest Among the Amorite Kingdoms." *Ebla to Damscus: Art and Archaeology of Ancient Syria.* Washington, D. C.: Smithsonian Institution.

Wolf, W.
 1924 Voflaufer der Reformation Eschatons. Zeitschrift fur Agyptische Sprache und Altertumskunde 59: 109-19.a

The Amarna Letters and the "Habiru"

Ronald Youngblood

The first cache of the Amarna tablets, the only cuneiform documents to emerge thus far from the sands of Egypt, was found accidentally by an Egyptian peasant woman in 1887 while she was digging in the ruins of Tell el-Amarna in Middle Egypt for a supply of nitrous soil.[1] Not knowing their value, she sold them to a neighbor for a pittance. Eventually her find, after changing hands several times, drew the attention of archaeologists and antiquities experts, who were attracted to the Amarna site itself. Subsequent excavations have produced to date a cumulative total of 380 published documents,[2] some of which are very fragmentary. Unfortunately, as many as two hundred additional tablets may have been completely destroyed shortly after the discovery of the original hoard, whether deliberately or through rough handling.

Thirty of the 380 known Amarna tablets include syllabaries, lexical lists, and practice copies of sections of Akkadian mythological texts for the training of apprentice scribes.[3] The other 350 are epistolary and constitute part of the diplomatic correspondence of the Egyptian pharaohs Amunhotep III, Amunhotep IV (Akhenaten) and, perhaps in one case, Tutankhamun.[4] Forty-four[5] of the letters were written to and from the kings of Babylonia, Assyria, Mitanni, Hatti, and Alashia (biblical Elishah, probably Cyprus), and the remaining 306[6] were written to, from and among Egyptian officials and vassals in Syria (ancient Aram) and Canaan. One can only speculate as to whether future excavations at Amarna, Thebes, or elsewhere in Egypt will unearth additional portions of this diplomatic archive. What we already have, however—especially the 350 letters—has helped to make the Amarna age one of the best-known periods in ancient history.

The Amarna documents were written in approximately the second quarter of the fourteenth century BC (c. 1375-1350).[7] Most of the letters in the archive reveal a turbulent state of affairs in Syria and Canaan, belying the facade of unity implied by Egyptian domination of the Levant. The deterioration of the Egyptian empire in Syro-Palestine, already in process during the reign of Amunhotep III, continued under Akhenaten, who was distracted by domestic matters for much of his reign. The resultant lowering of morale among the vassal rulers of the Canaanite city-states drove them to intercity bickering that often escalated into hostility and, on occasion, open warfare. Their Amarna correspondence is full of mutual accusations of treason against the Egyptian royal house and of disloyalty toward each other. So unsettled a

133

situation made them vulnerable to attack by rebellious elements within their own domains and by enemies from without. In their letters to the Egyptian court we often read their desperate pleas for fresh contingents of archers to reinforce their own depleted troop strength. The pharaohs met all such requests for help with a stony silence.

Each of the Syro-Palestinian princelings ruled a city-state that often held sway over a rather large region. The two most important city-states in the north were Hazor and Megiddo. The hill country was dominated by Shechem and Jerusalem, and Gezer and Lachish maintained extensive holdings in the Shephelah and the south. Mediterranean coastal cities such as Byblos, Beirut, Sidon, Tyre, Acco and Ashkelon are also represented in the 306 Syro-Palestinian letters, which constitute the bulk of the Amarna archive and supply us with essential information about the effects of Egyptian decline in that part of the world during the Amarna age.

One of the most persistent and enduring truisms of human history is the fact that disrupting forces will attempt to undermine or overthrow the dominant sociopolitical order. If the power structures of our current age fear its terrorists, hijackers, guerrillas and other subversives, ancient ruling houses guarded their own fiefs with equal nervousness. Of particular concern to political custodians in the Near East during the entire second millennium BC was the presence of groups of displaced persons who existed on the fringes of society, either fleeing from the dominant order or preying upon it. Malcontents and/or misfits, the most important of these elements are sometimes popularly referred to as "Habiru." No major Near Eastern epigraphic find of the second millennium, from Ur III Mesopotamia to New Kingdom Egypt, fails to mention them. Their existence is attested in Akkadian, Hittite, Egyptian and Ugaritic sources.

Who were the "Habiru"? It is now universally agreed that the terms *ḫabiru* (or, more precisely, *'apiru*) and SA.GAZ were interchangeable and referred to the same population group or groups. To the average modern American the word Sagaz, if it means anything at all, is the name of a company with offices in Miami, Florida. Several years ago I wrote to the owners asking who they were and what they did, and a lady with a pleasant voice called me on the phone to answer my questions. She told me that Sagaz is a company that manufactures automobile seat covers in standard sizes. Would I like to buy a set for my car, she wanted to know. I don't believe so, I told her, at least at the present time. Not to worry, she responded. "In San Diego, where you live, Sagaz distributes through Pep Boys and Chief Auto Parts, among others." Further questioning on my part revealed that she did not know the origin of the word Sagaz. I didn't have the heart to tell her that, in ancient times at least, the primary meaning of SA.GAZ was "robber" or "thief."

Technically speaking, in lexical lists Sumerian (LÚ)SA.GAZ was equivalent to Akkadian *ḫab-ba-tum*, which means "robber, plunderer."[8] It had long been suspected, however, that SA.GAZ was not a true Sumerian logogram, since variants such as SA.GA.AZ and SAG.GAZ occur as well, indicating that the writing was phonetic. This in turn led to the conclusion that SA.GAZ was a pseudo-ideogram for Akkadian *šaggāšu,* "destroyer, murderer."[9] Add to this the fact that SA.GAZ and its variants are freely interchangeable with *'apiru* in second-millennium texts and it would seem plausible to assume that *'apiru* meant "robber, plunderer, destroyer, murderer."

Although some *'apirū* indeed fit such a description, it was by no means suitable for all of them. The most that can safely be said about the word *'apiru* in general is that it was "a social apellative with an unfavorable meaning."[10] The *'apirū* were outcasts,[11] outsiders[12]—outlaws,[13] if you will—but not all of them were thieves and killers. During hopelessly desperate times they might turn to brigandage and murder, but under ordinary circumstances they were for the most part "uprooted, propertyless persons who found a means of subsistence for themselves and their families by entering a state of dependence in various forms."[14]

It is fortunate, then, that milder and less innocuous secondary meanings are attested for the verbal roots that underlie both *ḫabbātu* and *šaggāšu.* In certain contexts the first means "to wander, to migrate" and the second means "to be restive."[15] Such connotations are far more suitable for the bulk of the *'apirū,* who were usually not nearly so aggressive or belligerent as the primary meanings of *ḫabbātu* and *šaggāšu* require. Is this perhaps the reason that one group of Amarna letters frequently shortens SA.GAZ to simply GAZ[16]—as if to say, "They may consider themselves SA.GAZ, 'restive people,' but I call them GAZ, the 'murderers' that they really are"?[17]

Several lines of evidence lead to the conclusion that Akkadian *ḫa-bi-ru* should be normalized as *'apiru* and that the word is of West Semitic origin. Egyptian texts always spell the word *'pr* (plural *'pr.w*), and Ugaritic texts likewise always spell it *'pr* (plural *'prm*). If the word were Akkadian in origin, the first syllable would be *a-* or *e-* but not *ḫa-* (*ḫ* was the conventional Akkadian way of representing *'ayin* in words of West Semitic provenance). In Egyptian texts, *'pr.w* are always Asiatics, often imported to supplement the native labor forces.[18]

A total of almost two hundred second-millennium documents refers to SA.GAZ/ *'apiru.* Among the numerous intersecting lines of evidence that equate the two terms is the appearance of SA.GAZ[ru] twice in a single Akkadian text from Ugarit.[19] Of the nearly two hundred texts mentioned, almost a third (sixty-two in all) are found among the Amarna letters, making them the largest single group of documents relating to the SA.GAZ/*'apirū.* Of the total, fifty-seven use the pseudo-ideogram SA.GAZ or a variant, while five (all from Abdi-Ḫeba, prince of Jerusalem) spell the word *'a$_x$-pi-ru,* the West Semitic equivalent. Fully half of the sixty-two letters were produced by the harried scribes of the hard-pressed Rib-Haddi, prince of Byblos.[20]

What kinds of activities did the Amarna-age SA.GAZ/*'apirū* engage in to deserve such frequent mention? Let the texts speak for themselves:

It is said of the (SA.)GAZ twenty-five times that people and towns and lands "turn themselves over to, go over to, are made into, become" ([*nēpušu*] *ana*) them.[21] The SA.GAZ are frequently called an "army." They are "(very) hostile against" (*dannat* [*danniš*] *nukurtu muḫḫi*) authority (six times).[22] They form part of certain "auxiliary forces" (*tillatu*). They "set their faces against, turn upon, oppose" (*nadānu panīšunu ana*) authority.[23] They "take" (*leqû,* twice),[24] they "seize" (*ṣabātu,* often), they "fall upon, attack" (*maqātu muḫḫi*),[25] "make war against" (*epēšu nukurta muḫḫi*, twice),[26] "plunder" (*šalālu*, often), "set on fire" (*uššuru/šarāpu ina išāti*, often), "raid" (*šaḫātu*),[27] "rise up against" (*našû ina*),[28] are "strong against" (*dannu muḫḫi*, twice),[29] "put an end to" (*gummuru*)[30] people and towns and lands. They can also, less menacingly, "be on the side of" ([*bašû*] *itti*, twice),[31] "bring messages" (*šūrubu*),[32] "report to" (*erēbu ana maḫar/muḫḫi*, often), "send word to" (*šapāru ana*),[33] "depart, defect" (*namāšu*).[34] At the same time, princes and/or others can "muster, gather" (*puḫḫuru*, five times)[35] (SA.)GAZ, "become like" (*bašû kīma*) them,[36] "drive (them) away from" (*šumruru ištu*),[37] "be friendly toward, love" (*râmu/ra'āmu*) them (in the sense of being allied with them),[38] "station, place" (*šakānu*) them in a city or land,[39] "pay money/a stipend" (*nadānu kaspē/aqruta*) to them,[40] "dwell among" (*ašābu ina libbi*) them,[41] "stand with" (*itṣubu itti*) them,[42] "do battle with" (*epēšu tāḫāza ina*) or be "at war with" (*nukurtu ina*) them,[43] "kill" (*dâku*, twice) them,[44] "give up, surrender" (*nadānu*, three times) them,[45] "give to" (*nadānu ana*, often) them, "flee to" (*nābutu/ḫalāqu ana*, three times) them,[46] "deliver over to" (*uššuru ana*) them,[47] "restore to. . . from" (*turru ana . . . ištu*) them,[48] "drive (them) out" (*puṭṭuru*),[49] march "with . . . toward" (*qadu . . . ana pani*) them,[50] "rescue (them) from the hand(s) of" (*ekēmu ištu qāt*[*ē*], twice),[51] "associate with" (*atallaku itti*) them,[52] "desert to" (*paṭāru ina*, twice) them,[53] "pledge oneself to" (*nadānu qātēšu ana*) them,[54] or "save them from the hands of" (*šūzubu ištu qātē*).[55] Finally, something can "be lost to" (or, alternatively, someone can "rebel among")[56] (*ḫalāqu ina*) them.[57]

It will now be instructive to turn to the five Abdi-Ḫeba letters:

It is said of the *'apirū* that people "turn themselves over to, go over to, are made into, become" (*nēpušu ana*) them,[58] "give (land or cities) to" (*nadānu* [*ana*], twice) them,[59] "desert to" (*paṭāru ana*, twice) them,[60] and "are friendly toward, love" (*râmu/ra'āmu*) them (in the sense of being allied with them).[61] As for the *'apirū,* they "take" (*leqû*) a city.[62] It will be noted that the (SA.)GAZ of the fifty-seven letters do everything that the *'apirū* of the five letters do—and then some. There is only one exception: The *'apirū* "plunder"—but the the verb is not *šalālu*, as in the (SA.)GAZ examples, but *ḫabātu*[63] (an obvious Abdi-Ḫeba pun on *ḫabbātu*). The fifty-seven letters use only (SA.)GAZ, never *'apiru*, while the five letters use only *'apiru* never (SA.)GAZ. But it is quite evident that what is said of the *'apirū* in the five is said of the (SA.)GAZ in the fifty-seven—*prima facie* evidence, if such were needed, that the two groups are identical. Further corroboration of this fact is seen in that although Abdi-Ḫeba himself never uses the term SA.GAZ, Shuwardata (another city-state ruler) does, and in one passage he says, "I and Abdi-Ḫeba are at war with a SA.GAZ man."[64] Had Abdi-Ḫeba been writing, he would doubtless have stated that they were at war with an *'apiru* man.

An especially fascinating text now demands our attention. Dagantakala, a prince from southern Canaan, asks the pharaoh to save him from his "powerful enemies, from the SA.GA.AZ, the *ḫabbātu* and the Sutū."[65] SA.GA.AZ, an equivalent of *'apiru* in these texts, is here separated from *ḫabbātu*—or at least so it seems to me.[66] In any event the Sutū, or nomads, are isolated as a separate group of troublemakers. On several occasions the post-determinative element $^{-KI}$ is added to SA.GAZ and *'apiru*,[67] perhaps indicating that the SA.GAZ/*'apirū* originate from, are related to, or are quartered in specific recognizable places (perhaps even in cities). It must immediately be stated, however, that although their origin may be urban, they are not permanently settled in cities or towns.[68]

The Shuwardata reference above indicates that individuals, as well as groups, could be designated by the term SA.GAZ/*'apiru*. Lab'aya, a southern chieftain, bears the hallmarks of the Amarna *'apiru*, as does his northern counterpart, Abdi-Ashirta—or at least they do so in the eyes of loyalists Abdi-Ḥeba and Rib-Haddi respectively. At the same time, as might be expected, Lab'aya and Abdi-Ashirta both affirm their vassalage to the pharaoh in their own letters to him. Indeed, Abdi-Ashirta is not loath to declare his subservience to the pharaoh by referring to himself as "the slave of the king, a dog in his palace."[69] And Rib-Haddi does not shrink from using similar terminology of Abdi-Ashirta by calling him "the slave, the dog," on five or six different occasions.[70] The unknown author of a badly damaged letter says that one of his antagonists, perhaps Aziru son of Abdi-Ashirta, is like SA.G[A]Z.ZA^{MES} *kalbu ḥal-qú*—like "the *'apirū*, a runaway dog."[71] It is to be observed, incidentally, that there is no known case of a SA.GAZ/*'apiru* calling himself a SA.GAZ/*'apiru*—a term of opprobrium always applied to someone else.

From information in the Amarna letters and in other second-millennium documents that supplement them we are able to characterize the SA.GAZ/*'apirū* with reasonable confidence. The term *'apiru* itself, whose etymological origin remains uncertain, is nevertheless almost certainly a West Semitic word.[72] It is not an ethnicon, despite sporadic attempts to prove otherwise;[73] we simply observe here that the plural form of Ugaritic *'pr* is *'prm,* not *'prym* (which we would expect if a normal Ugaritic gentilic were intended). The SA.GAZ/*'apirū* occupied a dependent, subordinate status, only rarely becoming a recognizable element in the sociopolitical power structure. Though often foreigners (a debatable point, however), they were not invaders from the outside. Probably of urban origin, they were not a desert people. Not restricted to the hill country, they were at least comfortable in the presence of chariots and, in some periods at least, adept at chariot warfare.[74] No discernible united purpose may be divined in their activities, nor were they structured in tribal units. Their numbers were frequently augmented by desertions of natives to them. Judging from the requests for help from Amarna-age city-state rulers, groups of SA.GAZ/*'apiru* troops rarely, if ever, amounted to more than a few hundred.[75] If the Amarna *'apirū* appear to have been somewhat more obstreperous than their namesakes at other times and in other places, that fact may be a "correlative of local instability."[76] During the Amarna age, the SA.GAZ/*'apirū* seem for the most part to have been military mercenaries. Lacking that employment opportunity, others became renegade robbers. Virtually nothing in the above description augurs well for a wholesale identification of the Amarna-age (or other) *'apirū* with the Hebrews of the exodus and conquest (or other periods).

Nevertheless, scarcely had the Amarna letters been examined by epigraphers before it was noticed that the syllabic writing ḪA-BI-*ru*—first attested in these documents—bore a striking resemblance to the word "Hebrew."[77] Since the archive dates to the first half of the fourteenth century BC, the possibility that the vassal correspondence was reporting the Hebrew invasion of the promised land from the Canaanite viewpoint was too tempting to resist. One of the letters even gives us the proper name *Ya-šu-ia,*[78] which a few scholars dutifully claimed was the cuneiform spelling of "Joshua" (the last syllable of which, however, would have had to be written with a *ḥ* phoneme in order properly to have represented the *'ayin* in Joshua's Hebrew name). Although "the question of the entry of the Israelite tribes into Palestine must . . . be distinguished from that of the relationship between Ḫâbirū and Hebrew,"[79] and although most would now agree that the words *'apiru* and *'ibrî* ("Hebrew") are not completely interchangeable in every context, the possibility of an etymological connection between them[80] warrants a brief survey of the occurrences of *'ibrî* (and its feminine counterpart *'ibrîyâ*) in the OT.

It is not often noted that *'ibrî* appears only thirty-four times in the entire OT—less than one-third the number of times that SA.GAZ/*'apiru* occurs in the Amarna corpus alone. The term is found twenty-two times in the Torah, twelve times in the Prophets, and not at all in the Writings. It is attested in only six books: Genesis, Exodus, Deuteronomy, 1 Samuel, Jeremiah, and Jonah. We observe immediately that *'ibrî* does not appear in either Joshua or Judges. In fully twenty-five of the instances it is an ethnicon, a gentilic, either clearly or by implication.[81] In six of the remaining nine cases an Egyptian (during the patriarchal and exodus periods) or a Philistine (during the late judges and early monarchy periods) uses the term—sometimes, but not always, pejoratively—in a way that does not reject the possibility of a gentilic interpretation.[82] Two other occurrences are closely related in context to two of the above thirty-one and should therefore be understood in a similar way.[83] This leaves us only 1 Samuel 14:21: "Those Hebrews who had previously been with the Philistines and had gone up with them to their camp went over to the Israelites who were with Saul and Jonathan." If ever *'ibrîm* looked like a nonethnic term coinciding with the kind of *'apirū* that appear in the Amarna letters, it is here. And the LXX, which translates *'ibrî* by *Hebraios* twenty-eight out of thirty-four times, renders *'ibrîm* as *douloi,* "servants/slaves," in this passage. Nevertheless, since only ten verses earlier *'ibrîm* is a gentilic (so recognized by the LXX: *Hebraioi*), the word cannot be totally discounted as an ethnicon even in 1 Samuel 14:21.

In an important if controversial article,[84] Mary P. Gray understands *'ibrî* as a nonethnic appellative throughout and contends that it did not become a gentilic until post-biblical times (i.e., until after the OT was completed). It might therefore be helpful to briefly examine, as typical, her arguments concerning the first and last occurrences of *'ibrî* in the OT.

In Genesis 14:13 we read of "Abram the Hebrew." Among Gray's many arguments, here is the most critical: "The Greek translation of the passage uses the word *ho perátēs,* meaning 'the wanderer, the transient, the one who crosses or passes through.' In other words, the translators of the Septuagint understood the word in this case to be appellative rather than gentilic, and rendered it as such."[85] True enough—

but what she passes over in silence is that Abram is called *hā'ibrî*, "the Hebrew," in the same verse in which his associate Mamre is called *hā'ămōrî*, "the Amorite," a term that is surely understood as an ethnicon throughout the OT. Why take away from "Hebrew" what we willingly grant to "Amorite"?

In Jonah 1:9 the prophet says, "I am a Hebrew." His statement is in response to a series of questions: "Where do you come from? What is your country? From what people are you?" It would seem, then, that Jonah uses "Hebrew" as an ethnicon. Gray, however, prefers the LXX reading—*Doulos kuriou egō eimi* ("I am a servant of the Lord")—which assumes, instead of an original consonantal *'bry*, the reading *'bd yhwh*, later abbreviated to *'bd y* and then misread and miscopied as *'bdy*.[86] But three pages later, in support of her contention that "Hebrew" began to be used ethnically only in the intertestamental period, she states: "The ethnic sense of the term *Hebraios* appears in Judith 10.12. In response to a question and challenge from the Assyrian guard, 'Of what people are you, and from where are you coming, and where are you going?' Judith answers, *Thygátēr eimi tōn Hebraiōn*, 'I am a daughter of the Hebrews.' "[87] Again I ask: Why deny Jonah what we allow Judith?

"The date of the exodus is one of the most debated topics in OT studies because of the ambiguous nature of the evidence."[88] I can personally attest to the truth of that statement, since I am in print in at least three different volumes in advocacy of a thirteenth-century date[89] and in at least three other volumes in support of a fifteenth-century date.[90] In most of those publications I had the good sense to say something like this: "In view of the difficulties surrounding this problem, I currently hold that the exodus took place at such-and-such a time—but without being dogmatic about it."

Although I presently believe that the exodus of the Israelites occurred during Egypt's eighteenth dynasty in the middle of the fifteenth century BC, it will be clear from what I have written above that I do not believe that the Amarna SA.GAZ/*'apirū* are identical with Joshua's invading armies or that the second-millennium SA.GAZ/ *'apirū* can be simply equated with the biblical *'ibrîm* without further ado. Given the present state of the evidence, perhaps the most that can be said about the relationship of the Amarna *'apirū* to the biblical account of the exodus and conquest is that *'apirū*-type elements appear in the book of Judges among Abimelech's hired "reckless adventurers" (Judg 9:4) and Jephthah's "group of adventurers" (11:3). At least twenty-five years too late for Joshua's sudden, sustained, strategic blitzkrieg if we assume an early date for the exodus, the Amarna SA.GAZ/*'apirū* could nevertheless have served as sociopolitical midwives for the restless malcontents who, in the succeeding centuries, followed in their train.[91]

NOTES

[1]For additional details concerning the discovery of the tablets and their subsequent history, consult Youngblood (1979).

[2]EA (i.e., el-Amarna [tablet]) 1-358 were transliterated, translated and described in admirable fashion in Knudtzon, Weber and Ebeling (1908-15); EA 359-379, discovered and/or identified too late for Knudtzon's edition, are similarly treated in Rainey (1978). A final tablet was

published by Walker (1979). Two virtually illegible Amarna fragments have been identified and have recently been given the numbers 380 and 381, with the result that the Walker tablet has officially been renumbered as EA 382 (for details see Moran [1992: xv]).

[3] EA 340-361, 368, 372-377, 379.

[4] See Campbell (1970: 57); Albright (1966).

[5] EA 1-44.

[6] EA 45-339, 362-367, 369-371, 378, 382.

[7] Cf. Campbell (1970: 62). The dates given assume that Amunhotep III ruled c. 1402-1363 and Akhenaten c. 1363-1347 as suggested in Hallo and Simpson (1971: 300); cf. similarly Bright (2000: 490). Dates higher by more than a decade (1377-1360) for Akhenaten are given by Redford (1992: 181), while dates lower by just about a decade (1352-1336) are proposed by Kitchen (1992: 329).

[8] Cf. CAD Ḫ, 13. See further Cazelles (1973: 6-7); Beitzel (1982: 586). Beitzel's article is the finest overall summary of all aspects of problems relating to the *'apirū*.

[9] Cf. Greenberg (1955: 88-90); Gray (1958: 142); Meek (1960: 10 n. 28).

[10] Cf. Veenhof (1986: 265); cf. also Greenberg (1955: 92).

[11] Greenberg (1970: 193).

[12] Walsh (1987: 185 n. 8); Gottwald (1979: 401, 405).

[13] Cf. Mendenhall (1973: 138); Campbell (1970: 73); Greenberg (1955: 86); Veenhof (1986: 265); Weippert (1971: 65); Moran (1987: 209-212). We are no closer to the etymology or meaning of *'apiru* now than we ever were, as recent scholarly disagreement so amply attests; cf. e.g. Lemche (1992: 7). The celebrated "dusty one = donkey caravaner" definition of Albright (1968: 74-75) has fared no better than other equally valiant attempts; cf. e.g. Beitzel (1982: 586-87).

[14] Greenberg (1955: 88).

[15] Greenberg (1955: 89). Cf. also Bottéro (1954); for further amplification see especially Na'aman (1986).

[16] For a representative listing see Gray (1958: 143 n. 41).

[17] So approximately Greenberg (1955: 90).

[18] Weippert (1971: 89-91); Veenhof (1986: 265-66); cf. Gray (1958: 165).

[19] *PRU*, 3. 16.03:5 (and perhaps also 16.03:6). See Gray (1958: 161).

[20] See Gray (1958: 139 nn. 11-12); cf. also Mendenhall (1973: 122-23). For translation of and commentary on all the Amarna letters that mention SA.GAZ/*'apirū* see Greenberg (1955); Bottéro (1954).

[21] EA 68:17-18; 73:28-29; 73:32-33; 74:19-21; 74:27; 74:35-36; 76:34-37 (cf. 76:42-43); 77:28-29; 79:19-20; 79:25-26 (cf. 79:42-44); 81:12-13; 85:72-73; 88:31-32; 88:32-34; 104:51-52; 104:53-54; 111:19-21; 116:37-38; 117:57-58 (omitting *nēpušu*); 117:94; 121:21-22; 144:24-26; 144:29-30; 148:45; 179:20-23 (omitting *nēpušu*—although perhaps in this case the intended expression is *gamāru ana*). For discussion of this idiom cf. e.g. Campbell (1970: 67-68); Weippert (1971: 71-72); Artzi (1964: 163 n. 4; 165-166).

[22] EA 68:12-14; 74:14; 75:10-11; 76:8-9; 81:7; 243:19-20.

[23] EA 79:10-11. Cf. Hebrew *ntn pnym b-*; for discussion see Youngblood (1961: 201).

[24] EA 83:17-18; 90:25.

[25] EA 91:24-25.
[26] EA 185:13-14; 246:9'-10'. In the latter text Gray (1958: 159) follows Knudtzon in reading *i-bi-r[u]*, perhaps at least partly because of her desire to derive *'apiru* from the root *'br*. The reading *i-pí-š[i]*, adopted by Greenberg (1955: 45), is clearly superior—although his insertion of *a-na* after *nukurta* on the defaced and broken section of the tablet is unnecessary in the light of 185:13-14.
[27] EA 185:42-43.
[28] EA 366:12-14.
[29] EA 299:18-19; 305:21-22.
[30] EA 299:24-25.
[31] EA 82:9; 185:50-51. For Hebrew parallels see Youngblood (1961: 228-229).
[32] EA 112:46.
[33] EA 273:18-21.
[34] EA 313:5-6. In light of all these references, I do not know what to make of Mendenhall's statements (1973: 134) that "SA.GAZ occurs as the subject of a verb only thirteen times in the Amarna letters" and that in every case "the verb used implies illegitimate seizure or violent action against the property of the king."
[35] EA 71:28-29; 76:17-18; 85:77-78; 91:23-24; 132:20-21.
[36] EA 74:28-29 (cf. 74:26).
[37] EA 77:24-25 (cf. 76:38-41; 85:80-82; 103:30).
[38] EA 85:40-41 (cf. 73:14-18; 83:49-51; 137:46-48; 138:71-73).
[39] EA 87:21-22.
[40] EA 112:45-46; 246:5'-7'.
[41] EA 130:37-38.
[42] EA 148:42-43.
[43] EA 185:44-45; 366:20-21.
[44] EA 185:46; 366:16
[45] EA 185:56; 185:61-62; 366:15.
[46] EA 185:63; 186:66; 186:68.
[47] EA 189:10'-11'.
[48] EA 189:15'-17'.
[49] EA 189:18'.
[50] EA 195:24-30.
[51] EA 271:13-16; 274:10-13.
[52] EA 254:33-35.
[53] EA 272:14-17; 273:13-14.
[54] EA 298:26-27. Greenberg (1955: 49) appropriately compares 2 Chr 30:8; Ezra 10:19.
[55] EA 318:8-11.
[56] Cf. Weippert (1971: 71 n. 62).
[57] EA 207:19-21; 215:13-15.
[58] EA 288:44.
[59] EA 287:31; 289:24.
[60] EA 290:12-13; 290:23-24.

[61] EA 286:18-19. For the covenant background of this terminology cf. Campbell (1976: 47)

[62] EA 288:38.

[63] EA 286:56.

[64] EA 366:20-21.

[65] EA 318:9-13.

[66] Cf. Veenhof (1986: 267); Weippert (1971: 73); Albright (1966); Artzi (1968: 166-68). Cf., however, Greenberg (1955: 50).

[67] EA 215:15; 289:24; 298:27. It surely does not mean that they "now had a land of their own," as Meek states (1960: 21).

[68] Gray (1958: 166-67); Greenberg (1955: 86-87).

[69] EA 60:6-7.

[70] EA 71:17-18; 76:12; 79:45; 85:64; 91:5; 117:36. In 76:12; 79:45; 91:5 the epithet "slave," though omitted in the texts themselves, is surely implied in the light of the parallels elsewhere. In 91:5 Abdi-Ashirta, though not mentioned by name, is clearly intended; see Youngblood (1961: 355); Greenberg (1955: 38).

[71] EA 67:16-17. Cf. Weippert (1971: 72). See Mendenhall (1973: 130) for a helpful discussion of the significance of the term *kalbu halqu*. Mendenhall translates it as "stray dog" (or "fugitive dog," 1973: 124) and considers it to be virtually a definition of SA.GAZ, the opposite of which is the faithful vassal, the obedient dog, who "hears his master's voice." Cf. further Gray (1958: 156-57); Walsh (1987: 38).

[72] Mendenhall (1973: 138-39); de Vaux (1968: 222); Greenberg (1955: 90). Contrast Cazelles (1973: 19), who leans toward a Hurrian origin for the word. For a brief rebuttal cf. Beitzel (1982: 586).

[73] Cf. e.g. de Vaux (1968), who distinctly favors an ethnic interpretation of the word—a viewpoint clearly in the minority, however; cf. Roberts (1985: 87); Gottwald (1979: 759 n. 311); Weippert (1971: 70).

[74] Cf. Greenberg (1955: 96). Gottwald (1979: 402-3) argues otherwise but unconvincingly.

[75] Cf. Greenberg (1955: 75 n. 71). These figures apply only to the Amarna *'apirū*. At other times and in other places much larger groups of *'apirū* are attested; cf. e.g. the 3,600 *'pr.w* mentioned by Greenberg (1955: 56). (The correct figure is given on p. 98—a fact not observed, unfortunately, by Bruce [1967: 8].)

[76] Greenberg (1970: 196); cf. also Greenberg (1955: 76, 86); Gottwald (1979: 402).

[77] Cf. Gray (1958: 135-37); Mendenhall (1973: 122); Weippert (1971: 84).

[78] EA 256:18. Cf. the observation by Bruce (1967: 17 n. 45).

[79] Gray (1958:195).

[80] Cf. esp. Loretz (1984). See also Campbell (1970: 63); Mazar (1986: 58-59); Walsh (1987: 37); Veenhof (1986: 267); Gottwald (1979: 401); Weippert (1971: 101). Kaiser apparently assumes a relationship between the terms but then clouds the issue in a decidedly confusing footnote (1983: 99 n. 6). Beitzel expresses serious doubts about any such connection (1982: 589-90).

[81] Gen 14:13; 40:15; 43:32; Exod 1:15; 1:16; 1:19; 2:11; 2:13; 3:18; 5:3; 7:16; 9:1; 9:13; 10:3; 21:2; Deut 15:12 (twice); 1 Sam 4:9; 13:3; 13:19; 29:3; Jer 34:9 (twice); 34:14; Jonah 1:9. Weippert (1971: 84) fails to observe that Jer 34:9 contains two occurrences of *'ibrî(yâ)* and

therefore gives the total number of occurrences in the Hebrew Bible as thirty-three.

[82] Gen 39:14; 39:17; 41:12; Exod 2:6; 1 Sam 4:6; 14:11.

[83] Exod 2:7; 1 Sam 13:7.

[84] Gray (1958).

[85] Gray (1958: 175).

[86] Gray (1958: 186).

[87] Gray (1958: 189).

[88] Shea (1982: 230). Cf. similarly Youngblood (1995a: 273-74, 424).

[89] Youngblood (1971: 12), (1974: 6), (1979: 107).

[90] Youngblood (1982: 58, 60), (1983: 16), (1995b: 83-4).

[91] Cf. Mendenhall (1973: 135-38); Greenberg (1970: 279 n. 12); (1955: 76 n. 73); Gottwald (1979: 490, 496-97). The recent attempt by Waterhouse (2001: 31-42) to equate at least some of the Amarna 'apirū with Joshua's Hebrews, while suggestive, falls far short of establishing the connection.

REFERENCES

Albright, W. F.
1966 The Amarna Letters from Palestine. *Cambridge Ancient History.* Chapter 20.
1968 *Yahweh and the Gods of Canaan.* Garden City: Doubleday.

Artzi, P.
1964 *'Vox Populi'* in the el-Amarna Tablets. *RA* 58.
1968 Some Unrecognized Syrian Amarna Letters (EA 260, 317, 318). *JNES* 27: 166-68.

Beitzel, B. J.
1982 Habiru. Pp. 586-87 in vol. 2 of *The International Standard Bible Encyclopedia = ISBE,* gen. ed. G. W. Bromiley. Grand Rapids: Eerdmans.

Bottéro, J.
1954 *Le problème des Ḫabiru à la rencontre assyriologique internationale. Cahiers de la Société Asiatique* 12: 191-98. Paris.

Bright, J.
2000 *A History of Israel* (4th ed.). Louisville: Westminster John Knox.

Bruce, F. F.
1967 Tell el Amarna. Pp. 3-20 in *Archaeology and Old Testament Study,* ed. D. Winton Thomas. Oxford: Clarendon.

Campbell, E. F., Jr.
1970 The Amarna Letters and the Amarna Period. Pp. 54-75 in *The Biblical Archaeologist Reader* 3, eds. E. F. Campbell, Jr., and David Noel Freedman. Garden City: Doubleday.
1976 Two Amarna Notes: The Shechem City-State and Amarna Administrative Terminology. *Magnalia Dei: The Mighty Acts of God: Essays on the Bible and Archaeology in Memory of G. Ernest Wright,* ed. F. M. Cross *et al.* Garden City: Doubleday.

Cazelles, H.
1973 The Hebrews. *Peoples of Old Testament Times,* ed. D. J. Wiseman. Oxford: Clarendon.

Gottwald, N. K.
1979 *The Tribes of Yahweh.* Maryknoll: Orbis.

Gray, M. P.
1958 The Habiru-Hebrew Problem in the Light of the Source Material Available at Present. *HUCA* 29.

Greenberg, M.
1955 The Ḫab/piru. AOS 39. New Haven: American Oriental Society.
1970 Vol. 2, *The World History of the Jewish People,* ed. B. Mazar. New Brunswick: Rutgers University.

Hallo, W. W., and W. K. Simpson
1971 *The Ancient Near East: A History.* New York: Harcourt Brace Jovanovitch.

Kaiser, W. C., Jr.
1983 *Toward Old Testament Ethics.* Grand Rapids: Zondervan.

Kitchen, K. A.
1992 Egypt, History of (Chronology). *ABD* II: 321-31.

Knudtzon, J. A., O. Weber and E. Ebeling
1908-15 *Die El-Amarna Tafeln.* 2 vols., Vorderasiatische Bibliothek 2/1-2. Leipzig: Hinrichs.

Lemche, N. P.
1992 Ḫabiru, Ḫapiru. *ABD* III: 6-10.

Loretz, O.
1984 *Habiru-Hebräer: Eine socio-linguistische Studie über die Herkunft des Gentiliziums 'ibrî vom Appellativum ḫabiru* (BZAW 160). Berlin/New York: de Gruyter.

Mazar, B.
1986 *The Early Biblical Period: Historical Studies,* eds. S. Aḥituv and B. A. Levine. Jerusalem: Israel Exploration Society.

Meek, T. J.
1960 *Hebrew Origins.* New York: Harper.

Mendenhall, G. E.
1973 *The Tenth Generation.* Baltimore: Johns Hopkins.

Moran, W. L.
1987 Join the *'apiru* or Become One? Pp. 209-12 in *"Working with No Data": Semitic and Egyptian Studies Presented to Thomas O. Lambdin,* ed. D. M. Golomb. Winona Lake: Eisenbrauns.
1992 *The Amarna Letters.* Baltimore: Johns Hopkins.

Na'aman, N.
1986 Habiru and Hebrews: The Transfer of a Social Term to the Literary Sphere. *JNES* 45/4: 271-88.

Rainey, A. F.
  1978 *El Amarna Tablets 359-379: Supplement to J. A. Knudtzon, Die El-Amarna Tafeln.* 2nd ed. rev. *AOAT.* Neukirchen-Vluyn: Neukirchener.
Redford, D. B.
  1986 History of the Ancient Near East to the Time of Alexander the Great. *The World of the Bible,* gen. ed. A. S. van der Woude. Grand Rapids: Eerdmans.
  1992 Amarna, Tell el. *ABD* I:181-82.
Roberts, J. J. M.
  1985 The Ancient Near Eastern Environment. *The Hebrew Bible and Its Modern Interpreters,* eds. D. A. Knight and C. M. Tucker. Philadelphia: Fortress.
Shea, W. D.
  1982 Exodus, Date of the. *ISBE* 2:230-38.
de Vaux, R.
  1968 *Le problème des Ḫapiru après quinze années. JNES* 27.
Veenhof, K. R.
  1986 History of the Ancient Near East to the Time of Alexander the Great. *The World of the Bible,* gen. ed. A. S. van der Woude. Grand Rapids: Eerdmans.
Walker, C. B. F.
  1979 Another Fragment from el-Amarna (EA 380). *JCS* 31: 249.
Walsh, J. P. M.
  1987 *The Mighty from Their Thrones.* Philadelphia: Fortress.
Waterhouse, S. D.
  2001 Who Are the Habiru of the Amarna Letters? *Journal of the Adventist Theological Society* 12/1: 31-42.
Weippert, M.
  1971 *The Settlement of the Israelite Tribes in Palestine* (SBT 21). Naperville: Allenson.
Youngblood, R. F.
  1961 *The Amarna Correspondence of Rib-Haddi, Prince of Byblos* (EA 68-96). Dropsie dissertation. University Microfilms.
  1971 *The Heart of the Old Testament.* Grand Rapids: Baker.
  1974 *Teacher's Manual for ... His Way Out.* Glendale: G/L.
  1979 Amarna Tablets. *ISBE* 1:105-8.
  1982 A New Look at an Old Problem: The Date of the Exodus. *Christianity Today* (December 17).
  1983 *Exodus.* Chicago: Moody.
  1995a Chronology, Old Testament, Pp. 273-74 in *Nelson's New Illustrated Bible Dictionary,* gen. ed. R. F. Youngblood. Nashville: Thomas Nelson.
  1995b Introduction: Exodus, Pp. 83-4 in *The NIV Study Bible (10th Anniversary Edition).* Grand Rapids: Zondervan.

The Prelude to Amarna

Dr. Charles Aling
Northwestern College at
St. Paul, Minnesota

The Eighteenth Dynasty Pharaoh Akhenaten (ca. 1348-1331 B.C.) is one of the strangest and most interesting kings of ancient Egypt. In his seventeen-year reign he led (evidently personally) a thorough religious revolution in Egypt, starting in his sixth year, which replaced the worship of Amon-Re with that of the raw disk of the sun, the god Aton (Aldred 1988 and Redford 1984). His reign was also accompanied by great change in artistic style, as has been revealed by the excavations at this king's new capital at Tell El Amarna. The Amarna style is characterized by a new and at times grotesque realism. The king himself is depicted with a long thin face, a prominent chin, thick lips, a thin neck, and fleshy thighs. Such depictions have led to speculation that Akhenaten was suffering from some disease, but without more evidence (such as the royal mummy) it remains unproven. Other art works show the king and his wife Nefertiti in pleasant familial poses, holding their daughters in pleasant embrace. Yet another innovation is the placing of small hands at the ends of solar rays reaching down from the sun disk. Amarna art is truly different, at least when the royal family is presented, from typical ways the Pharaoh and royal family are shown in ancient Egypt.

But the biggest change Akhenaten brought about was in the area of religion. First, let it be said that some of the popular conclusions that have been reached about the Amarna religious beliefs are not true. Akhenaten's new religion was not "monotheism." While it is true that he reduced the number of gods receiving official government support, he by no means reduced the number to one. The king himself remained a god, who was to receive worship from the people. In turn, Akhenaten would then worship Aton. Nor were all other religious beliefs totally destroyed. Outside the new capital, devotion to the old gods continued. Even the Amarna workmen themselves continued to inscribe prayers to Amon-Re in their village! Nor was Akhenaten the pacifist he is often credited with being. He and his wife are shown in the traditional pose of smiting their enemies with maces. On the positive side, the religion at Tell el Amarna viewed the sun as the ultimate creator who gives life to all things, by means of its rays, which were thought of as physical (Grimal 1992).

An intriguing question is why Akhenaten made all these changes, which could only have thrown the nation into profound confusion. The suppression of the cults of deities like Amon-Re and Osiris, god of the dead, must have been poorly received by many people. Perhaps Akhenaten had only pure spiritual devotion to his god and no other motives at all. If this was so, we will never know. Or perhaps, if we rely on the artistic representations of the king, Akhenaten was mentally unbalanced. After all, he looks very strange, and he was willing to disrupt his entire society and forsake Egypt's hard-won foreign empire by ignoring it. But would his officials and his army support a king of such unbalanced mind? And would foreign rulers correspond with him, as they most surely did as is proven by the Amarna Letters, diplomatic correspondence between the Pharaoh and his vassal kings in Syria-Palestine?

While it is not possible to examine Akhenaten's total motivation for changing conservative Egypt's religion, there is evidence that politics played a substantial role in the situation. It is the purpose of this paper to present that evidence, which stems out of prosopographical study of the officials of Akhenaten's two predecessors, Thutmosis IV and Amenhotep III. It seems that these two rulers attempted to reduce the wealth and power of the Amon cult by removing titles from the High Priest of Amon.

The High Priest of Amon had, over several generations, benefitted greatly from Egypt's conquests in Nubia and more importantly Syria-Palestine (Gardiner 1966: 188 ff and Grimal 1992: 213 ff).

As kings such as Thutmosis III (1504-1450 BC) returned from campaign after campaign, laden with the wealth of conquest, gift after gift was granted to the temple of Amon-Re at Karnak, and the High Priest became ever richer and more powerful, perhaps rivaling the position of the king himself. As they gained wealth, the High Priests also accumulated titles to go with that wealth. The two kings immediately before Akhenaten, Thutmosis IV (ca. 1415-1385) and Amenhotep III (ca. 1385-1348)[1], were evidently bothered by the growing wealth and power of their High Priests and made a concerted effort to remove three key titles from them, as we shall see. If these moves failed to sufficiently weaken the High Priest and subordinate him to royal control, a further and more extreme solution to the problem was necessary. That solution, taken by Akhenaten, was to change Egypt's religion, its capital city, and its ruling hierarchy. The office of High Priest of Amon was abolished, and the royal court at Tell el Amarna (which replaced Thebes as the capital of the empire) dedicated itself to the worship of the god Aton. It is not our purpose to examine the new faith. But let us look at the removal of those titles from the High Priest of Amon in the two generations before the great religious revolution of Akhenaten.

Overseer of the Cattle of Amon

In ancient Egypt cattle were an important aspect of wealth. The king and the great temples would presumably have large herds, supervised by high officials. Any attempt to list all of the holders of the title Overseer of the Cattle of Amon in Dynasty Eighteen would be incomplete since there are so many people who have the title in addition to any other positions they may hold. It is certain that more than one person held the title at any given time. I have compiled a list of twenty-eight men who were Overseer of the Cattle of Amon in Dynasty Eighteen (Aling 1976: 236-7, 241), and while it is not complete, it is surely representative. Some holders of the title had no other known job and were probably low-ranking functionaries; others were high officials such as Mayor of Thebes, King's Son of Kush (governor of Nubia) or High Priest of Amon. It is relatively common for the Chief Steward of the King, the man in charge of the royal estates, to hold this title as well. Evidently there were temple herds on these estates.

Among the High Priests of Amon, four in succession are also Overseers of the Cattle of Amon: Hapuseneb and Ahmose under Hatshepsut, Menkheperre-Seneb under Thutmosis III, and Mery under Amenhotep II, the father of Thutmosis IV (Aling: 241). After Mery, an interesting thing happens. The title is never again granted to a High Priest of Amon (Lefebvre 1929: 281). Mery's successor, Amenemhat, who became High Priest in the last years of Amenhotep II but whose career in the main belongs to the reign of Thutmosis IV, is not given charge over any of the temple cattle herds.

What happened to the title, if it was not granted to the new High Priest? The title Overseer of the Cattle of Amon appears in the reign of Thutmosis IV in different and unexpected hands. In this king's reign and that of his son, the governor of Nubia, the King's Son of Kush, becomes Overseer of the Cattle of Amon. Amenhotep, governor under Thutmosis IV and the famous Mermose, the governor of Nubia under Amenhotep III who has left many monuments, both were given this title. This indicated a royal willingness to take the title from the High Priest, but it is also natural, since the wars of Thutmosis IV and Amenhotep III were in Nubia and therefore new cattle coming into Egyptian possession were from that region (Aling 1976: 244). But geography alone cannot explain what is going on. Two military men, Kaemwaset and Horemhab (not to be confused with the general and later king of the same name), also receive the title (*Urkunden* IV, 1589-96 and *Urkunden* IV, 1633). The kings are obviously favoring their most trusted servants, military officials, with this title. We will see more of Horemhab[2].

Overseer of All the Priests of Upper and Lower Egypt

A second title removed from the High Priest is that of Overseer of All the Priests of Upper and Lower Egypt. While we do not know all the duties of this official, Wolfgang Helck has established that he had administrative responsibilities concerned with the appointment of priests of all the deities of Egypt and over the economic interests of provincial temples (Helck 1964: 33). Since few are recorded, we may assume that in all probability only one person held this post at any given time. I know of the following nine Overseers of All the Priests of Upper and Lower Egypt in Dynasty Eighteen:[2]

1. Hapuseneb. High Priest of Amon under Hatshepsut.
2. Menkheperre-seneb. High Priest of Amon under Thutmosis III.

3. Mery. High Priest of Amon under Amenhotep II.
4. Amenemhat. High Priest omon under Amenhotep II and Thutmosis IV.
5. Horemhab. General (Scribe of Recruits) under Thutmosis IV and Amenhotep III
6. Ptahmose. Vizier and High Priest of Amon under Thutmosis IV and Amenhotep III.
7. Thutmosis/Djehutymose. Prince and High Priest of Ptah under Amenhotep III.
8. Ptahmose. High Priest of Ptah under Amenhotep III.
9. Ramose. The well-known Vizier under Amenhotep III and the pre-Amarna years of Akhenaten.

It is obvious that this title, from its inception under Hatshepsut until the reign of Thutmosis IV, was reserved for the High Priest of Amon. But at some time after the death of Amenemhat, the title first went to someone other than a High Priest, the military official Horemhab. We have seen that this individual also had the title Overseer of the Cattle of Amon. He was obviously a trusted friend of his king. But note that Ptahmose, who was High Priest of Amon, also held the title. What are we to make of this? Since only one person can hold this title at a time, there are two possibilities. He had the post either before or after Horemhab. Since Ptahmose served as High Priest of Amon until nearly year twenty of Amenhotep III, it seems best to place Horemhab's term as Overseer of All Priests earlier. After all, Horemhab's career goes back to the reign of Thutmosis III. He would be very old indeed if he was still alive and active after year twenty of Amenhotep III! That Ptahmose received the title late in his career, after the death of the first non-priest to hold it (Horemhab), is supported by the absence of the title on all of Ptahmose's monuments except one.

A question may arise regarding the fact that Ptahmose was High Priest of Amon. If that is so, and it is, could it not be thought that the title Overseer of All Priests had, after Horemhab, again reverted to the High Priest of Amon? The answer is yes, but there are other factors bearing on the case. Ptahmose also has the title Vizier. There were at this period in Egyptian history two men with this title at a time, the Northern and the Southern Vizier. Ptahmose, we know from his full title Vizier in the Southern City (Thebes), was Southern Vizier. But the man's name, Ptahmose, is a strong indication of a northern origin, since the god Ptah was a northern deity with his major temple at Memphis in Lower Egypt. Normally, the post of Northern Vizier went to a man of northern origin, and the office of Southern Vizier went to a man of southern connections. Ptahmose is the first Southern Vizier in Egyptian history who we know came from the north (Aling, 1976: 62 ff. and 247 ff.). Since Thutmosis IV was raised in the north, it is tempting to see Ptahmose as a boyhood friend and loyal supporter of the new king who is brought south to Thebes, made vizier there, and also is granted the title High Priest of Amon. By combining these titles in the hands of a loyal man, Thutmosis IV is attempting to control temple wealth and power. It would be reasonable to also make his friend head of all priests of the entire land. The close ties between the two can also be seen in the fact that Ptahmose named his own daughter Mutemwia, after the wife of Thutmosis IV and mother of Amenhotep III. He was also the first Vizier to receive the honor of being called Fan Bearer on the King's Right Hand.

Ptahmose died some time before year twenty of Amenhotep III. We know that because there is a new Southern Vizier in that year, the famous Ramose. The new High Priest of Amon is one Mery-Ptah. At first, neither of these men holds the title Overseer of all the Priests of Upper and Lower Egypt. Instead, the title passes on to a son of king Amenhotep, Prince Thutmosis, who was High Priest of the god Ptah at Memphis (Gauthier II, p. 336). His successor in that post, another Ptahmose, also was Overseer of All Priests. These two successive appointments were the first times ever that a High Priest of Ptah was Overseer of All the Priests of Upper and Lower Egypt and can be seen as a direct snub to Mery-Ptah, the High Priest of Amon at Thebes. In this departure from custom, we can see a king (Amenhotep III) groping for a solution to the problem of a too powerful High Priest of Amon at Thebes.

The last Southern Vizier under Amenhotep III was Ramose, again a Northerner. This official, who had a beautiful tomb excavated for himself at Thebes (de Garis Davies 1941),[3] served on briefly into the reign of Akhenaten. The only peculiar thing about his titles is the presence of the title Overseer of All the Priests of Upper and Lower Egypt, a title not normal for a non-priest. It is probable that he received it late in the reign of Amenhotep III, since there must be time for the High Priests of Ptah mentioned above to hold the title. Also, none of Ramose's early monuments have the title. His non-funerary inscriptions at Soleb, Sehel, and Bigeh do not have this title, nor do his jar labels from Malqata, which are dated year thirty of Amenhotep III (Helck 1958: 442-3). The title occurs only in his magnificent Theban tomb, in which Ramose was buried some time before Akhenaten changed Egypt's religion and capital city in year six of his reign. A reasonable supposition would be that Ramose received the title from the new king, Amenhotep IV (Akhenaten's original name), before he abolished the High Priesthood of Amon. After the death of Ramose, no other person held this title in the period here under discussion.

Steward of the Amon Temple

The last title removed from the control of the priesthood was that of Steward of the Amon Temple.[4] The holder of this post was evidently the chief supervisor of the vast lands held by the Amon Temple complex throughout Egypt, and it can be seen as a kind of ecclesiastical counterpart to the office of Chief Steward of the King, who controlled the royal estates scattered through the land.

The following are the datable Stewards of the Amon Temple in Dynasty Eighteen that are known to me:[5]

1. Mery, the High Priest of Amon under Amenhotep II.
2. Amenemhat, High Priest of Amon under Amenhotep II and Thutmosis IV.
3. Ptahmose, High Priest of Amon and Southern Vizier under Thutmosis IV and Amenhotep III.

4. Kaemwaset, serving under Thutmosis IV.
5. Amonuser, Vizier under Hatshepsut.
6. Rekhmire, the well-known Vizier of Thutmosis III.
7. Senmut, the Chief Steward of Hatshepsut.
8. Sen-nefer, the Mayor of Thebes under Amenhotep II.
9. Sen-Djehuty, who served under Thutmosis III.
10. Nakht-sebek, who served under Amenhotep III.

Assuming, because of the relatively small number of men who held this office, that only one person held it at a time, our first task is to put the list in chronological order and determine what if any conclusions we may draw about the Stewards of the Amon Temple. The two earliest Stewards, Senmut and Amonuser, served under Hatshepsut, probably in that order (See note 5). Senmut seems to have been the first person to hold the office, and probably was followed by Amonuser when he was disgraced late in the reign of his queen. Amonuser was Vizier at the end of the reign of Hatshepsut and in the early years of Thutmosis III (Helck 1958: 292). He also only boasts of the title one time, in his tomb, thus making it probable that he did not have it for a long time (Helck 1958: 437). Next would come Rekhmire, who was also a Vizier, and who almost certainly inherited the title from his predecessor, Amonuser. The important thing to note here is that the title has not yet been given to a High Priest of Amon. In other words, the priesthood was not as fully in control of its lands as it would eventually be.

A problem arises at this point. Rekhmire continued to serve as Vizier into the reign of Amenhotep II, but late in the reign of Thutmosis III (year 43) a certain Sen-Djehuty is Steward of the Amon Temple (*Urkunden* IV: 1374). Did Rekhmire relinquish the title for some reason? Since Sen-Djehuty had the title in the last years of the earlier king, and since he never mentions serving under Amenhotep II, it seems likely that Rekhmire did give up the duties for some reason, while continuing to be Vizier.

Under Amenhotep II three men, Mery, Amenemhat, and Sennefer hold the title. The latest to be Steward must have been Amenemhat, since he served on as High Priest of Amon in the reign of the next king, Thutmosis IV. Mery, his predecessor as High Priest in the middle years of Amenhotep II, probably held the post of Steward immediately before Amenemhat, leaving the early years of the king for Sennefer. The key thing to notice here is that the title Steward of the Amon Temple has come into the hands of the High Priests of Amon for the first time, showing, I believe, a consolidation of economic power and control for the first time. Amenhotep II would have been the king who appointed the priests to this position, but what we have seen so far and what we will see indicate that the kings came to regret this decision.

In the reign of Thutmosis IV, two men held the post of Steward of the Amon Temple, Amenemhat the High Priest (in the king's early years) and Kaemwaset. Amenemhat had received the title under Amenhotep II, so little could be done to remove it from him without a visible disgracing of the High Priest, which the new king was probably not strong enough to undertake. But when Amenemhat died,

Thutmosis IV granted the title to Kaemwaset rather than to Ptahmose, the new High Priest. Of the early life and career of Kaemwaset, we know little. He had been a scribe on one of the king's personal estates (*Urkunden* IV: 1633).[6] His promotion to a previously ecclesiastical post supports what we have already seen: that Thutmosis IV was trying to remove power, particularly economic power, from the holders of the High Priesthood of Amon. The same king removed the title Overseer of the Cattle of Amon from the priesthood and gave it to the King's Son of Kush, and took the title Overseer of All Priests of Upper and Lower Egypt from the High Priest and gave it to a military man, Horemhab.

Amenhotep III had two attested Stewards of the Amon Temple, Ptahmose the Vizier and High Priest of Amon and Nakht-sebek. Their chronological sequence is easy to establish since Ptahmose was dead by year twenty of his king. He therefore served as Steward first, followed by Nakht-sebek late in the reign. This is supported by the mention of Nakht-sebek as Steward on a statue of Mery-Ptah, High Priest after Ptahmose (*Urkunden* IV: 1886). In the case of Ptahmose, the title here under consideration does revert to the priesthood, but it must be remembered that Ptahmose was a man particularly loyal to his king. Nakht-sebek also was the "king's man." He was a Northerner, and had served in the army, an institution that tended to be loyal to the king rather than to any of the priesthoods.

Summary of the Royal Religious Policy

We have seen that in the reign of Thutmosis IV and Amenhotep III there was a marked effort on the part of the kings to remove certain key administrative titles from the High Priests of Amon. As we have shown, no pre-Amarna High Priest of Amon after Amenemhat (with the exception of Ptahmose) held the titles Overseer of All Priests of Upper and Lower Egypt or Steward of the Amon Temple, and no High Priest at all was Overseer of the Cattle of Amon. Ptahmose, the vizier and High Priest under Amenhotep III, perhaps owed his position of favor to the king's mother, Mutemwia.[7] This woman was not queen during the reign of her husband, Thutmosis IV, being probably just a member of the harem. But she had the good luck to be the mother of the heir, and so she attained prominence in the reign of her son Amenhotep III. Since the king was very young at his accession, it seems likely that Mutemwia had an important role to play in the early years of the new monarch. Her importance in the monuments of Amenhotep III up to about year eleven of his reign supports the idea that she was a key person in those years.

A further important point to remember about the recipients of these titles is that they were men of proven loyalty to the throne. They were not men with backgrounds in the Amon priesthood. On the contrary, they were King's Sons of Kush, scribes from royal estates, military men, and men from the priesthood of the northern god Ptah of Memphis. From these backgrounds, two facts are immediately obvious. First, they come from occupations and organizations with strong ties of loyalty to the crown. Second, and this deserves a closer look, they often were Northerners.

Why is the northern origin of some of the officials we have considered important?

First, it needs to be observed that both Thutmosis IV and his son Amenhotep III had more than casual connections with the delta region of Egypt. The famous Sphinx Stele of Thutmosis IV seems to indicate that the youth of that future king was spent in the delta.[8] Also, when Thutmosis IV appointed officials, he many times selected men of probable or certain northern origin. The same went for Amenhotep III. Of thirty-four major officials of these two monarchs, thirteen are of northern origin while only five are of Theban or other southern origin, while the rest are not of identifiable origin.[9] Further, of the High Priests of Amon of Dynasty Eighteen in general, no certain Northerner held the post until Ptahmose. Since the cult of Amon-Re was headquartered in the south at Karnak, it stands to reason that Southerners would be prominent in it, and that is true so far as we know until the attempts of Thutmosis IV and Amenhotep III to exert more royal control over that cult and its wealth. Northerners would not have close ties to the Karnak temple bureaucracy, nor would they owe allegiance to the great families of the south. It should also be noted here that Ptahmose, again so far as we know, was the first Northerner to hold the southern Vizierate. When Ptahmose died, Amenhotep III continued the new policy by appointing Ramose, son of the mayor of the northern city of Memphis, to be southern vizier. Of the three Chief Stewards of the King known from the reign of Thutmosis IV and from the early years of Amenhotep III, two, both named Mery-Re but without doubt different individuals, were from the north, and the third, Tjenuwna, who began his career as a scribe of his predecessor, cannot be connected with any geographical region. Other key economic officials, such as Overseers of the Treasury and Overseers of the Treasure House (these are distinctly different posts), were also most commonly Northerners in the period under consideration.

But is there any evidence beside the removal of these titles from the High Priests of Amon that the roots of the Amarna religious revolution extend back to the days of Thutmosis IV? We know that the worship of the god Aton does go back well before Akhenaten (See also Wolf, W. 1924).[10, 11] A most interesting text does exist which may hint at some of the problems behind what has been discussed above. One of the boundary steles from Tell el Amarna, though unfortunately badly broken, quotes Akhenaten as saying that something (perhaps involving priests) was "More evil than that which I heard in year four." He goes on to say "It was more evil than that which Thutmosis IV heard" (Helck 1964: 32-3).[12] The implication here is that something considered bad by Akhenaton, and important enough to be mentioned on a boundary stele at his new capital, pertained to the reign of Thutmosis IV. Akhenaten is perhaps telling us that the open struggle with the High Priests of Amon dates back to the very reign where key titles are first shifted to other, non-priestly people.

In conclusion, let it be said that we believe there is enough evidence to suspect that the Amarna revolution was more than just the product of the deep devotion of Akhenaton to a different god, sincere and devout as he may have been. There were without much doubt serious issues involving power and economics, issues stemming back to the wars of conquest of Thutmosis III and the resultant growth of the wealth of the temple establishment of Amon-Re. Kings Thutmosis IV and Amenhotep III resented that wealth and saw the growing power of the High Priest of Amon as a threat to royal power. They attempted to check their rival's wealth and power by removing key titles from the high priests. Evidently, this solution was not totally successful. When Akhenaten, a devout worshiper of Aton, became Pharaoh, he decided for both religious and economic reasons to take a more radical step, which involved the elevation of Aton to the position of primary god of Egypt, the elimination of the position of High Priest of Amon at Thebes, and the construction of a new capital at Tell el Amarna (Akhetaten), away from the influence of the powerful Theban families and the hometown of the god Amon-Re. Although drastic, these changes did not long outlive their maker. After the death of Akhenaten, the capital of Egypt reverted to Thebes and the old religion again became the supreme faith of the land. In the following years of Egyptian history, the High Priests of Amon became, as nearly as we can tell, even more wealthy and powerful than they were before the Amarna period. Thutmosis IV, Amenhotep III, and Akhenaten took steps to weaken that priesthood, but the ultimate victory belonged to Amon.

NOTES

[1] This chronology rejects a co-regency between Amenhotep III and Akhenaten.

[2] The nine Overseers of All the Priests of Upper and Lower Egypt in Dynasty Eighteen are as follows:

- a. Hapuseneb - High Priest of Amon under Hatshepsut (*Urkunden* IV, 471).
- b. Menkheperre-seneb - High Priest of Amon under Thutmosis III (*Urkunden* IV, 927).
- c. Mery - High Priest of Amon under Amenhotep II (Lefebvre, pp. 235-7).
- d. Amenemhet - High Priest of Amon under Amenhotep II and Thutmosis IV (Lefebvre, pp. 237-9).
- e. Horemhab - General (Scribe of Recruits) under Thutmosis IV and Amenhotep III. He is not to be confused with the general and later king of the same name (*Urkunden* IV, 1589-96).
- f. Ptahmose - Vizier and High Priest under Thutmosis IV and Amenhotep III (Lefebvre, pp. 241-3).
- g. Djehutymose/Thutmosis - Prince and High Priest of Ptah under Amenhotep III (Gauthier, II, p. 336).
- h. Ptahmose - High Priest of Ptah under Amenhotep III. (Aling, pp.132-4).
- i. Ramose - The well-known Vizier under Amenhotep III and the pre-Amarna Years of Akhenaten (Helck, *Verwaltung,* p. 292 and 437).

[3] For Ramose's monuments and titles see W. Helck's *Zur Verwaltung* 442-3.

[4] The title Chief Steward of the Amon Temple is attested once, in the case of Hatshepsut's favorite, Senmut. That this was, however, not a separate and higher title is shown by the fact that Senmut uses the titles Chief Steward and Steward of the Amon Temple interchangeably. See for example Cairo statue 579.

[5] The following are the datable Stewards of the Amon Temple in Dynasty 18 known to me.

a. On Mery: see note 2 above.

b. On Amenemhet: see note 2.

c. On Ptahmose: see note 2.

d. On Kaemwaset: see note 6.

e. On Amonuser: see Helck, *Verwaltung,* pp. 436-437.

f. On Rekhmire: see Helck, *Verwaltung,* 437-439.

g. On Senmut: see *Urkunden* IV, 403.

h. On Sen-nefer: see *Urkunden* IV, 1437.

i. On Sendjehuty: see *Urkunden* IV, 1207.

j. On Nakht-Sebek: see *Urkunden* IV, 1886-9.

[6] This fact supports our conclusion that he served as Steward late in the king's reign, since in his early career he was a relatively low ranking but presumably very loyal scribe on one of the estates of the same king, Thutmosis IV.

[7] For a full study of this important woman, consult Aling (Aling pp. 19ff).

[8] For evidence of the estate of Thutmosis IV at Giza, see Breasted, *Ancient Records,* II, Par. 1043.

[9] For a tabulation of this see Aling, chart 11.

[10] A scarab exists from the reign of Thutmosis IV naming Aton as a distinct deity.

[11] Consult the work of M. and J. Doresse.

12 Check M. Sandman for Stele X. Also see Helck's *Einfluss,* pp. 32-3.

REFERENCES

Aldred, C.

    1988 *Akhenaton, King of Egypt.* London: Thames and Hudson.

Aling, C.   Prosopographical Study of the Reigns of Thutmosis IV and Amenhotep III. 1976 Unpublished Ph.D. Thesis, University of Minnesota, 1976.

Breasted, J.H.

    1962 *Ancient Records of Egypt,* II (New York, Russell & Russell Inc. , par. 1043).

de Garis Davies, N.

    1941 *The Tomb of the Vizier Ramose.* London: Egypt Exploration Society.

Doresse, M. and J.

    1941-2 Le Cult d'Aton sous la XVIIIe avant le schisme Amarnien. *Journal Asiatique* 233.

Gardiner, A. H.

    1966 *Egypt of the Pharaohs.* Oxford and New York: Oxford University Press.

Gauthier, H.

    1912 *Le Livre Des Rois D'Egypte.* 5 Vols. Cairo: Memoires publies par les membres. de l'institut Francais d'archeologie orientale. II.

Grimal, N.

    1992 *A History of Ancient Egypt.* Oxford: Basil Blackwell.

Helck, W.

    1958 *Zur Verwaltung des Mittleren und Neuen Reichs.* Leiden: E. J. Brill.

1964 *Der Einfluss der Militaerfuehrer in der 18. Aegyptischen Dynastie.* Hildesheim: George Olm Verlagsbuchhandling.

Lefebvre, G.

1929 *Histoire des Grands Pretres D'Amon de Karnak:* Paris: Libraire Orientaliste Paul Geuthner.

Redford D. B.

1984 *Akhenaten the Heretic King:* Princeton: Princeton University Press.

Sandman, M.

1938 *Texts From the Time of Akhenaton.* Brussels: Bibliotheka Aegyptiaca.

Sethe, K. and Helke, W. eds.

1903-58 *Urkunden IV, Urkunden der 18.* Dynastie. Leipzig.

Wolf, W.

1924 Volaufer der Reformation Echnatons. *Zeitschrift fur Agyptische Sprache und Altertumskunde* 59.

Testing the Factuality of the Conquest of Ai Narrative in the Book of Joshua

Peter Briggs

Abstract

Summary of the problem.

The gamut of views concerning the conquest of Ai narrative in the 7th and 8th chapters of the Book of Joshua can be summarized as follows: the narrative is *factual*, having the weight of eye witness testimony; or, it is an *aetiological legend*, compiled long after the fact, either just before or during the Babylonian exile for the purpose of justifying Israel's presence in the land of Canaan; or, it is a *pernicious myth*, deceptively and skillfully fabricated to correspond with the material time-space context in which it is alleged to have occurred. Is there a method that is capable of objectively arbitrating among these three views?

Summary of the method.

The theory of True Narrative Representations propounded by John W. Oller provides the basis for an analytical test of the factuality of the narrative in question, and thereby an arbitration among the three views summarized above. The analytical process begins with the derivation of a fourteen-parameter *criterial screen* from careful exegesis of the biblical text in the Book of Joshua. The criterial screen is the analytical tool whereby the correspondence of the biblical narrative to its material time-space context can be empirically assessed. The first three parameters of the screen form a *predicate criterial screen*, which is applied to the three candidate sites for Joshua's Ai that emerge from past research; namely, et-Tell, Kh. Nisya, and Kh. el-Maqatir. Even this very limited three-parameter screen is sufficiently explicit that only one of the candidate sites, Kh. el-Maqatir, meets all of its requirements. The remaining eleven parameters of the more elaborate and still more demanding criterial screen are then applied to that one surviving site, which entails a careful and detailed correlation of the text of Joshua 7 and 8 with the archaeological, geographical, and topographical context of the site. By this means, the conformity of the narrative in question with the determinacy, connectedness, and generalizability properties of true narratives is empirically tested. Included in the analytical process is the postulation of viable engagement scenarios for the two battles of Ai.

Summary of the conclusion. The result of the analytical process is that, of the three candidate sites for Joshua's Ai, only Kh. el-Maqatir satisfies all fourteen parameters of the criterial screen, thus providing conclusive evidence that the conquest of Ai narrative is a True Narrative Representation and that Kh. el-Maqatir is the site of the fortress of Ai conquered by Joshua. Key aspects of the evidence include the geographical/topographical context of Kh. el-Maqatir, the configuration of its defensive system, its size, its archaeology, and its total conformity with the requirements of the text in Joshua 7 and 8. The view that the conquest of Ai narrative is factual is thereby vindicated, and the aetiological legend and pernicious myth views are refuted.

The Conquest of Ai Narrative: Fact or Myth

The Bible as Historical Narrative

The Bible is essentially an historical narrative concerning the nation of Israel, by means of which *Yahweh*, the God of Israel presents his character, his purposes, and his requirements with respect to human personalities. In his introduction to the commentary on the Book of Joshua in (Boling 1982: 5), G. Ernest Wright captures the Jewish concept of history and knowledge as follows:

> Israel had no idea of a two-realm theory of knowledge, one of a supernal, universal Good and one of the world of human beings where they live. There was only one realm where significant knowledge was obtainable. That was their own, their own life as a people in the midst of the nations with whom they had contact. Yet in this world they indeed affirmed that God is good, but they meant by this that definitive actions in their history exhibited a mysterious Power who for his own reasons had acted toward them with remarkable graciousness.

According to Kaiser (1987: 61-79), a substantial cross-section of scholars would agree that the Bible's theological truth claims are suspended on a cable of historical factuality. Moreover, according to the theory of true narratives propounded by John W. Oller [Oller (1996: 199-244); Oller & Collins (2000); Collins & Oller (2000)], only true narratives can support and sustain generalizations. Thus, for valid theological truth to be derived from the Bible, it is essential that the Bible's historical content be true. If the Bible's historical content is fictional or false, as the critics of the Bible would claim, then the theory of true narratives affirms that the theological truth claims of the Bible must be invalid.

Historical Factuality of the Old Testament

Since the focus of this paper is upon a portion of the Conquest episode recorded in the Book of Joshua, how has the factuality or non-factuality of the Old Testament been viewed from antiquity to the present? The straightforward manner in which

Jesus handled, referred to, and taught from the Old Testament writings demonstrates that he regarded them as not only theologically true but also historically factual. For example, consider the following statement by Jesus as he was teaching in the temple in Jerusalem toward the very end of his ministry:

> ... Upon you may fall the guilt of all the righteous blood shed on earth, from the blood of righteous Abel to the blood of Zechariah, the son of Berechiah, whom you murdered between the temple and the altar. [Matthew 23:35, NASB [2]]

Concerning this statement by Christ, the following quotation is especially instructive:

> Indeed, from one end of Scripture to the other there was a trail of martyred prophets that included *all* the martyred prophets! For Jesus, therefore, the canon began with Genesis and ended with 2 Chronicles, just as it does in the traditional Hebrew order of the OT, and so the dynamic equivalent of Jesus' expression, considering our present English order of the OT books, would be: "all the righteous blood . . . from Genesis to Malachi" (Kaiser 1987: 46).

In like manner, the apostles Peter and Paul regarded the Old Testament scriptures to be God-breathed according to 2 Peter 1:20-21 and 2 Timothy 3:15.

Hayes & Miller (1977: 1-69) trace the evolution in historiography concerning the nation of Israel from the Hellenistic period to the modern era. Through the period of the Reformation, that is, until the middle of the 17th century with the dawn of the Enlightenment, a consensus generally prevailed among biblical and historical scholars that the historical sections of the Old Testament were factual. Moreover, until this time the provenance of biblical interpretation had resided within the community of the church, albeit a church now fragmented by the polemics of the Reformation. However, by the middle of the 18th century, the provenance for critical analysis of the biblical text had been decisively wrested from the community of the church and had come to reside within the community of philosophical and scientific scholars. The momentous shift in scholarly attitude toward the Old Testament text culminated in the Graf-Wellhausen Documentary Hypothesis. Cassuto (1983: 9-11) cites the work of a succession of scholars who contributed to the development of this hypothesis, including the following: Witter (ca. 1711); Astruc (ca. 1753); Eichhorn (ca. 1783); Vater (ca. 1805); Stähelin, Ewald, et al. (ca. 1820-1830); Lachmann (ca. 1840); Hupfeld (ca. 1853); and Graf (ca. 1865). All of this past research was brilliantly combined, further developed, and persuasively articulated by Julius Wellhausen in a series of works published ca. 1876-1901. Wellhausen affirmed the Jahwist-Elohist-Priestly-Deuteronomist multi-source model developed by his predecessors. Moreover, he asserted that the theocratic organization of Israel and the priestly laws of the Pentateuch reflected post-exilic Judaism rather than the state of Israel at the time of

Moses. Furthermore, according to Wellhausen, the earliest date for the codification of portions of the Old Testament was the 8th century BC beginning with the prophecy of Amos and his contemporaries. However, according to Wellhausen, the Hebrew text of the Old Testament in its present form was first compiled and integrated during the post-exilic period. Wellhausen dogmatically asserted that the account of the patriarchs in Genesis was entirely legend, being substantially, if not totally, divorced from historical reality. Because the same sources were detected in the Book of Joshua, the idea of the Hexateuch emerged from Wellhausen's research.

According to Cassuto (1983: 1-7), Wellhausen's literary analysis of the Old Testament was so rigorously executed and effectively presented that it came to be regarded as unassailable fact. Having embraced Wellhausen's research, a biblical scholar would be driven to the conclusion that the earliest point at which the historical narrative of the Old Testament could be trusted as essentially factual corresponded to the establishment of the monarchy under Saul. This is exactly the conclusion manifested in the following quotations from Miller & Hayes:

> Literary analysis reveals that this whole Genesis-2 Kings account, from beginning to end, is composite. In other words, many originally independent items (stories, songs, genealogies, collections of laws, and so on), each with its own issues and problems of interpretation as well as historical implications, have been combined to produce the overall account. These various items have been edited, so the resulting composite account has a degree of unity and coherence. Many ragged edges remain, however, which raise glaring questions for the serious reader and which in some cases present what appear to be blatant contradictions [Miller & Hayes (1986: 61)].

> We decline any attempt to reconstruct the earliest history of the Israelites therefore, and begin our treatment with a description of the circumstances that appear to have existed among the tribes in Palestine on the eve of the establishment of the monarchy. Our primary source of information for this purpose will be narratives in the Book of Judges [Miller & Hayes (1986: 79)].

Bright (1981: 129-130) directs attention to the apparent contradictions in the account of the Conquest found in Joshua and Judges. On the one hand, the Book of Joshua describes a concentrated sequence of military campaigns by a unified Israelite army under Joshua that brought at least the central hill country under Israel's control. On the other hand, the Book of Judges describes a fragmented and only partially successful effort by the twelve tribes to subdue the entrenched Canaanites in their various allotments. Factors such as this have motivated most biblical scholars to attribute the account of the Conquest found in Numbers 13:1-Judges 18:31 to multiple literary sources and traditions. The majority opinion in regard to the contour of the actual conquest episode favors the "fragmented model" in Judges over the "unified model" in Joshua. Following is Bright's assessment of these two competing views of the Conquest:

> Both views doubtless contain elements of truth. But the actual events that established Israel on the soil of Palestine were assuredly vastly more complex than a simplistic presentation of either view would suggest [Bright (1981: 130)].

In his chapter on the Israelite occupation of Canaan [Hayes & Miller (1977: 213-221)], J. Maxwell Miller summarizes the two dominant positions of modern biblical scholarship in regard to the Conquest narrative: (a) the Hexateuch model according Wellhausen, et al., which held that Genesis-Joshua is the product of a unified literary tradition; and, (b) the Deuteronomistic History model according to Alt, Noth, and Von Rad, which held that Deuteronomy-2 Kings is the product of a unified literary tradition. According to both models, the historical sections of the Old Testament are the product of multiple authors, compilers, and redactors who integrated oral traditions and fragments of literary and historiographic material to create a more or less coherent biblical history of Israel. Miller's concluding assessment follows:

> Obviously, the final word is yet to be said on the matter, but two conclusions hold regardless of whether one thinks in terms of a 'hexateuch' or a 'Deuteronomistic history'. First, it is clear that the biblical account of the conquest in Numbers 13-Judges 1 is a highly composite construction. Second, when one attempts to disentangle the various literary strata which compose this account, it becomes increasingly apparent that older traditions which seem unaware of an initial conquest of the whole land of Canaan by a unified Israel have been incorporated into later materials which do. In fact, the concept of an initial conquest by all Israel appears to be largely Deuteronomistic... [Hayes & Miller (1977: 220-221)].

The Conquest of Ai Narrative

John Bright's reconstruction of the Conquest episode [Bright (1981: 140-143)] bears the imprint of literary and historical criticism of the biblical text as well as that of archaeological research by Kelso & Albright at Beitin [Kelso & Albright (1968)], Kenyon at Jericho [Kenyon (1957); Kenyon (1960: 195-220 & 331-332)], and Callaway at et-Tell [Callaway (1970: 10-12)]. Bright envisages a complex, protracted, and multilateral penetration of Israelite elements into Canaan, even including Hebrew elements that had possibly remained in Canaan during the sojourn of the Israelites in Egypt. His analysis reflects the tension created by the apparently contradictory results of archaeological research. In particular, excavations at et-Tell place in evidence the fact that the Early Bronze city at that site was destroyed ca. 2400 BC, and the site remained unoccupied until a small Iron Age village was established ca. 1200 BC.

Commenting upon the apparent conflict between the archaeological data and the biblical narrative, Bright makes the following statement in regard to the conquest of Ai:

> This has led some to question the location, others to regard the story as legendary, and still others to adopt other expedients. Far the most plausible suggestion is that the story of Josh., ch. 8, originally referred to the taking of Bethel, of which we are told in Judg. 1:22-26, but which is not mentioned in Joshua [Bright (1981: 131)].

Bright's reconstruction may seem reasonable in the light of the fragments of evidence, some of which may appear to be mutually contradictory. However, the reader is strongly motivated toward the conclusion that the narrative in Joshua is a vast oversimplification of the Conquest episode and far removed from a straightforward, factual account. In particular, the conquest of Ai narrative in Joshua 7 and 8 is either legendary, or it actually describes a campaign against another location such as Bethel. In either case, the conquest of Ai narrative is substantially nonfactual.

The Emergence Theory

Within the framework of the Finkelstein & Na'aman emergence theory, Na'aman proposes a more radical view of the conquest of Ai narrative.

> In the light of the nonhistorical character of the conquest tradition in the Book of Joshua, one should raise a fundamental question: Where did the author derive the material for his narratives? We have yet to establish whether a vague memory of past events was retained in some stories. It is clear, however, that most of the conquest narratives are devoid of historical foundation. One may assume that the author designed the past descriptions in the light of the reality of his time; since he was well acquainted with the sites and the environment portrayed by him, he composed narratives that outwardly appear authentic (save for the conquest miracle of Jericho). This assumption may be supplemented by another: In order to add a sense of authenticity to his narratives, the author borrowed military outlines from concrete events that had taken place in the history of Israel.

> Scholars have suggested that the conquest by stratagem of Ai is a literary reflection of the historical episode of the battle of Gibeah (Judges 20). Unfortunately, the literary relationship between the two narratives was not examined in detail, and it is not clear whether the author of Joshua 8 worked the narrative of Judges 20, or vice versa. The author of the story of Ai was certainly impressed by the prominent ruins of the site (Kh. et-Tell), assuming that it was conquered by the Israelites when they occupied the country. To give this story of the capture of Ai an aura of authenticity, he used military

elements of either the capture by stratagem of Gibeah or the conquest of another unknown site, transplanting them within a new environment that he knew very well from personal acquaintanceship. The conquest story of Ai did not emerge from an authentic historical memory of the event, but is rather the outcome of a reworking and adaptation of a conquest story relating to another site [Na'aman 1994: 249-251)].

Thus, Na'aman proposes that not only is the conquest of Ai narrative nonfactual, but that the author of the narrative intentionally and deceptively cloaked it with an "aura of authenticity" based upon his knowledge of the geographical and topographical context of the site in question combined with the artifice of borrowing data from other historical episodes. The site around which Na'aman's hypothetical author formulated the conquest of Ai narrative was the prominent ruins of et-Tell. In his discussion of the literary background of the conquest of Ai narrative, Na'aman proposes that it was actually compiled either in the late 7th century BC, just prior to the conquest of Jerusalem by the Babylonians, or in the early 6th century after the Israelites had been deported to Babylon. In either case, the most ancient historiographic fragments upon which the narrative was based dated to the 10th century BC, that is, the time of David and Solomon [Na'aman (1994: 218-230)]. Moreover, if the composition of the narrative actually took place in the 6th century BC, its author would have been physically insulated from the site, and therefore he would have been forced to rely entirely upon memory for all archaeological, geographical, and topographical detail [Briggs (2004: 48-51 & 77-83)].

Alternative Views of the Conquest of Ai Narrative

Aetiological Legend View

The aetiological legend view of the conquest of Ai narrative that emerges from the tradition of Albright, Callaway, Kenyon, Bright, et al., can be summarized as follows:

a.   The first attempt to codify the Joshua narrative occurred during the divided monarchy toward the end of the 10th century BC. Subsequently, it was revised one or more times, ca. 640-540 BC.

b.   The narrative of chapters 7 and 8 of Joshua actually derives from the conquest of nearby Bethel and was later applied to the city of Ai by either the original 10th century BC narrator or by one of the later redactors.

c.   Thus, the conquest of Ai narrative can be accurately characterized as a nonfactual aetiological legend compiled long after the events in question.

d.   The legend was loosely built around the ruins at et-Tell, the supposed site for the city of Ai, and nearby Bethel.

e.   The original compilation of the legend together with its later revisions was strongly motivated by political and theological concerns.

The aetiological legend view of the conquest of Ai narrative probably represents the majority opinion of modern biblical scholars.

Pernicious Myth View

The pernicious myth view of the conquest of Ai narrative that derives from the work of Na'aman can be summarized as follows:

a. The formulation of the content of the book of Joshua occurred at approximately the time of the Babylonian exile, that is, either at the end of the 7th century or during the 6th century BC.
b. The fragments of historical data upon which the composition was based dated no earlier than the 10th century BC, that is, to the time of David and Solomon.
c. The author of the conquest of Ai narrative possessed considerable knowledge of the Benjamin hill country context of the battle of Ai, and he employed this knowledge to deceptively impart to the narrative an aura of authenticity.
d. In particular, the author of the narrative in question crafted the story of the conquest of Ai around the prominent ruins of et-Tell.
e. Moreover, this author even borrowed the contours and outlines of certain historical battles of antiquity to further enhance the credibility of the conquest of Ai story.

Eyewitness Account View

In contrast to the above, by far the most straightforward explanation for the incredible amount of detail in the conquest of Ai narrative is that it was compiled during the lifetime of Joshua and was based upon direct, eyewitness contact with the places and events in question.

Statement of the Problem

The problem addressed in this paper is the arbitration among the three alternative views of the conquest of Ai narrative summarized above. This is accomplished by testing the correspondence between the narrative in question and the material time-space context it purports to represent. The analytical method is based upon the theory of True Narrative Representations (TNRs) propounded by John W. Oller [3].

Theological Significance

Given the prevailing scholarly opinion concerning the Conquest narrative in general, and the conquest of Ai narrative in particular, the research summarized in this paper is of great relevance to the ongoing debate concerning the factuality of the historical sections of the Old Testament, and, therefore, the theological truth value that is contained therein. Because the Conquest narrative in Joshua is the historical fulfillment of *Yahweh's* unconditional covenant with the patriarchs Abraham, Isaac, and Jacob to give the land of Canaan to their descendants, the integrity of *Yahweh*, the God of Israel is either established or impugned depending on whether the Conquest narrative in Joshua is factual or nonfactual.

Definition of Terms

Numerical Values

Military force element sizes in the conquest of Ai narrative, and, in fact, throughout the Hebrew Bible, are expressed in terms of אֶלֶף or its plural form, אֲלָפִים (transliterated 'eleph and 'elephîym, respectively). Hereafter in this paper, these two Hebrew terms are denoted *eleph* and *elephim* without diacritical markings. Furthermore, the point of controversy is over the numerical equivalence of *eleph* and *elephim*, not over their literary meaning. Therefore, to further simplify the discussion, the numerical equivalent of *eleph* and *elephim* is designated **E**.

This research is narrowly focused on the meaning and numerical equivalence of *eleph* and *elephim* when the terms are used to describe military forces, such as in the military censuses of Numbers 1 and 26 and the conquest of Ai narrative in Joshua 7 and 8. Within the sphere of this specific use of *eleph* and *elephim*, the customary gloss corresponding to **E** = 1,000 men is employed throughout the Hebrew Bible. According to Gottwald (1979: 270), this equivalence is appropriate to the time of David. However, according to the research of Briggs (2004), Fouts (1992, 1997), Gottwald (1979), Humphreys (1998, 2000), Mendenhall (1958), Petrie (1931), and Wenham (1981), the equivalence **E** = 1,000 men may not be appropriate to the time of Moses and Joshua. In particular, Briggs (2004: 55-57) discusses a number of problems precipitated by **E** = 1,000. With regard to the conquest of Ai narrative, the most serious problem is that if the army of Israel was actually of the order of 600 thousand men in accordance with the customary rendering of Numbers 1:46 & 26:51, then it would have been the mightiest fighting force in the ancient world. Compared with the number of Canaanites killed at Ai, Israel would have possessed a 50-to-1 numerical advantage!

The results of past research concerning the meaning and numerical equivalence of *eleph* can be summarized as follows:

a.   Within the sphere of the military application, there is general agreement that *eleph* designates a troop of men under command of a leader. The customary gloss of **E** = 1,000 corresponds to the assumption that a troop size of 1,000 applies consistently throughout the Hebrew Scriptures.

b.   According to Gottwald, one *eleph* would have been the contribution to the national military muster deriving from a particular tribal subdivision. A troop size of **E** = 1,000 applies to the time of David, but not necessarily to the time of Moses and Joshua.

c.   According to Humphreys, the problematically large size of the army of Israel according to the censuses of Numbers 1 and 26 results from a conflation of terms in the Hebrew text. The value of **E** in both censuses is tribe-dependent and lies in the range of 5 to 17 men with an average value of approximately 10. This means that the army of Israel was actually of the order of 6 thousand men during the time of Moses. Gottwald, Mendenhall, Petrie, and Wenham would probably agree with Humphrey's result, although not necessarily with his method for obtaining it.

d. Fouts argues for a hyperbolic use of numbers in the two censuses to ascribe glory to *Yahweh* as the reigning monarch over Israel. Since the Israelites employed a decimal numbering system, Fouts suggests that the equivalence **E** = 1,000 incorporates a divine force multiplication factor of 10, which means that **E** should be quantified as 100^4.

e. Because of the consistency with which **E** = 1,000 is assumed throughout the Hebrew Bible, and because of the Pauline reference to a plague incident in 1 Corinthians 10:8, this researcher favors a third resolution to the *eleph* problem; namely, a representational view according to which Moses, as an inspired writer of Scripture, was consistently directed to assume a divine force multiplier of 100 to represent the invincibility of the army of Israel so long as they remained faithful to the covenant with *Yahweh*.

Considering the proposed resolutions to the *eleph* problem, there exists a two-order of magnitude range of uncertainty applicable to the value of **E**. That is, **E** lies within the range of 10 to 1000. Data from the Conquest narrative in Joshua is brought to bear later in this paper in order to shrink the uncertainty band for **E** applicable to the time of Joshua.

Archaeological Periods

Archaeological periods pertinent to analysis of the conquest of Ai narrative in this paper are defined in Table 1. The dates and nomenclature have been synthesized from LaSor (1979), Amiran (1970), and Finegan (1998). The archaeological period nomenclature and dates defined in Table 1 are used throughout this paper.

Testing the Factuality of the Conquest of Ai Narrative

Table 1. Archaeological Periods

Archaeological Period	Dates	Biblical Correspondence
Early Bronze Age (EBA) / Intermediate Bronze Age (IBA)	3000-1900 BC	Post-diluvian patriarchs
Middle Bronze Age (MBA)	1900-1550 BC	Abraham, Isaac, Jacob, and Joseph
Late Bronze Age (LBA)	1550-1200 BC	
LB I	1550-1400 BC	Moses
LB II	1400-1300 BC	Joshua
LB III (or, IIB)	1300-1200 BC	Early Judges
Iron Age (IA)	1200-586 BC	
IA I	1200-1000 BC	Later Judges and Saul
IA IIA	1000 - 900 BC	David and Solomon

Regnal Periods of 18th and 19th Dynasty Pharaohs

There is a tight linkage between the regnal periods of the Egyptian pharaohs and the dating of archaeological finds in Palestine. Both the 13th century date for the Exodus favored by the majority of scholars, and the 15th century date that obtains from the biblical timeline fall within the LBA and also within the time frame of the 18th and 19th dynasties. Authoritative sources for the names and regnal periods of the 18th and 19th dynasty pharaohs include the following: Hayes (1975), Wente & Van Siclen (1977), and Kitchen (1992, 1996). In Briggs (2004: 18-20) these multiple sources are compiled into a single table by means of a weighted average technique.

The Fortress of Ai

In the Hebrew text of chapters 7 and 8 of Joshua, the site in question is characterized by the Hebrew word עִיר ('îr), normally translated 'city'. Frick (1977) and Hansen (2000: 36-42) present detailed analyses of this word, the central aspect of whose meaning is a fortified site. In terms of size, 'îr could designate a broad range of occupied sites from a watchtower or citadel to a fortified city. The configuration of the site described in Joshua 7 and 8 was probably a citadel surrounded by an outer fortification wall and gate system. The term that is selected for most precisely defining the meaning of 'îr in regard to the site of Ai is 'fortress'.

The Site of Kh. el-Maqatir

This is one of the candidate sites for the fortress of Ai conquered by Joshua. It is located 3.5 kilometers east-northeast of the modern city of El Bireh, 1.6 kilometers southeast of the modern village of Beitin, and 1.1 kilometers west of et-Tell. The precise spelling of the Arabic name for this location is as follows: Khirbet el-Maqāṭir. Throughout this paper, the diacritical marks are omitted for the sake of convenience and the name of the site is denoted Kh. el-Maqatir.

167

Definition of a Narrative

For purposes of this paper, a narrative is a verbal description of an event or an event sequence that is alleged to have taken place in a given material time-space context. An event sequence is designated an *episode*. Note that a delimitation is inherent in the definition; namely, only narratives that are known or alleged to be factual are considered. A fictional narrative is invented or imagined by its author; therefore, it is not known to be factual, and its author makes no claim as to its factuality. Two additional delimitations are imposed as follows: this paper only considers narratives that are, (a) written down, and, (b) linguistically coherent, that is, well-formed in terms of syntax and grammar. Thus, the gamut of narratives to be considered include factual narratives, traditions, legends, myths, and lies. All of these terms are employed in accordance with their normal definitions. A kind of legend that is especially germane to this paper is an *aetiological legend*, that is a story, perhaps partially or even substantially factual, that seeks to define a cause that lies behind an observable effect (e.g., the presence of Israel in the land of Palestine, the prominent ruin of et-Tell, etc.). A kind of myth that is especially germane to this paper is a *pernicious myth*, which is a nonfactual story whose author intentionally and deceptively cloaks with an aura of authenticity in order to make it appear to be factual.

Definition of True Narratives

The *True Narrative Representation*, or TNR, is the perfected and limiting case of a factual narrative, and it is distinguished by a triad of properties: determinacy, connectedness, and generalizability in accordance with [Oller (1996); Oller & Collins (2000); Collins & Oller (2000)]. These properties derive from the fact that a competent observer/narrator maps an episode consisting of a sequence of one or more empirical time-space events into a linguistic representation. According to the delimitations imposed above, only true narratives that are written down are considered. The triad of TNR attributes are defined as follows:

a. Determinacy. Through the perceptive and cognitive faculties of the narrator, the empirical particulars of the episode are mapped into language. Therefore, the surface form of the linguistic representation of the episode is motivated by the material facts of the episode as they are perceived by the narrator, and the linguistic representation determines those material facts in the sense of characterizing them and imparting meaning and relationship to them. In fact, apart from a TNR, the material facts of the episode are empty and meaningless, that is, indeterminate.

b. Connectedness. There are three aspects of this attribute. First, the components of the narrative are connected by the cognitive and linguistic faculties of the observer/narrator to the events that make up the episode. Second, the trajectory of the episode, which is embodied in the dynamic connections among the events that comprise the episode, is mapped into recognizable components of the narrative. Third, and because of the above, even as the episode is couched in a particular material time-space context, in like manner the TNR and its components are rooted in and tightly coupled to that context. Therefore, all TNRs that describe episodes that have occurred in a given material time-space context accurately reflect the particulars of that context, even though they may describe different episodes. Furthermore, since the episode of which the TNR is a mapping unfolded from event to event, with event-to-event transitions that are physically realizable, correspondingly the TNR accurately describes physically realizable event-to-event transitions.

    c.   Generalizability. Unlike any other kind of narrative, only TNRs are capable of supporting and sustaining generalizations. Such generalizations encompass the attributes and behaviors of any and all of the entities included in the episode, ranging from material objects to human personalities. For example, the genesis of the law of gravity undoubtedly originated with a TNR that described the falling of an object from a height.

Necessary Correspondence

This is a property of true narratives that derives from the formal properties of determinacy and connectedness defined above. In particular, a true narrative necessarily corresponds with the material time-space context of the episode that it describes.

Empirical Correspondence

Because of the property of necessary correspondence, there ought to be an observed or empirical correspondence between a TNR and the material facts it purports to represent. Whereas necessary correspondence exists by definition, empirical correspondence is subject to the uncertainties that unavoidably attend any operation of quantitative measurement [Oller (1996: 227-229)]. Hereafter in this paper, where the term 'correspondence' is employed without qualification, it shall be understood as empirical correspondence rather than as necessary correspondence.

Criterial Screen

This is the particular measure of empirical correspondence that is selected for use in the present research. Through valid and correctly applied hermeneutical procedure, the parameters of the criterial screen are derived from the text of the narrative. Each of the parameters describes an aspect of the material time-space context of the narrative which must be true if the narrative is a TNR. For example, the fact that the fortress of Ai was a small site with area less than 7 acres is a criterial screen parameter which derives from the statement in Joshua 10:2 where the area of the fortress of Ai is compared with that of Gibeon.

Extending the argument to the general condition, if any given narrative is true, then all of the criterial screen parameters derived from it must also be true. In general, the greater the detail contained in the text of the narrative, the larger the number of criterial screen parameters that can be derived from the text, and, therefore, the greater the confidence factor that is associated with the result of testing the criterial screen against the material time-space context of the narrative.

Mutual Independence

Not only are the parameters of the criterial screen conditions which can be either true or false, but they are also mutually independent. That is, no parameter in the screen is functionally linked or statistically correlated with any other parameter.

Probabilities and Confidence Factors

Suppose that it were possible to assign a probability to each of the parameters in the criterial screen. Considering the example above, one could examine a source for the sizes of Bronze Age settlements in the Benjamin hill country and determine the ratio of the number of sites whose areas are less than 7 acres divided by the total number of sites. This ratio would approximate the probability that any Benjamin hill country site selected at random would be smaller than 7 acres. If a number of parameters in the screen are found to be true, then, in accordance with the product rule for Bernoulli trials [Feller (1957: 183-198)], the joint probability of the combined event is equal to the product of the probabilities associated with each of the individual screen parameters. In fact, the result is the probability that the confluence of factors resulting in multiple screen parameters being true is a purely random occurrence. Generally, as the number of screen parameters that are true increases, the probability that such a confluence of factors is a random occurrence decreases to the point of becoming vanishingly small. In the case of a criterial screen that contains 10 parameters with a probability of 0.5 arbitrarily assigned to each, the probability that all 10 are true as a random occurrence is $2^{-10} = (1 / 1,024) = 0.000977$. Thus, the probability that the 10 parameters being true is not a random occurrence is $1 - 2^{-10} = 0.999023$. This exemplifies the logic that is applied later in this paper to develop a confidence factor for the result of the present research.

Reenactment

A corollary to the connectedness and generalizability properties of TNRs is this: a TNR uniquely enables the spatial reenactment of the event sequence of which the episode is comprised. In the case of the conquest of Ai narrative, the gamut of reenactment possibilities range from a detailed, "cast of thousands" portrayal of the battle to the reconstruction of one or more scenario models that fit the narrative's description of the battle. In effect, a true narrative can be generalized back upon itself and relived in the spatial, but not the temporal, context in which the episode it describes originally occurred. This is true provided that the spatial context of the narrative can be identified and that it has not changed significantly over time. Thus, the ability to reenact the episode described in a narrative is an approach to rigorously testing the correspondence property.

Limited Cases of Reenactment

How does the reenactment property of TNRs apply in the case of the conquest of

Ai episode? If the biblical narrative is a TNR, then it is possible to formulate one or more engagement scenarios involving the Israelite and Canaanite force elements described in the narrative. In particular, the traversal on foot of the routes and distances described and in the times allotted would be feasible. Thus, in the case of the conquest of Ai narrative, it is possible to probe the plausibility that a campaign such as that described in the narrative could have been carried out in actuality through a combination of analytical modeling and ground surveys of the topography in question.

Representational Uncertainty

This is a general term that includes the factors of imprecision, approximation, ambiguity, and a finite level of detail. Representational uncertainty has nothing to do with necessary correspondence, as defined above, but only with empirical correspondence. In particular, representational uncertainty can be structured and defined in terms of the criterial screen defined above. In general, the more precise and detailed a narrative, the greater the number of criterial screen parameters that can be derived from it and the lower the uncertainty. Therefore, the more precise and detailed the narrative, the greater the degree to which its factuality can be tested through comparison of its criterial screen with the material time-space context that the narrative purports to represent. The lower the precision and detail, the less amenable the narrative is to testing by this means. The level of precision and detail contained in the conquest of Ai narrative permits the formulation of a 14-parameter criterial screen.

Uncertainty Band

Representational uncertainty is encountered in deriving and evaluating the parameters of the criterial screen. For example, based upon available data, the area of LB I Gibeon is estimated to have been 11 ±4 acres [Briggs (2004: 123-125)]. In this particular case, the median value of 11 acres is the expected value or best estimate of the size of LB I Gibeon. The variation around the median value of ±4 acres is a measure of the representational uncertainty present in the estimate of the area of LB I Gibeon.

Conclusiveness of the Evidence

The larger the number of parameters in the criterial screen, the more conclusive the evidence in favor of a given factuality test result. In the case of the 14-parameter criterial screen derivable from the conquest of Ai narrative in Joshua 7 and 8, if all 14 parameters are found to be true in connection with one of the candidate sites of Joshua's Ai, then the evidence in favor of that being the correct site and the biblical narrative being factual would be conclusive beyond reasonable doubt. On the other hand, if few or none of the parameters are found to be true, then either the site has not been correctly identified, or the biblical narrative is nonfactual, that is, either an aetiological legend or a pernicious myth.

Derivation of the Numerical Equivalent of *eleph*

Range of Uncertainty From Past Research

The meaning of *eleph*, together with its plural form *elephim*, is one of the most baffling interpretive issues facing scholars of the Hebrew Bible. For the sake of convenience and simplicity of nomenclature, the symbol **E** is used to designate the numerical equivalent of either *eleph* or *elephim*. In the immediate context of the military censuses of the non-Levitical tribes recorded in Numbers 1 and 26, it has been concluded from the analysis of past research that, *eleph* = Troop of fighting men. However, as to the numerical equivalent of **E**, the uncertainty band is very large, extending over two orders of magnitude from **E** = 10 to **E** = 1,000. Since the sizes of the various Israelite and Canaanite force elements that were involved in the two battles of Ai are described in terms of **E**, a central issue to correctly interpreting the conquest of Ai narrative is an accurate understanding of the numerical equivalent of **E**. Exegesis of the biblical texts pertinent to the conquest of Ai is brought to bear upon estimating the magnitude of **E** that was appropriate to the time of Joshua, and thereby narrowing the band of uncertainty to something in the order of ±50%.

The Army of Israel

The military force mustered at the command of *Yahweh* in Joshua 8:1-3 is described as follows: "Take all the people of war with you." In other words, Joshua was to muster the whole army of Israel, evidently equivalent to that enumerated in the second military census of Numbers 26. Employing the analytical model of Humphreys (1998)[5] as a working hypothesis, the magnitude of **E** under the leadership of Moses was approximately 10. At the time of the census of Numbers 26, the army of Israel numbered 5,730 fighting men organized into 593 troops, each of which consisted of between 5 and 17 men. This was the size and organizational structure of the army of Israel as it was poised on the plains of Moab opposite Jericho prior to the death of Moses. Thus, in accordance with Humphreys' model, the number of fighting men that Joshua took with him for the second battle of Ai was 5,730. However, did Joshua organize his army with the same troop size, that is, with **E** approximately 10, or with a different troop size? In particular, does the text in the Book of Joshua provide clues as to the value of **E** that was appropriate to the time of Joshua?

In fact, clues as to the numerical equivalent of **E** can be derived from the spies' report in Joshua 7:2-3 combined with the size of Ai as compared with that of Gibeon in accordance with Joshua 10:2.

Content of the Spies' Report

In Joshua 7:2-3, the spies commissioned by Joshua assessed the size and defensive capability of Ai in terms of the size of the attack force needed to conquer the fortress. Their recommendation was that a force of only 2**E** or 3**E** would be adequate. While it is later suggested that the spies underestimated the size of Ai, it is reasonable to assume that they had in mind a significant numerical advantage in Israel's favor.

Therefore, their estimate of the number of military-aged males at Ai would have been of the order of 1**E** so as to provide Israel with a 2-to-1 or 3-to-1 numerical advantage. Assuming that the median age of the male population of Ai was 20 years in agreement with Humphreys, the total number of males in the population of Ai would have been 2**E**. Assuming that the population of Ai was equally divided between males and females, the total population of Ai, according to the spies' assessment, would have been of the order of 4**E**.

Implications of the Spies' Report

The implications of the spies' report with respect to the population and size of Ai depend upon the value selected for **E**. Table 2 presents the results that obtain from three values of **E**: $E_1 = 10$, the minimum value associated with the range of values appropriate to the time of Moses; $E_2 = 1,000$, corresponding to the customary gloss for *eleph* throughout the Hebrew Bible; and $E_3 = 100$, which is the geometric mean between E_1 and E_2. For each value of **E**, the total population of Ai according to the spies' report is listed in Table 2. The size of Ai is estimated from the population by application of a population density of 162 persons per acre [Broshi & Gophna (1986)].

Table 2. Population and Size of Ai According to the Spies' Report and for Three Values of E

Value of E	Population of Ai	Size of Ai (acres)	Comments
10	40	0.25	Population and size are implausibly small.
1000	4000	24.7	Size exceeds the maximum value for the estimated area of LB I Gibeon by 65%.
100	400	2.5	Size is 36% of the minimum value for the estimated area of LB I Gibeon.

Size of Ai According to the Spies' Report

According to Joshua 10:2, Ai was smaller than Gibeon. Based upon available data, the area of LB I Gibeon is estimated to lie between a minimum value of 7 acres and a maximum value of 15 acres, that is, 11 ±4 acres [Briggs (2004: 123-124)]. The equivalence of $E_1 = 1,000$ persons yields an area estimate for the fortress of Ai which exceeds the maximum value by 65%, and, therefore, which blatantly contradicts the statement in Joshua 10:2. Accordingly, the value of **E** appropriate to the time of Joshua must be smaller than $E_1 = 1,000$.

If the biblical requirement in Joshua 10:2 is interpreted to mean that the maximum value for the area of Ai must be less than the minimum value for the area of LB I Gibeon, that is, the uncertainty bands for the two areas must be disjoint with that for Ai falling below that for Gibeon, then the maximum value for **E** can be derived as follows:

(1) $E_{MAX} = (162 \times 7) / 4 = 283.5$, or approximately 300 [6]

As noted in Table 2, $E_1 = 10$ yields a population and area of Ai that is implausibly small. Therefore, the value of **E** applicable to the time of Joshua must lie between 10 and 300. Suppose that the minimum value for the area of Ai is taken to be 10% of its maximum value of 7 acres, that is, 0.7 acres. Based upon available data concerning the area of the candidate sites of Ai, this value appears to be very conservative, that is, much smaller than a minimum plausible area for the fortress of Ai. Nevertheless, employing it to calculate a minimum value of **E** according to the pattern of equation (1),

(2) $E_{MIN} = (162 \times 0.7) / 4 = 28.4$, or approximately 30

Thus, the uncertainty band for the value of **E** applicable to the time of Joshua is estimated to be from a minimum value of **E** = 30 to a maximum value of **E** = 300. The geometric mean of 30 and 300 is

(3) $E_{MEAN} = (30 \times 300) = 94.9$, or approximately 100

Referring to Table 2, the value $E_{MEAN} = E_3 = 100$ yields 2.5 acres for the area of the fortress of Ai, that is, 36% of the maximum allowable value of 7 acres. The areas of the two most plausible candidates for Joshua's Ai, Kh. Nisya and Kh. el-Maqatir, lie within the range of 3 to 6 acres; therefore, the value of 2.5 acres is plausible, albeit on the small side. In conclusion, **E** = 100 is selected as the best estimate for the value of **E** applicable to the time of Joshua.

Size of Ai According to the Canaanites Killed in the Second Battle
According to Joshua 8:25, the total number of Canaanites killed in the second battle was 12**E**. From Joshua 8:17, this number included the entire population of Ai plus, evidently, the fighting men from Bethel, who had joined the men of Ai in pursuing Israel. How can the constituent parts of the 12**E** be estimated? Let us assume that the spies underestimated the population of Ai by 50% so that there were actually 1.5**E** fighting men there, and the total population, including women, children, and aged men was 6**E**. This yields an area of 3.7 acres for the fortress of Ai, which accords very well with the measured sizes of Kh. Nisya and Kh. el-Maqatir. As a byproduct, the fighting men from Bethel would have numbered 6**E**.

Conclusion with Respect to the Magnitude of E
The equivalence **E** = 100 is adopted as being appropriate to the time of Joshua. This equivalence is subject to an estimated uncertainty band of ±50%. That is, the value of **E** is considered to range from a minimum value of **E** = 50 to a maximum value of **E** = 150 at the time of Joshua. While the size of the army that Joshua inherited

from Moses was 5,730 fighting men, he organized this force into troops of 100, each under its own leader. The attack force deployed in the first battle of Ai was $3E = 300$ men, and the attack force that Joshua personally led into the second battle was 5,730, or approximately $57E$. The primary ambush force that Joshua deployed according to Joshua 8:3-9 was $30E = 3,000$ men, that is, 53% of the entire force. The secondary ambush force mentioned in Joshua 8:12 was $5E = 500$ men. The residual attack force that Joshua led to a place of encampment north of Ai according to Joshua 8:10-13 was $22E = 2,200$ men or 39% of the total force. The total number of Canaanites that were killed in the second battle numbered $12E = 1,200$ people, including the following constituent parts according to the reasoning presented above: (a) fighting men of Ai $= 1.5E = 150$; (b) remaining population of Ai, including women, children, and aged men $= 4.5E = 450$; and, (c) fighting men of Bethel $= 6E = 600$.

The Biblical Timeline

Material facts of all kinds, including artifacts from an archaeological locus, are devoid of meaning, that is, they are indeterminate. Meaning is ascribed to them solely by a narrative representation of a determinate kind [Oller (1996: 216); Oller & Collins (2000); Collins & Oller (2000)]. Thus, archaeological research should always operate within the framework of a determinate narrative, that is, a TNR. In the case of archaeological research of the Bronze Age Canaanite cultures in Palestine, and because of the paucity of epigraphic or historiographic material unearthed from these cultures, the Bible assumes the role of the primary source of historical data. There simply is no other source of comparable scope and integrity.

The Contribution of the Biblical Timeline to the Criterial Screen

A necessary component of the criterial screen is the establishment of the temporal location of the conquest of Ai according to the biblical narrative. The conquest of Ai, as recorded in chapters 7 and 8 of Joshua, would have occurred near the beginning of the Conquest. Therefore, the date of the conquest of Ai would be determined in relationship to that of the Exodus. As summarized in Briggs (2004: 64-71), the selection of the date for the Exodus is the object of intense debate, much of which is precipitated by archaeological findings. However, for determining the temporal location of the conquest of Ai we must insist on allowing the Bible to speak for itself and prevent the confounding of biblical data by archaeological data. This is true because the parameters of the criterial screen must be in strict accord with the biblical text.

Date of the Exodus

An Exodus date of ca. 1450 BC derives from the following biblical sources: (a) 1 Kings 6:1; (b) the letter from Jephthah to the king of Ammon summarized in Judges 11:26; (c) the genealogy of Heman in 1 Chronicles 6:33-43; and, (d) chronological data dispersed throughout the books of Judges and 1 & 2 Samuel. The fourth source for the date of the Exodus is not weighted significantly. An uncertainty band of ± 10 years reflects the scatter in the three primary sources of biblical information [Briggs (2004:

64-68)]. Steven Collins has carefully analyzed the historical synchronism between the account in the Book of Exodus vis-a-vis the profiles of the pharaohs of the 18th and 19th dynasties in Egypt [Collins (2002)]. He demonstrates the substantial correlation that exists with the profile of the reign of Tuthmosis IV as the Pharaoh of the Exodus. In contrast, correlation with the reigns of 19th dynasty pharaohs, which would be needed to corroborate a 13th century BC date for the Exodus, is conspicuously lacking.

Timeline of the Wilderness Journey

According to Numbers 33:3, the Israelites set forth from Egypt on the 15th day of the 1st month, that is, the day after Passover. According to Exodus 19:1, the Israelites arrived at the base of Mt. Sinai on the 15th day of the 3rd month, that is, 2 months after leaving Egypt. From Exodus 40:17, they received the law and directions for constructing the tabernacle through Moses, and they completed the construction of the tabernacle by the end of the 1st year. According to Exodus 40:17, the tabernacle was actually erected in the 1st month of the 2nd year. From Numbers 10:11, the tribes of Israel broke camp and departed from Mt. Sinai exactly 13 months and 5 days after their departure from Egypt. Based upon available chronological data in the Book of Numbers, the date of the Israelites' arrival at Kadesh Barnea is placed in the 15th month after their departure from Egypt. The estimate of 2 months for the duration of their trip from Mt. Sinai to Kadesh Barnea is partially based on the fact that, according to Numbers 11:20ff, the people received the miraculous visitation of quail to satisfy their hunger for meat over a period of 1 month.

The Kadesh Barnea Episode

The Kadesh Barnea episode is recorded in chapters 13 and 14 of Numbers. While encamped at Kadesh Barnea, Moses dispatched the twelve spies to survey the land, the spies returned with their report, and the people responded to the report by refusing to trust the promise of *Yahweh* that he would give them victory over the tribes of the Canaanites. The apostasy of the people at Kadesh Barnea precipitated the period of wilderness wanderings, which, according to Deuteronomy 2:14, consumed 38 years. By the end of the 38 years, the entire generation which had experienced the Exodus from Egypt had died. Chronologically, the key event in the Kadesh Barnea episode is the promise given to Caleb, which is stated in Numbers 14:24. According to this promise, he would survive the 38 years of wandering in the wilderness and would enter the land of Canaan. Allowing 2 months for completion of the spies' reconnoitering mission, the timing of the promise to Caleb is placed in the 17th month after the Exodus.

Timeline of the Wilderness Wanderings

From Exodus 7:7, Moses was 80 years old at the time of the Exodus, and from Deuteronomy 34:7, he was 120 years old when he died while the Israelites were encamped on the plains of Moab opposite Jericho. Another data point is derived from Exodus 16:35, where the period of the people's dependence on manna is stated to be 40 years. According to Joshua 5:10-11, the Israelites observed Passover after having crossed the Jordan and just prior to the attack on Jericho. This Passover was precisely 40 years after the one observed at the time of the Exodus. According to Joshua 5:12, the daily provision of manna ceased at the same time. Thus, the period of time from the Exodus until the people were encamped at Gilgal nearby Jericho and ready to initiate the Conquest is determined to be precisely 40 years.

Timeline of the Conquest

On the basis of the chronological data summarized above, the Conquest would have commenced 40 years after the Exodus from Egypt, that is, ca. 1410 BC. In Joshua 14:10, Caleb states that 45 years had elapsed from the time of *Yahweh's* promise to him at Kadesh Barnea to the conclusion of the Conquest. Based on the estimate above that the promise to Caleb was delivered in the 17th month after the Exodus, the end of the Conquest would have occurred approximately 46 years after the Exodus. Therefore, the duration of the Conquest was 6 years. This would place the Conquest near the end of the LB I archaeological period [7].

Implications of the Biblical Timeline

In accordance with our analytical method for deriving the criterial screen for the conquest of Ai narrative, the biblical timeline is postulated to be true from the Exodus until the beginning of the Conquest. This establishes the temporal context for the conquest of Ai narrative as lying near the end of the LB I archaeological period in accordance with Table 1. The conquest of Ai narrative is then subjected to a detailed analysis based upon the TNR formalism, and, in particular, upon empirical correspondence as manifested in the criterial screen. If it turns out that all of the criterial screen parameters are satisfied, then the narrative is determined to be factual. As a byproduct of this determination, the biblical timeline would be confirmed. It would then be possible to move forward or backward along the biblical timeline to consider other narratives where a similar analytical approach could be applied. On the other hand, if the conquest of Ai narrative is found to be nonfactual, then at least that portion of the Bible should be regarded as either a remarkable, erroneous conception or worse: a deliberately and maliciously fabricated myth which is tantamount to a lie. Furthermore, the credibility of other portions of the Bible that rely upon the conquest of Ai narrative would be called into serious question.

Derivation of the Criterial Screen

The criterial screen derived from exegesis of the conquest of Ai narrative is the measure of empirical correspondence between the narrative and the material time-space context it purports to describe. In fact, the criterial screen is the desired end-product of the exegesis of the text. Table 3 defines each parameter of the criterial screen, including a symbolic definition of the associated probability and the principal passage in the text from which it is derived. The following paragraphs summarize the derivation of each of the fourteen criterial screen parameters from the biblical text[8].

Table 3. Criterial Screen for the Conquest of Ai Narrative

Number	Parameter	Probability	Derivation
1	Site located in the Benjamin hill country and occupied during LB I	P_1	The biblical timeline
2	Small site with area less than 7 acres	P_2	Joshua 10:2
3	Fortified site with wall and gate	P_3	Joshua 7:5, 8:1-2 & 8:11-13
4	Gate facing north to northeast	P_4	Joshua 8:11-13
5	High ridge north of the fortress within 2 kilometers and intervening shallow valley north of the fortress within 1 kilometer	P_5	Joshua 8:11-13
6	Ambush hiding place approximately southwest of the fortress within 3 kilometers	P_6	Joshua 8:3-9
7	Suitable location for feigned retreat maneuver north or northeast of fortress within 3 kilometers	P_7	Joshua 8:14-17
8	Viable egress route with descent and *shebarim* within 3 kilometers	P_8	Joshua 7:3-5 (refer to page 31)
9	Trafficable routes to location	P_9	Joshua 8:9-11
10	Viable engagement scenarios	P_{10}	Joshua 8:14-17
11	Ceramic artifacts appropriate to small highland fortress	P_{11}	Joshua 7:3
12	Object artifacts appropriate to small highland fortress	P_{12}	Joshua 7:3
13	Convenient line-of-sight to Bethel	P_{13}	Joshua 8:17
14	Evidence of conflagration	P_{14}	Joshua 8:19 & 28

Predicate Criterial Screen

The first three parameters of the criterial screen in Table 3 form a predicate criterial screen. These particular parameters constitute the minimum set that is capable of discriminating between viable and non-viable sites for Joshua's Ai. Even though the predicate screen consists of only three parameters, it is sufficiently explicit that only one of the three candidate sites for Joshua's Ai survive its application. That single site is then subjected to the still more demanding requirements of the remaining eleven parameters of the criterial screen.

Explanation of the Criterial Screen
The following paragraphs describe the derivation of each of the parameters of the criterial screen listed in Table 3.

Site located in the Benjamin hill country and occupied during LB I. This first parameter is of primary importance, for it culls out from further consideration all candidate sites for Joshua's Ai that are not properly located in space and time according to the biblical text. Spatially, Joshua's Ai was situated in the Benjamin hill country of Israel. (Refer to Figure 1 on page 184 for a more precise definition of the portion of the Benjamin hill country indicated by the biblical text and the results of past research.) Temporally, Joshua's Ai was occupied during LB I. On what basis is this temporal requirement asserted? According to the biblical timeline presented above, the Conquest began ca. 1410 BC and concluded 6 years later, ca. 1403 BC. In particular, the conquest of Ai occurred near the beginning of the 6 year period of the Conquest. Therefore, in accordance with traditional archaeological periods for dating (see Table 1), the conquest of Ai took place at or near the end of the LB I period.

Small site with area less than 7 acres. According to Joshua 7:2-3, the fortress of Ai appeared to be so small that the spies recommended that only a contingent of $2E$ or $3E$ would be sufficient to take it. In accordance with Joshua 10:2, the area of Ai was smaller than that of Gibeon. Analysis of the area of LB I Gibeon presented in Briggs (2004: 123-125) based upon available data in Broshi & Gophna (1986: 82) and Finkelstein & Magen (1993) yields the estimate of 11 ±4 acres, that is, its area lay between a minimum value of 7 acres and a maximum value of 15 acres. Accordingly, the requirement that the area of the fortress of Ai be less than that of Gibeon is interpreted to mean that the maximum value for the area of the fortress of Ai must be less than the minimum value for the area of LB I Gibeon, that is, 7 acres.

Fortified site with wall and gate. There is no specific and direct biblical statement that Ai was fortified. However, a number of statements in the text of Joshua 7 and 8 present conclusive evidence that it was indeed fortified. In particular, the lines of evidence supporting fortification are as follows:

a. In Joshua 7:5, the flight of the Israelites after the first battle of Ai is described as having started from before or in front of the gate of the fortress. The existence of a gate implies that of a wall as well.
b. An unfortified location would not have a "front" face. The fact that Joshua 8:11 describes the residual attack force under Joshua's command as "arriving in front of the city" is only reasonable if the Israelites acquired a position that was before or in face-to-face opposition to the principal wall face and gate of the fortress of Ai.
c. The divinely mandated ruse is not reasonable unless it was necessary for

the Israelites to trick the Canaanites to leave the fortress open. If the site of Ai was unfortified, the overwhelming Israelite offensive force (5,730 versus a Canaanite defensive force estimated to be 750, a 7.6-to-1 numerical advantage) could have entered it with impunity from any direction without employing a feigned retreat and ambush strategy.

The result of applying the predicate criterial screen. If **S** is the set of all sites in Israel, without regard to geographic location or period of occupation, then the parameters of the predicate criterial screen progressively narrow the set of candidate sites for Joshua's Ai. As a result of requiring that a candidate site for Joshua's Ai be located in the Benjamin hill country, the set **S** is reduced to **S'**. How should the set **S'** be represented for purposes of calculating a probability associated with the first criterial screen parameter? The approach adopted in what follows is to define the set of six sites that have been considered at one time or another as candidates for Joshua's Ai as being representative of **S'**. As a result of completing the application of the first parameter, the set of potentially viable candidates is reduced to S_1, the sites in the Benjamin hill country that were occupied during LB I. Application of the second parameter narrows the set of candidates further to S_2, those members of S_1 that are smaller than 7 acres. Application of the third parameter narrows the set of candidates still further to S_3, those members of S_2 that were fortified with wall and gate. In fact, as is demonstrated in the next section, S_3 is populated by just one site. The function of the parameters of the criterial screen which follow, that is, the 4th through the 14th, is to confirm the correct identification of that one site as Joshua's Ai. For purposes of calculating a number of the probabilities P_4 through P_{14} associated with the remaining 11 criterial screen parameters, the candidate sites for Joshua's Ai are treated as a representative microcosm of the set of all fortified Benjamin hill country sites occupied during the LB I.

Gate facing north to northeast. According to Joshua 8:11, the residual attack force "arrived in front of the city, and camped on the north side of Ai." Thus, the principal gate of the fortress, or perhaps the only gate, was in the north or northeast face of the wall.

High ridge north of the fortress within 2 kilometers and intervening shallow valley within 1 kilometer. According to Joshua 8:11, most of the 22E residual attack force was encamped north of the fortress in a location which was hidden from the view of the men of Ai. Joshua 8:11 further states that there was an intervening valley between this camp and the fortress. Hence, the Israelite camp must have been located on a high ridge, probably forested, which lay north of Ai. Moreover, Joshua and his immediate subordinates would have required an elevated location close to the fortress of Ai from which to direct the battle. The value of 2 kilometers is set for the threshold of proximity of the high ridge relative to the fortress. Ridges that were more distant than this could not satisfy all of the biblical requirements. Furthermore, according to

Joshua 8:13, Joshua made his camp and "spent the night in the midst of the valley," probably taking with him a small detachment of men from the residual attack force. Thus, from Joshua 8:11-13, two separate but related aspects of the topography north of Ai are derived. First, there must have been a high ridge north of the fortress, and then there must have been an intervening valley where Joshua and his men spent the night. The fact that the valley in question was shallow is indicated by Joshua 8:14, which states that the king of Ai was able to observe all of Joshua's movements and the place where he and his men set up camp. The value of 1 kilometer is set for the threshold of proximity of the valley relative to the fortress.

Ambush hiding place approximately southwest of the fortress within 3 kilometers. While the Canaanites were fixated on Joshua's visual presentation of the detachment from the residual attack force on the north side of the fortress [9], it was essential that the 30E primary ambush force of Joshua 8:3-9 remain hidden from view. The topography surrounding the site of Ai had to be such that the primary ambush force could not be seen from either Ai or Bethel, the neighboring Canaanite city to the west. Based upon the combination of mildly contradictory directional indicators provided in the text ("behind" Ai, to the west of Ai, and "between" Ai and Bethel), it is concluded that the place of ambush was approximately southwest of the fortress [Briggs (2004: 105-106)]. A proximity factor of 3 kilometers is selected because Joshua instructed the primary ambush force to acquire a position that was not far from the fortress according to Joshua 8:4.

Suitable location for the feigned retreat maneuver north or northeast of the fortress within 3 kilometers. According to Joshua 8:14ff, the Israelite force deployed frontally against the north-facing wall and gate of the fortress allowed itself to be driven back as in the first battle of Ai, and it feigned retreat toward an "appointed place before the desert plain," that is, a location which commanded a view of the Jordan valley to the east [Briggs (2004: 110-112)]. The location was such that once the men of Ai had been drawn into pursuit of the Israelites, they would have been prevented from quick return to their fortress, thus opening a significant window of opportunity for the primary ambush force to penetrate the fortress and set a fire. Accordingly, the topography to the north and northeast of Ai would have been characterized by an expanse suitable for maneuvering armies, a view of the Jordan valley, and a natural barrier obstructing the rapid return of the Canaanites to their unprotected fortress. A proximity factor of 3 kilometers is selected for this parameter since the location in question could not be so far to the east as to obscure Joshua's raised weapon signal in accordance with Joshua 8:18.

Egress route with descent and shebarim within 3 kilometers. According to Joshua 7:5, the Canaanites chased the fleeing Israelites as far as a specific location or landmark designated 'the Shebârîym', a term which is unique to this passage. Based upon available lexical data, this term denotes a prominent feature characterized by broken

181

or jointed rock, quarrying, or possibly a ruin. To simplify nomenclature, the specific landmark spoken of in Joshua 7:5 is denoted 'the *Shebarim*' without diacritical marks, and candidate features observable in the region that may correspond to this specific one are denoted '*shebarim*' or '*shebarim* formations'. According to Joshua 7:5, the features of a descent and the *Shebarim* were present along the egress route traversed by the Israelites in the first battle of Ai described in Joshua 7:4ff. Since these features characterized the route along which the men of Ai pursued the fleeing Israelites, they would necessarily have to exist within a short distance of Ai. A proximity factor of 3 kilometers is selected [10].

Trafficable routes to location. According to Joshua 8:3, Joshua and the entire army of Israel left the camp at Gilgal near Jericho and marched to a staging encampment close to the fortress of Ai. According to Joshua 8:9, the 30E primary ambush force initiated a nighttime march toward their assigned place of ambush close to and southwest of the fortress. In fact, they probably completed their ingress under cover of darkness to minimize observability from actual or potential enemy positions. The next morning, according to Joshua 8:10-11, Joshua led the residual attack force along a different route to a point north of the fortress, a march that was completed in a single day. Thus, there needed to be a well-defined, trafficable route, such as an existing road or a wadi network, to support each of these three marches.[11]

Viable engagement scenarios. The battle strategy described in the conquest of Ai narrative must be viable with respect to the geographical and topographical context of the site of Joshua's Ai as well as with respect to the military technology possessed by the Israelite army [12]. The key elements of the strategy are the feigned retreat maneuver, Joshua's raised weapon signal, the role of the secondary ambush force of Joshua 8:12, and the primary ambush force assault described in Joshua 8:14-17. While the biblical text is unusually detailed, certain aspects of the engagement are not specifically addressed. This can be overcome by formulating an engagement scenario model that effectively interpolates the missing detail between the data points supplied by the text. It is essential that the engagement scenario model be realizable in its topographical context, given times, distances, available lines-of-sight, degree of forestation, etc. In particular, there must have been a viable means for Joshua's raised weapon signal to be relayed to the 30E primary ambush force, and the ambush force must have been able to quickly penetrate the unprotected fortress once the signal was delivered. A key aspect of the Israelite's military technology was the fact that they were neither trained nor equipped for siege warfare. In other respects, their military technology and strategy would have been a derivative of that manifested in the campaign of Tuthmosis III against Megiddo, ca. 1479 BC.

Ceramic artifacts appropriate to a small highland fortress. Not only must the ceramic artifacts be diagnostic to LB I, but the kinds of wares represented must be appropriate to a small military outpost, that is, principally large storage vessels and common wares for cooking and serving food. One would not expect to find exotic imported wares at the fortress of Ai.

Object artifacts appropriate to a small highland fortress. In addition to the appropriate kinds of ceramic artifacts, one would expect to find objects that attest to a military location, such as gate post socket stones, sling stones, and possibly flint arrow and spear heads.

Convenient line-of-sight to Bethel. Since, according to Joshua 8:17, the fighting men of Bethel joined those of Ai in pursuing the Israelites, there must have been a means for the king of Ai to signal his counterpart at Bethel. The location of the fortress and the topography between it and Bethel would have allowed signal passing between the two locations.

Evidence of conflagration. According to Joshua 8:19, the 30E primary ambush force set a fire as soon as they had penetrated the fortress. Moreover, according to Joshua 8:2 & 28, the Israelites burned the entire fortress after they had removed "its spoil and its cattle," making it a permanent heap of ruins. Therefore, evidence of a conflagration would be expected.

Application of the Predicate Criterial Screen

Three candidate sites for Joshua's Ai emerge from past research as follows: (a) the traditional site, et-Tell; (b) Kh. Nisya; and, (c) Kh. el-Maqatir. Depicted in Figure 1 is the portion of the Benjamin hill country of interest to this research (namely, the 16 square kilometer tract bounded by grid coordinate 144,000 on the south, 148,000 on the north, 171,000 on the west, and 175,000 on the east) and the location of the three candidate sites for Joshua's Ai with respect to each other and other geographical and topographical features in the vicinity [13] [14]. The predicate criterial screen consists of the first three parameters listed in Table 3, of which the first is of primary importance. These three parameters constitute the minimum set which suffices to cull out the non-viable candidates for Joshua's Ai, leaving only a single, viable candidate.

Figure 1. Locations of the Three Candidate Sites For Joshua's Ai

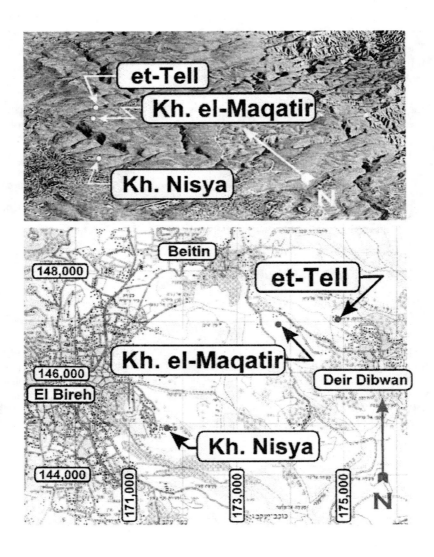

Application of the Predicate Criterial Screen to et-Tell

While et-Tell is properly located in the Benjamin hill country, there is universal agreement among archaeologists that the site was not occupied during LB I (Callaway 1993: 39-45); therefore, it fails to satisfy the first critical screen parameter. Moreover, the area of the EBA city at et-Tell is 27.5 acres, that is, nearly 4 times the screen value of 7 acres. In fact, it is nearly twice the size of the maximum estimated area of LB I Gibeon, that is, 15 acres. Finally, while the EBA city at et-Tell was fortified, the only exposed gate structures are in the south or southeast sectors of the city, which contradicts the fourth parameter of the criterial screen in Table 3. Hence, the site of et-Tell satisfies, at best, only one out of three predicate criterial screen parameters, and therefore it is not a viable candidate for Joshua's Ai.

Callaway's hypothesis. Joseph Callaway postulates that the conquest of Ai described in chapters 7 and 8 of Joshua actually took place during IA I [Callaway (1968: 312-320)]. He identifies the small, unwalled IA village that was situated on the acropolis of et-Tell as the Ai of Joshua, the area of that site being approximately 3 acres and thus satisfying the second criterial screen parameter. While Prof. Callaway is free to speculate on a skirmish at the site of et-Tell which might have occurred during the IA, such does not correspond with the battle described in Joshua 7 and 8. Rather than taking liberties with the biblical text in an attempt to harmonize it with archaeological evidence, the present analysis is directed toward identifying a site that corresponds precisely with the biblical text as written.

Zevit's hypothesis. Zevit (1985) postulates a battle scenario for the conquest of Ai as it might have played out at the site of et-Tell. Actually, there are a number of factors in the topography surrounding et-Tell which fail to correspond with the narrative of Joshua 8. In particular, there is no suitable hiding place for the 30E ambush force southwest of the site in accordance with Joshua 8:2-9 [15]. While there is a high ridge to the north, the intervening valley is the Wadi el-Gayeh, which is deep and steep-walled at that point. Thus, the topography north of the site precludes the playing out of the battle scenario as described in Joshua 8:9-28.

Application of the Predicate Criterial Screen to Kh. Nisya

There are a few artifacts that have been unearthed at Kh. Nisya that suggest some occupation during LB I. Moreover, the size of the site satisfies the screen parameter of being less than 7 acres. However, there is absolutely no evidence that the site was fortified during LB I [Livingston (1999: 13-20)]. Hence, the site of Kh. Nisya satisfies two of the three predicate criterial screen parameters. Because it fails to satisfy all three, it is not a viable candidate for Joshua's Ai.

Livingston's hypothesis. According to Livingston (1999: 15), the topography surrounding the site of Kh. Nisya perfectly matches the biblical requirements. While there is a valley to the west of the site for the 30E primary ambush force to lie in wait, the head of that valley is adjacent to the spring at El Bireh, which Livingston (1970, 1971, 1994) identifies as the location of ancient Bethel. Moreover, the ingress of the ambush force would have been visible from the site of Kh. Nisya itself. While there is a high ridge to the north of the site with a shallow intervening valley, there is no suitable place for the playing out of the feigned retreat maneuver in accordance with Joshua 8:14-17 because the deep and steep-sided Wadi Sheban lies immediately beyond the ridge in question to the east [16].

Application of the Predicate Criterial Screen to Kh. el-Maqatir

According to Wood (2000a, 2000b, 2000c), evidence of LB I occupation at Kh. el-Maqatir is abundant, the area of the site satisfies the screen parameter of being smaller than 7 acres, and the LB I fortification system is truly impressive, especially along the north face where the foundations of the gate have been exposed. Therefore, of the three candidate sites, only Kh. el-Maqatir unequivocally satisfies all three predicate criterial screen parameters, and it is subjected to the detailed analysis in the following section.

Application of the Criterial Screen to Kh. el-Maqatir

The formulation of engagement scenario models for the first and second battles of Ai provides the framework in which the empirical correspondence between the biblical text and the archaeological, geographical, and topographical contexts of the site of Kh. el-Maqatir can be tested [17]. The test is actually carried out by subjecting Kh. el-Maqatir and its context to the rigors of the remaining 11 parameters of the 14-parameter criterial screen of Table 3. The results of applying the full 14-parameter criterial screen of Table 3 to Kh. el-Maqatir are summarized in Table 4.

Criterial Screen Analysis

In the following paragraphs, the satisfaction of each of the criterial screen parameters is addressed, and, to the extent possible, the associated probability defined in Table 3 is evaluated. All of the estimated probability values are listed in Table 4. For each of the criterial screen parameters, the associated probability reflects the likelihood that the satisfaction of that parameter could occur accidentally, that is, at a randomly selected site in the Benjamin hill country. Thus, the product of the 14 probability values represents the likelihood that the confluence of satisfaction of all 14 parameters of the screen is the result of a random event, that is, akin to 14 consecutive coin tosses producing 14 heads. This, in fact, is the probability that Kh. el-Maqatir is not Joshua's Ai.

Preliminary discussion of the selection of probabilities. While there are available data to support the estimation of probabilities for a number of criterial screen parameters, the rigorous estimation of probabilities for others would have required archaeological, geographical, and topographical data that has been inaccessible since September 2000 due to the serious state of unrest in Israel. In particular, access to the region of the Benjamin hill country defined in Figure 1 for continuing archaeological and topographical research has been prevented. However, in every case, a probability value is selected based upon available data, but not necessarily with the rigor that this aspect of the analysis deserves.

Table 4. Probability That Kh. el-Maqatir Is Not Joshua's Ai

Parameter	Satisfied?	Probability	Combinatorial Probability
Site located in Benjamin hill country and occupied during LB I?	Yes	0.1667	0.1667
Small site with area less than 7 acres?	Yes	0.7778	0.1297
Fortified site with wall and gate?	Yes	0.7692	0.09973
Gate facing north to northeast?	Yes	0.1250	0.01247
High ridge to north within 2 kilometers with intervening shallow valley within 1 kilometer?	Yes	0.6667	0.008312
Ambush hiding place approximately southwest within 3 kilometers?	Yes	0.1250	0.001039
Suitable location for feigned retreat maneuver to north or northeast within 3 kilometers?	Yes	0.1250	0.0001299
Viable egress route with descent and *shebarim* within 3 kilometers?	Yes	0.6667	0.0000866
Trafficable routes to location?	Yes	0.6667	0.0000577
Engagement scenarios viable?	Yes	0.3333	0.00001924
Ceramic artifacts appropriate?	Yes	0.5000	0.000009620
Object artifacts appropriate?	Yes	0.5000	0.000004810
Convenient line-of-sight to Bethel?	Yes	0.3333	0.000001603
Evidence of conflagration?	Yes	0.3333	0.0000005343

Site located in the Benjamin hill country and occupied during LB I. An abundance of ceramic artifacts diagnostic to LB I have been unearthed at Kh. el-Maqatir. A total of 6 Benjamin hill country sites have been considered at one time or another as candidates for Joshua's Ai [18]. Of these, only Kh. el-Maqatir manifests substantial LB I occupation. On this basis, P_1 is estimated to be 1/6 = 0.1667.

Small site with area less than 7 acres. The estimated area of the LB I fortress that existed at Kh. el-Maqatir is 3.1 acres [Briggs (2004: 123-125 & 137-141)], which is believed to be accurate to within ±62%. To calculate a probability for this parameter, the MB II sites listed in Table 7, Judea Sites, of Broshni & Gophna (1986: 82) are analyzed. Both Bethel (i.e., Beitin) and Gibeon are included in this table. Of the 44 entries in the table, 8 are cemeteries, leaving 36 occupied sites. Of these, 8 are equal to or larger than the threshold value of 7 acres. On this basis, P_2 is estimated to be (36-8)/36 = 0.7778.

Fortified site with wall and gate. Very substantial LB I fortification walls have been unearthed at Kh. el-Maqatir. In fact the foundation of the wall on the north face of the fortress is an impressive 4 meters thick. Based upon a customary 3-to-1 height-to-width ratio, this translates to a mudbrick superstructure that would have risen to a height of 12 meters (i.e., approximately 40 feet). Hansen (2000: 80-172) presents a comprehensive analysis of the fortification status of LBA sites in Palestine. In particular, on page 171 of Hansen's work, a summative table is presented, on page 172 a map identifying the location of the sites is presented, and on pages 80-166 an analysis of all the sites is set forth. Of the sites examined, 13 are situated in the central hill country, and of these 13, 10 were fortified during the LBA. On this basis, P_3 is estimated to be 10/13 = 0.7692.

Gate facing north to northeast. The foundations of a chambered gate have been exposed on the north side of Kh. el-Maqatir [Briggs (2004: 137-141)]. Sealed loci adjacent to the gate foundation stones date to LB I. On the assumption that the direction in which city gates face is uniformly distributed over a range of 0-360°, the value of P_4 is estimated to be 45°/360° = 0.125.

High ridge to north within 2 kilometers and intervening shallow valley within 1 kilometer of the site. The summit of Jebel Abu Ammar, the highest point in the local area, is 1.4 kilometers due north of the gate of Kh. el- Maqatir [Briggs (2004: 137-141 & 159-160)]. The valley in question is the mouth of the Wadi el-Gayeh, lying immediately east of the modern village of Beitin [Briggs (2004: 159-160)]. It is broad and shallow north of Kh. el-Maqatir, lying within 0.8 kilometer of the site. How should one go about estimating the probability, P_5, associated with this parameter? The most logical approach, given the available data, is to employ the three candidate sites for Joshua's Ai as representative of Benjamin hill country sites in general. While all three have high ridges to the north of them, only Kh. Nisya and Kh. el-Maqatir have shallow intervening valleys. On this basis, P_5 is evaluated as $2/3 = 0.6667$.

Ambush hiding place approximately southwest within 3 kilometers of the site. The probable location of the primary ambush force encampment has been determined by means of ground surveys of the Wadi Sheban [Briggs (2004: 154-155)]. It is located 2.6 kilometers south-southwest of the gate structure. It can reasonably be assumed that most sites in the Benjamin hill country would be characterized by an ambush hiding place within 3 kilometers. Furthermore, it can reasonably be assumed that the direction in which an ambush hiding place would be located relative to a randomly selected site is uniformly distributed over a range of 0-360°. Therefore, the value of P_6 is estimated to be $45°/360° = 0.125$.

Suitable location for the feigned retreat maneuver to north or northeast within 3 kilometers of the site. The location in question lies 2.2 kilometers east-northeast of Kh. el-Maqatir and commands an unobstructed view of the Jordan Valley [Briggs (2004: 155-156)]. The probability of finding such a location nearby a randomly selected site in the Benjamin hill country is judged to be no greater than $45°/360° = 0.125$. Accordingly, P_7 is evaluated as 0.125.

Viable egress route with descent and shebarim within 3 kilometers of the site. With respect to Kh. el-Maqatir, two candidate egress routes have been defined [Briggs (2004: 146-149)]. Both are characterized by a descent and *shebarim*. In the case of the first option, the *shebarim* formation lies 2.8 kilometers southeast of the site, and in the case of the second option, it lies approximately 2 kilometers east of the site. As was done with P_5, the three candidate sites for Joshua's Ai are regarded as a representative microcosm of randomly selected Benjamin hill country sites within the tract depicted in Figure 1. In the case of both Kh. Nisya and Kh. el-Maqatir, viable egress routes characterized by descents and *shebarim* formations exist within 3 kilometers. However, in the case of et-Tell, egress back toward Jericho from the north side of the site would have required a precipitous descent down the steep walls of the Wadi el-Gayeh, which is not regarded as particularly viable, either for the defending Canaanite force or for the fleeing Israelites. Hence, P_8 is evaluated as $2/3 = 0.6667$.

Trafficable ingress routes to location. The trafficability of ingress routes to Kh. el-Maqatir has been verified by ground surveys conducted by the author and colleagues from the Kh. el-Maqatir excavation project. As was done with P_5 and P_8, the three candidate sites for Joshua's Ai are regarded as a representative microcosm of randomly selected Benjamin hill country sites within the tract depicted in Figure 1. Trafficable ingress routes are available in the case of both Kh. Nisya and Kh. el-Maqatir. However, approach to et-Tell from the north is complicated by the steep walls of the Wadi el-Gayeh. Accordingly, P_9 is evaluated as $2/3 = 0.6667$.

Engagement scenarios viable. With respect to Kh. el-Maqatir, all aspects of the engagement scenarios for both battles are militarily viable, given the assets Joshua had at his disposal. However, such is not the case for either Kh. Nisya or et-Tell. In the case of Kh. Nisya, the ingress of the primary ambush force to its place of encampment would have been visible from enemy positions. In the case of et-Tell, an attack from the north of the site is not viable on account of the steep walls of the Wadi el-Gayeh. Hence, P_{10} is evaluated as $1/3 = 0.3333$.

Ceramic artifacts appropriate. The LB I pottery that has been unearthed at Kh. el-Maqatir is suited to a small military outpost, including large, commercial-grade pithoi for storage of grains, water, and olive oil, and common ware for cooking and table service [Briggs (2004: 161)]. For purposes of evaluating P_{11}, Kh. Nisya and Kh. el-Maqatir are considered to be a representative microcosm of LB I sites in the Benjamin hill country. Since the pottery unearthed as Kh. el-Maqatir is representative of a small highland fortress, while that unearthed at Kh. Nisya is not, P_{11} is evaluated as $1/2 = 0.5$.

Object artifacts appropriate. By the end of the 2000 excavation season at Kh. el-Maqatir, more than 100 slingstones and 3 gate post socket stones have been unearthed [Briggs (2004: 161-162)]. Employing the same approach to evaluating P_{12} as was applied to the evaluation of P_{11}, the probability of finding this combination of objects at a Benjamin hill country site picked at random is judged to be no greater than 1/2. Hence, P_{12} is evaluated as $1/2 = 0.5$.

Convenient line-of-sight to Bethel. A direct line-of-sight exists from the hilltop above Kh. el-Maqatir to El Bireh, the probable location of Bethel. Moreover, at a height of 12 meters, the parapet of the wall near the westernmost extremity of the wall perimeter would have afforded line-of-sight contact with Bethel = El Bireh from the protection of the fortress [Briggs (2004: 162-163)]. In fact, this is true even if one should insist that Bethel = Beitin. However, the topography surrounding et-Tell and Kh. Nisya denies equivalent line-of-sight contact with either of the candidate locations for Bethel. On this basis, the probability of a randomly selected site in the Benjamin hill country affording a convenient and direct line-of-sight to Bethel is judged to be no greater than 1/3. Accordingly, P_{13} is evaluated as $1/3 = 0.3333$.

Evidence of conflagration. During the 1999 excavation season at Kh. el-Maqatir, materials derived from Area G, that is, the area of the gate structure and an LB I context, were subjected to testing for remanent magnetization, which is an indication of superheating. Three of the samples manifested statistically significant levels of remanent magnetization, affording positive evidence of a conflagration in antiquity. Also during the 1999 season, an ash layer was exposed in square G24 that lies 80 meters southeast of the gate. Continued work in G24 and neighboring F24 during the

2000 excavation season revealed an extended ash layer superimposed on what appears to be an LB I pavement. The thickness of the ash layer was 10 centimeters (= 4 inches) in some places. In square R14, which lies 17 meters west of the gate, a similar condition was uncovered, including a thin layer of ash (2 to 3 centimeters) along with clumps of burned and flaking limestone. Also during the 2000 excavation season, widespread evidence of a conflagration was uncovered in the form of superheated and calcined limestone bedrock and LB I pottery that had been subjected to superheating to the point of metallic hardness [Wood (2000c: 68-69)]. The probability of finding evidence of an LB I conflagration at a Benjamin hill country site picked at random is judged to be no greater than 1/3. Accordingly, P_{14} is evaluated as $1/3 = 0.3333$.

Factors militating against preservation of ash layers. Militating against finding extensive ash layers at Kh. el-Maqatir is the fact that the entire site has been exposed and under cultivation for centuries. Furthermore, over most of the site, the soil depth above bedrock is no more than a meter and in many places bedrock is actually exposed. With such shallow stratification and extensive and ongoing cultivation, the probability that extensive ash deposits would be preserved *in situ* is remote.

Concluding remarks on the selection of probabilities. Based upon available data, values for probabilities P_1 through P_{14} have been selected that are believed to be reasonable and generally somewhat conservative. That is, the combinatorial probability result of 5.343×10^{-7} is probably larger than the value that would result from a rigorous analysis with unrestricted access to all necessary archaeological, geographical, and topographical data concerning Benjamin hill country sites. The primary objective of this aspect of the analytical process has been to demonstrate a method for estimating a confidence factor associated with the factuality test result. This objective has been achieved. A secondary objective has been to select probability values with adequate credibility to demonstrate the high degree of confidence that can be placed in the result of the analysis. Refinement of the probability values is an important goal of future research.

Concluding remarks on the combinatorial probability result. Given the selected probabilities for the set of criterial screen parameters, the computed value for the probability of all 14 parameters being satisfied by a single site selected at random in the Benjamin hill country of Palestine is 5.343×10^{-7}, that is only 1 chance in almost 2 million. If a randomly selected site could satisfy the criterial screen, then there would be no basis for asserting that a particular site, Kh. el-Maqatir, is Joshua's Ai. The complement of the above probability is the confidence factor placed in the assertion that Kh. el-Maqatir is Joshua's Ai; that is, $(1 - 5.343 \times 10^{-7}) = 0.9999994657 = 99.99994657\%$.

Conclusions
The result of applying the 14-parameter criterial screen of Table 3 to the

archaeological, geographical, and topographical context of Kh. el-Maqatir is summarized in Table 4. In particular, evidence has been brought forward that Kh. el-Maqatir is Joshua's Ai. Moreover, this same body of evidence demonstrates that the conquest of Ai narrative is a TNR. The strength of evidence is judged to be conclusive beyond reasonable doubt based on the probability values selected for the 14 criterial screen parameters. Accordingly, the eye-witness account view of the conquest of Ai narrative is confirmed, and the aetiological legend and pernicious myth views are both refuted by this analysis.

In addition to demonstrating a method for testing the factuality of the conquest of Ai narrative in the Book of Joshua, a method has been mapped out for calculating an associated confidence factor. The confidence factor is based upon probability values that represent the likelihood of an accidental satisfaction of the criterial screen parameters. Based upon available data, all 14 probabilities are evaluated, but not necessarily with the desired rigor in a number of cases. Thus, the more precise evaluation of some of the probabilities and the rigorous working out of confidence factor calculation is relegated to future research. While some of the probabilities may need to be increased above their presently estimated values, such adjustments should not be expected to materially affect the overall conclusion, however. Even if the combinatorial probability result in Table 4 were to be increased by a factor of 10, the confidence factor associated with the result of this research is still virtually 100%.

Finally, this research has demonstrated the appropriate method for allowing interaction between biblical and archaeological data. Because archaeological findings are almost always indeterminate, they inherently rely upon a determinate narrative for interpretation. Therefore, one should always proceed from the narrative to the archaeological data instead of the reverse.

REFERENCES

Amiran, R.
1970   *Ancient Pottery of the Holy Land*, p. 12. Rutgers University Press.
Boling, R.G.
1982   *The Anchor Bible: Joshua*. New York: Doubleday.
Briggs, P.
2004   *Testing the Factuality of the Conquest of Ai Narrative in the Book of Joshua*, 3rd ed. Academic Monograph Series, AR-1. Albuquerque, New Mexico: Daystar Systems. Contact **Daystar@swcp.com** to order a copy.
Bright, J.
1981   *A History of Israel*, 3rd ed. Philadelphia: Westminister Press.
Broshi, M. & Gophna, R.
1986   Middle Bronze Age II Palestine: its settlements and population. *Bulletin of American Schools of Oriental Research*, Vol. 261, pp. 73-95.
Callaway, J. A.
1968   New evidence on the conquest of Ai. *Journal of Biblical Literature*, Vol. LXXXVII, No. III, pp. 312-320.

Callaway, J. A.
1970   The 1968-1969 'Ai (et-Tell) excavations. *Bulletin of American Society for Oriental Research*, Vol. 198, pp. 10-12.

Callaway, J. A.
1993   Article on Ai in, *The New Encyclopedia of Archaeological Excavations in the Holy Land*, Stern, E. (Ed.), pp. 39-45. New York: Simon & Schuster.

Cassuto, U.
1983   *The Documentary Hypothesis and the Composition of the Pentateuch.* Translated by I. Abrahams. Jerusalem: Magnes.

Collins, S.
2002   *Let My People Go: Using Historical Synchronisms to Identify the Pharaoh of the Exodus*, AMS/TSU AR.1. Albuquerque, New Mexico: Trinity Southwest University Press.

Collins, S. & Oller, J. W., Jr.
2000   Biblical history as true narrative representation. *The Global Journal of Classical Theology*, Vol. 2, No. 2. Visit **www.trinitysem.edu/journal/journalindex.html**.

Feller, W.
1957   *An Introduction to Probability Theory and Its Applications.* New York: John Wiley & Sons, Inc.

Finegan, J.
1998   *Handbook of Biblical Chronology*, p. xxxv. Peabody, Massachusetts: Hendrickson Publishers, Inc.

Finkelstein, I. & Magen, Y. (Eds.)
1993   *Archaeological Survey of the Benjamin Hill Country*, p. 46. Jerusalem: Israel Antiquities Authority.

Fouts, D. M.
1992   *The Use of Large Numbers in the Old Testament, With Particular Emphasis on the Use of elep.* Doctoral dissertation, Dallas Theological Seminary, Dallas, Texas.

Fouts, D. M.
1997   A defense of the hyperbolic interpretation of large numbers in the Old Testament. *Journal of the Evangelical Theological Society*, Vol. 40, No. 3, pp. 377-388.

Frick, F. S.
1977   *The City in Ancient Israel*, pp. 25-55. Missoula, Montana: Scholars Press.

Gottwald, N. K.
1979   *The Tribes of Yahweh*, pp. 270-276. Maryknoll, New York: Orbis Books.

Hansen, D. G.
2000   *Evidence for Fortifications at Late Bronze I and II Locations in Palestine.* Unpublished doctoral dissertation, Trinity College & Seminary, Newburgh, Indiana.

Hayes, W. C.
1975   Chronological tables (A) Egypt. *Cambridge Ancient History*, Vol. II, No. 2, p. 1038.
Hayes, J. H. & Miller, J. M. (Eds.)
1977   *Israelite and Judean History*. Philadelphia: Trinity Press International.
Humphreys, C. J.
1998   The number of people in the Exodus from Egypt: decoding mathematically the very large numbers in Numbers I and XXVI. *Vetus Testamentum*, Vol. 48, pp. 196-213.
Humphreys, C. J.
2000   The numbers in the Exodus from Egypt: a further appraisal. *Vetus Testamentum*, Vol. 50, pp. 323-328.
Kaiser, W. C., Jr.
1987   *Toward Rediscovering the Old Testament*. Grand Rapids, Michigan: Zondervan Publishing House.
Kelso, J. L., & Albright, W.F.
1968   The excavation of Bethel. In Kelso, J.L. (Ed.), *Annual of American Schools of Oriental Research*, Vol. XXXIX, Cambridge.
Kenyon, K. M.
1957   *Digging Up Jericho*. London.
Kenyon, K. M.
1960   *Archaeology in the Holy Land*. London: Benn.
Kitchen, K. A.
1992   History of Egypt (chronology). *The Anchor Bible Dictionary*, Freedman, D. N. (Ed.), Vol. 2, pp. 322-331. New York: Doubleday.
Kitchen, K. A.
1996   The historical chronology of ancient Egypt: a current assessment. *Acta Archaeologica*, Vol. 67, pp. 1-13.
LaSor, W. S.
1979   Article on archaeology in, *The International Standard Bible Encyclopedia*, Bromiley, G. W. (Gen. Ed.), Vol. One, pp. 235-244. Grand Rapids, Michigan: Eerdmans Publishing Company.
Livingston, D. P.
1970   Location of Bethel and Ai reconsidered. *Westminister Theological Journal*, Vol. 33, pp. 20-24.
Livingston, D. P.
1971   Traditional site of Bethel questioned. *Westminister Theological Journal*, Vol. 34, pp. 39-50.
Livingston, D. P.
1994   Further considerations on the location of Bethel at El-Bireh. *Palestine Exploration Quarterly*, Vol. 126, pp. 154-159.
Livingston, D. P.
1999   Is Kh. Nisya the Ai of the Bible? *Bible and Spade*, Vol. 12, No. 1, pp. 13-20.

Mendenhall, G. E.
1958   The census of Numbers 1 and 26. *Journal of Biblical Literature*, Vol. 77, pp. 52-66.
Miller, J. M. & Hayes, J. H.
1986   *A History of Ancient Israel and Judah*. Philadelphia: The Westminister Press.
Na'aman, N.
1994   The 'Conquest of Canaan' in the Book of Joshua and in History. In Finkelstein, I. & Na'aman, N. (Eds.). *From Nomadism to Monarchy*. Washington: Biblical Archaeology Society.
Oller, J. W., Jr.
1996   Semiotic theory applied to free will, relativity, and determinacy: or why the unified field theory sought by Einstein could not be found. *Semiotica*, Vol. 108, No. 3 & 4, pp. 199-244.
Oller, J. W., Jr. & Collins, S.
2000   The logic of true narratives. *The Global Journal of Classical Theology*, Vol. 2, No. 2. Visit **www.trinitysem.edu/journal/journalindex.html**.
Petrie, W. M. F.
1931   *Egypt and Israel*, pp. 40-46. London: Society for Promoting Christian Knowledge. Originally published in 1910.
Wenham, G. J.
1981   *Numbers: An Introduction and Commentary*, pp. 56-66. Downers Grove, Illinois: Inter-Varsity Press.
Wente, E. & Van Siclen, C., III
1977   A chronology of the New Kingdom, Table 1, p. 218. *Studies in Ancient Oriental Civilization No. 39*. Chicago: The Oriental Institute.
Wood, B. G.
2000a   Khirbet el-Maqatir, 1995-1998. *Israel Exploration Journal*, Vol. 50, pp. 123-130. Jerusalem: Israel Exploration Society.
Wood, B. G.
2000b   Khirbet el-Maqatir, 1999. *Israel Exploration Journal*, Vol. 50, pp. 249-254. Jerusalem: Israel Exploration Society.
Wood, B. G.
2000c   Kh. El-Maqatir 2000 Dig Report. *Bible and Spade*, Vol. 13, No. 3, pp. 67-72.
Zevit, Z.
1985   The problem of Ai: new theory rejects the battle as described in the Bible but explains how the story evolved. *Biblical Archaeology Review*, Vol. XI, No. 2, pp. 58-69.

NOTES

[1]This paper is derived from the doctoral dissertation, Briggs (2004).

[2]Scripture quotations in this paper are taken from the New American Standard Bible (abbreviated

NASB), Copyright © 1960, 1962, 1963, 1968, 1971, 1972, 1973, 1975, 1977 by the Lockman Foundation. Used by permission.

[3]For a fuller discussion of TNR theory and its application to testing the factuality of the conquest of Ai narrative, refer to Briggs (2004: 22-26 & 72-76).

[4]Refer to Briggs (2004: 60-61) for a definition of *Force Multiplication*.

[5]Refer to Appendix A in Briggs (2004: 183-190) for a critical analysis and review of Humphreys' model.

[6]In this equation, 162 persons per acre is the population density from Broshi & Gophna (1986), 7 acres is the maximum value for the area of Ai, and 4 is the multiple of E that represents the total population of Ai according to the spies' estimate.

[7]In Briggs (2004: 126-127) the factors contributing to temporal uncertainty are analyzed, which leads to the conclusion that the tolerance band associated with the date of the Exodus, and therefore that of the Conquest, is ±50 years.

[8]Refer to Briggs (2004: 89-120) for the detailed exegesis of the biblical text in support of the formulation of the criterial screen.

[9]This detachment, denoted the *ruse attack force*, was perhaps $3E$ in size to emulate the attack force of Joshua 7. It is noteworthy that if the king of Ai had accurately assessed the magnitude of the threat to the north, he would have secured the fortress and forced the Israelites to engage in a prolonged siege, for which they were neither trained nor equipped. Thus, Joshua would have kept most of the residual attack force hidden from view.

[10]Refer to Briggs (2004: 102-104) for illustrations of candidate *shebarim* formations; refer to Briggs (2004: 146-149) for candidate engagement scenarios for the first battle of Ai.

[11]Refer to Briggs (2004: 150-157) for the postulated engagement scenario for the second battle of Ai.

[12]Refer to Briggs (2004: 60-63) for a review of ancient military technology pertinent to this research.

[13]For additional detail concerning the results of past research in regard to the site of Joshua's Ai, refer to Briggs (2004: 51-53).

[14]For additional detail concerning the locations and topographical contexts of the three candidate sites for Joshua's Ai, refer to Briggs (2004: 129-141).

[15]For the detailed exegesis of the biblical text in regard to the location of the encampment of the primary ambush force, see Briggs (2004:105-106). The combination of directional indicators in the text require that this encampment be approximately southwest of the fortress of Ai.

[16]For further discussion of Livingston's hypothesis and the topographical context of Kh. Nisya vis-a-vis the requirements of the biblical text, see Briggs (2004: 134-137).

[17]For the details of the engagement scenarios, refer to Briggs (2004: 145-157).

[18]In addition to the three candidate sites for Joshua's Ai examined in this paper, the following three sites have been considered as candidates at one time or another in past research: Kh. Khaiyan, Kh. Khudriya, and Kh. Raddana. Refer to Briggs (2004: 51) for a summary of the archaeology of these three sites.

EB I - MB IIA at Abila
Based on A Paper Presented
to the Near East Archaeological Society
Dr. Glenn A. Carnagey, Sr.

The EBI - MBIIA Ceramic Horizon at Abila of the Decapolis

Introduction

Abila was an enormous city for a large portion of its historical existence. Based on the seasoned evaluation of some 14 years of excavation, it was one of the largest Early Bronze cities in all of Palestine (1.5 kilometers north-south by .5 kilometers east-west). Its closest rival would have been et-Tell on the Cis-Jordanian side of the Jordan River. It seems to have maintained its population from Early Bronze I all the way through EBII, EBIII, EBIV and well towards the end of MBIIA when for some reason not yet determined, habitation ceased on the site until the Late Bronze Age (Only a smattering of graves and grave goods have been recovered from the MBIIB and MBIIC periods).

A very thin layer of Late Bronze materials without any architectural remains (about 10-15 cm) but with an impressive variety of imported pottery styles precedes a much larger presence of Iron I and Iron II pottery and a wall stub that runs some 7 meters across part of Area AA and is preserved to a height of 8 courses, though again, no domestic architecture appeared. A small amount of Persian period remains followed by a constantly increasing quantity of first Greek, then Early and Late Roman and finally Early and Late Byzantine materials testify to a period of great growth and prosperity for the site. Even after the Umayyad conquest the city continued to flourish during much of the Arab Period, including the Umayyad, Abbasid, Ayyubid and Mamluk Periods. The site appears to grow smaller after the Umayyad Period, though the artifacts suggest strongly that the site continued as a city through the Abbasid and Mamluk Periods. Today, it is used almost entirely by farmers, Bedouin, shepherds and archaeologists.

The purpose of this paper is to give an overview of recent excavation at Abila and to suggest some reasons why the finds at the site are especially important.

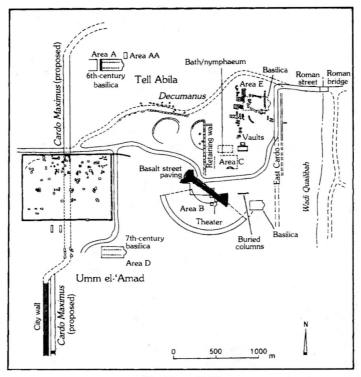

Site Map of Abila

Areas of the Tell

Area AA — Tell Abila (North Tell)

As Area Supervisor of Area AA, my job has been to excavate a 1.c. Test Trench down to bedrock on Tell Abila, the north tell of this twin-telled site. Consequently, except for two or three small probes in Area A (also on Tell Abila) and in Area D (located on the South Tell) none of the other areas have been excavated deep enough to reach the early levels of the site.

It has been my good fortune to discover an unbroken sequence of domestic levels beginning at least as early as EBI and continuing without a break through EBII, EBIII, EBIV, MBI, MBIIA, MBIIB, and MBIIC. Except for Tell el-Hayat, excavated by Bonnie Magness-Gardiner and Steven Falconer in central Trans-Jordan (Magness-Gardiner, B. and Falconer, S., 1983-4) this particular sequence is nearly unique. It shows that at Abila the city managed to survive the transition from EBIII to MBIIA without a break in occupation. Because the exposure is limited (2 squares down through MBIIA and only one square penetrating the 4 EB levels) caution is indicated in interpretation, but

198

several additional squares have been brought down to a point at which we should soon be able to broaden the exposure considerably. At least three rooms of an MBIIA house have been uncovered, including its kitchen. In the room adjacent to the kitchen an infant pithos burial under the stone wall corner with attendant burial pottery (a grey-burnished juglet and a red-burnished small cup) and the remains of a small fire, probably used to burn incense, testify to the practice of sacrificing an infant and burying it under the wall or the door to insure the blessing of the gods upon the new house (I Kings 16:34). Our osteologist identified the infant remains as those of a 0-6 month old baby.

Also, the delay of the publication of the MBIIA will allow us to peruse the MBIIA-IIB remains of Dhahrat 'ed Dhrah in southern Jordan, found and excavated by Dr. Stephen Falconer, whose earlier work is legendary for the MBII period, since it was from a North Central site, Tell el Hayat. That will give us the North-Central Assemblage of MB, while Abila provides the most Northern Assemblage of Ceramics.

Late Bronze remains are restricted to a 10-12 cm layer above the Middle Bronze house and below the Iron I-II wall. This wall, some 7 meters in length and preserved to a height of eight courses, continues to be somewhat of a mystery. As yet no additional structures have been found to connect with it. We hope to find additional Iron age remains in adjacent squares. The volume of Iron I and Iron II pottery found in Area AA along with the wall suggests strongly that there was an iron age village on part of the site. Unfortunately, the portion of the tell which has the highest concentration of Iron Age sherds is located on an area of the tell which belongs to a local farmer who is not at all interested in letting us excavate his field!

Aside from a burial and a few isolated sherds (north side of AA002), no remains from the Persian (Iron III Period) have been discovered. However, Robert Smith did find a Hellenistic-Roman wall complex in Square AA01. The walls were apparently built during the Hellenistic Period and then a rebuild was carried out during the Early Roman Period. These walls were quite solid, because the Early Byzantine inhabitants anchored their walls to them.

Extensive remains of the Late Byzantine domestic quarters attached to the Basilica on Tell Abila adjacent to this site and to the east and south of Area AA have slowed the pace of vertical excavation somewhat, but have provided valuable information concerning water resource management and structural activity during the Byzantine Period. This includes an extensive water channel system with mortared interior used to collect water and deposit it in an as-yet-undiscovered cistern near the North Apse of the Basilica. Most of the building blocks used for buildings at this level have been robbed out and used for other building projects by later inhabitants, but a few foundation courses of worked stone for building corners and walls are still visible after excavation in the 1994 season. A workshop and several tabuns (ovens) lined up down the north-south balk between Squares AA04 and AA05 suggest that this was a very active part of town during the Byzantine era.

Large amounts of glass fragments and some partial vessels of glass discovered in the fill of the water channels continue to tantalize us with the possibility of a major glass production facility somewhere in the vicinity.

Area A — Tell Abila (North Tell)

Coin evidence from the Roman era shows a Roman Temple at Abila, and Schumacher's survey suggested that the visible remains on Tell Abila were that temple. However, John Wineland, Area A Supervisor, did not find the temple when he excavated this section of the tell. Instead, he found a sixth century triapsidal basilica.

Excavation of the church revealed a central nave and two side aisles, all with opus sectile red and white flooring. A base of one iconostasis white marble column was discovered and numerous fragments of what must have been the screen. Many large column fragments were found, along with bases and capitals, but they appeared to have been mutilated in antiquity and broken into small segments. Many of them vanished between seasons, apparently to grace local gardens.

To the west of the east-west lying basilica lies an atrium associated with the entry. It extends out almost 15 meters. Its mosaic floor was also uncovered and conservation steps were taken to consolidate it. The mosaic decoration was geometric and composed of red and black diamonds with crosses in the center. After drawing and photography, it was re-covered with dirt for its protection. Several whole artifacts were discovered in one square, including a lovely glass bottle, a lamp and a Byzantine cookpot.

Excavation where the atrium south edge approaches the edge of the tell revealed at least two additional mosaic floors below the current one with much more intricate and colorful decoration. A portion of the south city wall also was uncovered.

One of the most exciting finds was the result of clearing debris and fill away from the north wall of the basilica. A life-sized sculpture made of white marble of the Greek goddess Artemis (Roman Diana) was uncovered. Although the head and arms and one leg were missing, 1.64 meters of the statue was preserved.

Area B — Central Saddle

The most spectacular find so far in what was supposed to be the theater has been the two roads uncovered. A limestone Roman road and a basalt Byzantine road have been found and exposed for a considerable distance. A number of associated Roman structures have been excavated as well.

The Mamluks built a structure on top of the Roman remains to the south of the road near the cavea. A stairway to what would have been the second story of the Mamluk building is complete, though the second story is completely gone. Inside the room, which has an arched doorway leading into the cavea fill is a beautiful checkerboard floor, made of alternating white and black diamonds.

During the 1994 season a large statue niche was found about halfway up the cavea and the process of clearing it was begun. Dr. Bastiaan Van Elderen, the Area B Supervisor, also uncovered a white marble column with a Byzantine cross clearly inscribed in the center of the column.

Area C — Central Saddle

Dr. Jack Lee, Area C Supervisor, has been excavating what was a massive rock tumble when he began. With the help of the Department of Antiquities crane and front loader it has been possible to clear enough space to make several important discoveries. Area C is located directly across the modern road to the north of Area B. It has been proposed that this area is a Bath-Nymphaeum complex. Supporting evidence for this hypothesis emerged with the excavation of two water sluices which carried the Umm el-'Amad aqueduct's water into a large vaulted settling basin east of the vaulted dome in the east facade of the complex. Further east from this first settling basin, a second basin was found along with two basalt sarcophagi reused as smaller distribution containers. South of this and extending far back under the structure yet a third vaulted settling tank was discovered.

The vaulted dome-shaped room discovered in the east facade of the complex is one of the more interesting items discovered in Area C. It is entered by an arched doorway and is 3.5 meters in diameter. Excavation of the interior revealed a hemispherical room with excellent flagstone paving. Pottery sherds found inside the room suggest that it was built and used by the Mamluks.

Area E — Saddle Depression

Area E, under the direction of Dr. Clarence Menninga, continued clearing the large basilica found to the north and east of Area C. The major discovery here was that the basilica was cruciform in shape with four apses (N, S, E, and W). It is almost square in shape and is about 25-26 meters in both width and length.

The first full inscription to be discovered at Abila came to light inscribed on the bottom section of a long granite column which had been reused in the church. Composed in the late second century A.D., it began with the well-known "Agathe Tuche" (O Good Tyche!), and went on to express thanks for something the donor believed Tyche had done for him.

Area D — Umm El 'Amad (The South Tell)

Excavations in Area D were under the direction of Dr. Wilkie Winter, upon whose untimely death Robert Clark, and then David Vila, assumed the role of Area Supervisor, were concentrated in two areas. Additional squares southwest of the 7th century basilica revealed additional flooring with white tessarae and occasional geometric designs of red and black. The additional flooring suggests an extended area of "work" or "service" rooms along the south wall of the basilica. A beautiful red granite column was found and pictures taken, but someone took it between seasons.

The second area of concentration was to the northwest of the entrance to the church on the west end across the modern road. Here a threshold to some early building to the north and a water drain under a pavement leading to the previously discovered cistern were found. Mosaics from two floor levels were found here as well.

Area DD — Umm El 'Amad (The South Tell)

Area DD is a new area, opened in 1994 as a result of the discovery in 1992 of the apse of a basilica across the modern road to the west of the porch of the seventh century basilica in Area D. Inside this apse was found an inscribed mosaic floor of geometric design. Under the direction of David Vila, Area Supervisor, the team discovered two additional apses, thus showing that this earlier basilica was triapsidal.

Inscribed mosaic floors were found in all three apses. In excavations south of the south apse the south wall of the basilica was found and patches of mosaic floor of circular pattern were revealed west of the three apses (the church runs East to West). Found in this same area was a group of glass lamp fragments together with one complete glass lamp with projecting glass stem. These were most likely used in an elaborate system of ceiling-hung circular chandeliers/candela (filled with glass lamps) used to illuminate the interior of the church. Found with the glass was an almost complete brass bottle with accompanying metal handle cast in the form of a leopard, probably used as a filling vessel to fill the glass lamps with oil. The altar area was uncovered with its foundation blocks and internal opus sectile flooring. On one of the blocks was a carefully incised cross within a circle.

Twelve meters west of the north apse the team excavated the church's five meter deep cistern, which produced large quantities of Late Roman to Ayyubid/Mamluk pottery. The cistern was apparently used by later inhabitants as a garbage dump.

The lack of any columns, capitals, bases or stylobates indicates that the builders of the seventh century basilica to the east used the structural elements of the DD basilica in their building activities.

Tomb Excavations — Area H

Robert Smith, Tombs Area Supervisor, and his crew excavated one or two small graves along with one small undisturbed tomb complex. One or two other robbed tombs were salvaged.

Much of the season was spent excavating and drawing the Area H36 pottery kiln found in 1992 (Roman pottery). No Bronze Age or other early graves were found.

The Ceramic Horizon

[Editorial note: Dr. Carnagey had continued the essay with a study of the ceramics recovered in Area AA, illustrated by sherds identified by loci, decorative elements, color, etc. The drawings, however, were not of publishable quality. Because of his lamented death, this problem could not be corrected prior to publication, so the descriptive text and plates are lacking. When the Abila materials reach final publication, this problem will be resolved and the information will be available. The final conclusions of this study, however, follow below.]

Conclusions

Because of its unique sequence of **Early Bronze IV** through **Middle Bronze IIA** strata, Abila should contribute an excellent ceramic horizon for comparison with other sites in Palestine, especially in Northern Jordan, from which no major site has yet been published. Since the **EBIV** levels are so clear at Abila, we suggest that Abila did not share the fate of other Early Bronze cities in Palestine, which were abandoned at the end of **Early Bronze III**. Instead, it continued to flourish as an urban site right on through the **Middle Bronze IIA** period before being temporarily abandoned until the Late Bronze period when population began to pick up again.

A second advantage derives from the variety of basilicas all found at the same site (four so far excavated): three triapsidal basilicas (Area A 6th-7th century basilica, Area D triapsidal basilica, Area DD triapsidal basilica) and the additional Area E cruciform basilica. The publication of these four churches should greatly enrich our knowledge of church architecture during the Umayyad rule of this area. Thirdly, Abila has one of the most extensive water tunnel systems in all of Palestine, stretching for miles in several directions. Additional examination and interpretation of the water management practices at Abila Area C along with a special season of survey in the summer of 1995 have contributed valuable information about Roman and Byzantine water management systems.

Wide exposure of the surface water channel system and building remains in the domestic area of Area AA Late Byzantine along with workshops found here and to the south of the Umm el 'Amad Basilica will help us to understand how water was collected and saved for use in the industrial and domestic quarters of Byzantine Abila. Aside from Jerash, the Roman/Byzantine road structure at Abila is one of the best preserved in Jordan. When its full extent is uncovered we will learn much about the traffic flow and how it was directed through and around the city.

Finally, an as-yet unexcavated Umayyad "Citadel" on Tell Abila plus Umayyad constructions in the Area DD church and the Area A church should increase our knowledge of Umayyad occupation of the site. The dome-shaped room in Area C together with the Mamluk building in Area B should shed considerable light upon the Mamluk Period in northern Jordan.

We are still in search of the Late Bronze and Iron Age domestic areas, the Hellenistic and Roman domestic and merchant sections and additional Arab Period structures that could expand our knowledge of that time span. Many of the questions have been solved, but the answers to the rest still lie beneath the ground!

REFERENCES

Albright, William F.
   1973   The Historical Framework of Palestinian Archaeology between 2100 and 1600 B.C. *BASOR* 209, 12-18.
Amiran, R.
   1961   Tombs of the Middle Bronze Age I at Ma'ayan Barukh, *'Atiqot* 3, 84-92.
   1969   *Ancient Pottery of The Holy Land*. Jerusalem - Ramat Gan: Masada Press Limited.
Dever, W. G.
   1973   Palestine in the Early Bronze Age. Pages 132-163 in *Near Eastern Archaeology in the Twentieth Century*. (Essays in honor of Nelson Glueck, ed. J. A. Sanders) New York.
   1973   The EB/MBI Horizon in Transjordan and Southern Palestine, *BASOR* 210, 37-62.

Kouri, R.
    2001   Rare Middle Bronze Age village near Dead Sea coast, *Artifax* 16, 9-10.

Falconer, S. E. and Magness-Gardner, B.
    1983   Preliminary Report of the First Season of the Tell el-Hayat Project, *BASOR* 255, 49-74.
    1984   1982 Excavations of the Tell el-Hayat Project, *ADAJ* 27, 87-104.

Hadidi, A.
    1982   An EB-MB Tomb at Jebel Jofeh in Amman, *ADAJ* 26, 283-6

Helms, S. W.
    1986   The EB-MB Cemetery at Tiwal esh-Sharqi in the Jordan Valley, 1983, *ADAJ* 27, 55-85.

Hess, P.
    1984   "Middle Bronze Tombs at Tell 'Artal" *BASOR* 253, 55-60.

Ibrahim, M., Sauer, J. and Yassine, K.
    1976   The East Jordan Valley Survey, 1975, *BASOR* 22, 241-66.

Lapp, P.
    1970   Palestine in the Early Bronze Age. Pages 100-131 in *Near Eastern Ar chaeology in the Twentieth Century*. (Essays in honor of Nelson Glueck, ed. J. A. Sanders), New York.

Prag, K.
    1971   A Study of the Intermediate Early Bronze - Middle Bronze Age in Transjordan, Syria and Lebanon. Unpublished D. Phil. thesis, Oxford.
    1974   The Intermediate Early Bronze - Middle Bronze Age: an interpretation of the evidence from Transjordan in *Levant* VI, 69-116.
    1980   Toward a Consensus of Opinion on the End of the Early Bronze Age in Palestine-Transjordan, *BASOR* 237,
    1985   Ancient and Modern Pastoral Migration in the Levant, *Levant* XVII, 81-88.
    1986   The Intermediate Early Bronze - Middle Bronze Age Sequences at Jericho and Tell Iktanu Reviewed, *BASOR* 264, 61-73.

Pritchard, J. B.
    1963   *The Bronze Age Cemetery at Gibeon*. Philadelphia: University of Pennsylvania Press, 1963.

Richard, Suzanne
    1980   Toward a consensus of opinion on the end of the Early Bronze Age in Palestine and Transjordan, *BASOR* 237, 5-34.
    1986   Excavations at Khirbet Iskander, Jordan, *Expedition* 28, 3-12.

Richard, Suzanne and Borass, R. S.
    1984   Preliminary Report on the 1981-1982 Season of the Expedition to Khirbet Iskander and its Vicinity, *BASOR* 254, 63-87.

Suleiman, Emsaytif
    1985   "An EB/MB Tomb at Tla' el-'Ali, *Annual of the Department of Antiquities of Jordan* XXIX, 179-80.

Tubb, Jonathan N.
  1985 Excavations in the Early Bronze Age Cemetery of Tiwal esh-Sharqi 1984, *Annual of the Department of Antiquities of Jordan.* Vol.XXIX.
Wightman, G. J.
  1988 An EBIV Cemetery in the North Jordan Valley, *Levant* XX, 139-159.

Index

Apostle 33, 36
apostle 33, 36
Apse 199
apse 31, 201, 202
Aqueduct 24
aqueduct 12
Aquila 100
Arab 2, 62, 71, 72,
 73, 197, 203
Arabia 60
Aram
 2, 60, 99, 117, 118,
 120, 121, 123, 124,
 126, 128, 129, 130,
 131, 133
Aram-Naharaim 117,
 118, 120, 121, 123,
 124, 128, 129
Aram-naharaim 99
Aramaic 38, 39, 40,
 44, 45, 48, 49, 50,
 51, 53, 57, 59, 62,
 103
Aramean 118
Ararat 66, 73
Archaeology 2, 3, 4, 5,
 6, 7, 8, 9, 11, 13,
 14, 15, 16, 19, 20,
 23, 25, 26, 29, 32, 34,
 49, 60, 61, 79, 80,
 84, 88, 91, 92, 166,
 167, 193, 197
archaeological 3, 5, 7,
 8, 9, 10, 12, 15, 20,
 21, 28, 29, 32, 33,
 35, 36, 64, 65, 68, 71,
 72, 78, 79, 80, 81, 82,
 83, 84, 87, 105, 128,
 157, 161, 162, 163,
 166, 167, 175, 177,
 179, 185, 186, 187,
 191, 192
archers 67, 134

arches 70
architects 7, 35
Architecture 12
architecture 12, 28,
 84, 197, 203
archons 54
arena 39
Armenia 123
Artemis 22, 200
artifacts 83, 84, 175,
 178, 182, 183, 185,
 186, 188, 190, 197,
 200
Artifax 25, 204
artisans 72
Arzawa 127
Asara/Terqa1 16
Asherahs 117
Ashkelon 86, 134
ashkenaz 66
Ashur-Nasirpal 35
Ashuruballit 72
Asiatics135
Assemblage199
assemblage33
Assyria 66, 107,
 109, 125, 133
Assyrians 64, 66, 67,
 73, 118, 124, 128
Astour 115
astrology 50
Astruc 159
Athens 28, 67
atrium 200
Attic 21
Augustine 54, 58
Averbeck 115
Avi-Yonah 62, 63, 64,
 67, 68, 71, 72, 73,
 74, 97, 102
ayin 135, 138
Ayyubid 197, 202
Azerbaijan 67

B
Babylon 66, 104, 105,
 106, 107, 109, 111,
 112, 163
Babylonia 51, 107, 133
Balatah 31
Balawat 36
balk 199
Baptism 56, 57, 58
baptism 52, 55
Bar-Nathan 68, 74
barbarism 66
Barthélemy 100, 102
basalt 8, 28, 69,
 200, 201
Basilica1 99, 203
basilica 8, 12, 28, 31,
 69, 200, 201, 202, 203
Bauer 55
Baumgarten 43, 44,
 46, 47
Bedouin 197
Beirut 28, 134
Beisan 62, 68
Beit-Shean 67
Beitin 86, 161, 167,
 188, 190
Beitzel 140, 142, 143
Bell 42, 44
Belzoni 35
Ben-Sasson 91
Ben-Tor 91
Beth-Shean/Scythopolis
 68
Bethel 86, 101, 162,
 163, 174, 175, 178,
 181, 183, 186, 188,
 190, 194
Bethesda 115
Billington 117, 124,
 130
Bimson 93, 94, 98,
 102

Index

213

Index